Marxis... and ...m...

UNIVER
WO

nd Culture

Michael Wayne and Esther Leslie

This new series aims to revive, renew and develop Marxism as an emancipatory tool for analysing media and cultural practices within capitalism and class society. The focus is on both contemporary popular culture and the high and avant-garde art of the past, brought into connection with a range of pressing issues, such as globalisation, ecology and nature, science, the family, identity, migration and asylum, war, inequality and oppression. Developments in new technologies, their relation to capital and the contradictory role of the intelligentsia within media and culture institutions represent other significant strands. The interplay of class relations with forms of identity – ethnic, gendered and sexual – may be addressed. We are also keen to consider proposals that address metatheoretical work on the history of Marxist cultural theory and rival theoretical outlooks.

Marxism and Media Studies

Key Concepts and Contemporary Trends

Mike Wayne

Pluto  Press

LONDON • STERLING, VIRGINIA

First pu̇ʟ ı ı   ꜱ̇³ ı
345 Archway Road, London N6 5AA
and 22883 Quicksilver Drive, Sterling, VA 20166-2012, USA

www.plutobooks.com

British Library Cataloguing in Publication Data
A catalogue record for this book is available from
the British Library

ISBN 0 7453 1914 9 hardback
ISBN 0 7453 1913 0 paperback

Library of Congress Cataloging in Publication Data
Wayne, Mike.
   Marxism and media studies : key concepts and contemporary
trends / Mike Wayne.
      p. cm.
   ISBN 0–7453–1914–9 (hard.) — ISBN 0–7453–1913–0 (pbk.)
   1. Marxian economics. 2. Commodity fetishism. 3. Mass
media—Economic aspects. 4. Mass media—Social aspects. I. Title.
   HB97.5 .W35 2003
   302.23'01—dc21
                                                    2003004707

10   9   8   7   6   5   4   3   2   1

Designed and produced for Pluto Press by
Chase Publishing Services, Fortescue, Sidmouth, EX10 9QG, England
Typeset from disk by Stanford DTP Services, Towcester, England
Printed and bound in the European Union by
Antony Rowe Ltd, Chippenham and Eastbourne, England

Education upholding the bourgeois state can be replaced by education critical of capitalist society. Instead of being trained to be obedient subjects and disciplined wage-earners dominated by the ideology of individual achievement, young people can be encouraged to think independently and to act in collective solidarity. It is self-evident that a practice of this kind must lead to serious conflicts with the ruling class and cannot in the long-run be reconciled with the normal workings of late capitalist society.

Mandel, *Late Capitalism*

For my son Jacob,
because change begins at home.

Contents

Acknowledgements		x
Introduction: From the Small Screen to the Big Picture		1
1	Class and Creative Labour	6
2	Mode of Production: Technology and New Media	38
3	Powers of Capital: Hollywood's Media–Industrial Complex	61
4	The State: Regulating the Impossible	87
5	Base–Superstructure: Reconstructing the Political Unconscious	118
6	Signs, Ideology and Hegemony	155
7	Commodity Fetishism and Reification: The World Made Spectral	183
8	Knowledge, Norms and Social Interests: Dilemmas for Documentary	220
9	Conclusion: Reflections on Key Concepts and Contemporary Trends	257
Notes		269
Bibliography		273
Index		283

Acknowledgements

My thanks to the following: Pluto Press for supporting both this book and the Marxism and Culture series, Graham Murdock for his early suggestions on structure and content, Brunel University for providing me with the sabbatical I needed to write this book, Peter Wissoker and Robert Glynn for their comments on Chapter 2, Peter Keighron for his observations and comments, Deirdre O'Neill for her support and thoughts throughout, Douglas Kellner for his reassurances during a moment of doubt, Laura Harrison for her careful copy editing and the readers of the *International Journal of Cultural Studies* and *Radical Philosophy* for their feedback on parts of Chapters 3 and 5 respectively. A version of Chapter 3 appears in the *International Journal of Cultural Studies* (volume 6, no. 1, 2003) under the title 'Post-Fordism, monopoly capitalism and Hollywood's media–industrial complex' and a version of parts of Chapter 5 appears in *Radical Philosophy* (no. 117, Jan/Feb 2003) under the title 'Surveillance and Class in *Big Brother*'.

Introduction: From the Small Screen to the Big Picture

Something very peculiar has happened to the end credits of television programmes in the UK. 'Where once they were slow-paced and full screen, increasingly end credits are being shrunk, split, sidelined and confined to boxes or speeded up to the point of being almost illegible.'[1] This comment comes from an article in the New Media section within the Media supplement of the *Guardian* newspaper. Such divisions and subdivisions of 'news' are typical of the dominant daily organs for the distribution of information concerning current events and trends. It is inconceivable, within such media practices, that there might be a relationship worth exploring between such a seemingly specialist topic or relatively trivial item as end credits and some larger more substantive world events. Yet is there a relationship between our *Guardian* news item and some of the events which unfold, with rather minimal analysis, on the nightly television news? What possible relationship could exist between this shrinking, splitting and boxing of end credits on the one hand and mass revolts against the imposition of International Monetary Fund policies (obsequiously followed by national politicians) in a modern metropolitan capital such as Argentina's Buenos Aires? How could it be that this shrinking, splitting and boxing is related in any way whatsoever to the West dropping bombs on this or that part of the developing world? Surely there is no connection between the peculiar fate of end credits and the slow state-sanctioned privatisation of public services such as transport, health and education in the UK? Could there be a connection between such a marginal aspect of our experience of the media and the structures of the media themselves? And is there anything linking all this to the forms and content of the media and the meanings they generate? Perhaps, like Neo in *The Matrix* (Andy and Larry Wachowski 1999 US), you are aware that the world is not quite right, but the reasons for why it is wrong do not disclose themselves in how the world appears. But where to begin sifting, sorting, analysing the bewildering complexity of events, processes, and debates?

As students of the media, we could do worse than start with our lead story. Those end credits. The problem you see is that the nature

1

of television's airtime has altered in recent years. Previously there was no problem in having the end credits, which register the involvement and roles of the people who made the product you have just watched, scroll past at a leisurely pace with the screen all to themselves. Today the ferocious competition for audiences between broadcasters (however they are funded) means that the end credits must now vie with promotions and announcements designed to keep the viewer watching their channel. This ferocious competition did not develop naturally within the television industry, but was carefully promoted and institutionalised by the state and corporate agents. Airtime now has an economic value which it never had previously. For something to become valuable for some people, it has to be made scarce for others. Once upon a time scarcity afflicted human kind because nature imposed certain limitations and visited certain cruelties upon us. We lacked the basic means by which to overcome these limitations and afflictions. Then, along came a new social and economic system, which gradually developed and matured and promised to conquer scarcity and provide food, health, material wealth and cultural riches never before obtained. Some of these promises were indeed delivered, although patchily, unequally and often in stunted and limited ways. For many, these promises were never delivered. This social and economic system, which came to be known as capitalism, did not in fact abolish scarcity. Rather, it introduced new forms of scarcity, scarcity that was artificially, or socially *designed*. Time is money, they say. And this is another way of saying that time has become a scarce resource. A value. So time is now *so* valuable on television, that broadcasters are toying with the idea of displacing the end credits altogether and relocating them on the Internet. This erasure of the labour that has produced the television programme has not best pleased the industry trade unions. In America, the idea was flighted by the Discovery channel only to be shot down by the Documentary Credits Coalition, which represented various filmmakers' organisations. Our newspaper report notes: 'Such was the backlash that Discovery was branded as "greedy" and "un-American" in the US press, a reaction that seems to have frozen management on both sides of the Atlantic.'[2] The logic of competition and the drive to accumulate audiences and therefore profits from the advertisers (or sustain audience share if publicly funded) are thus resisted, which indicates one important facet of the social and economic system. It does not go unchallenged. The fact that this resistance has been supported by the American press, a capitalist press funded by advertisers, calling the television industry 'greedy' points to another facet: the social and economic scene is full of contradictions, with individual and collective agents espousing values at one level that are contradicted by their practices at another. We should also note that the internationalisation of commercialisation very often takes the route implied here: exported from America, onto Britain, and then the rest of the world. Our own newspaper article is rather keener on the idea of relocating end credits, judging by the many quotes from industry sources supporting the idea which pepper the article. One commentator suggests that 'There's no evidence to suggest that consumers are that interested in them.' There is, on the other hand, plenty of evidence that audiences get irritated and frustrated with adverts. Of course, that kind of consumer response is not something the industry wants to do anything about since that would threaten its very existence.

Now you may understandably be unmoved by all this and feel that it is hardly a matter of life and death to have an opinion either way. The point, however, is to imagine what a world would look like if it was organised entirely around such principles as artificial scarcity, competition for profits, the marginalisation of labour, the use of new technology to 'solve' problems in a way that is beneficial to capital and so forth. Of course you do not have to have a BA in Imagination Studies to do this because this is in fact the world we live in. The penetration of the forces of capital into every area of our lives, every interaction we have, extends all the way from those end credits to wars over oil supplies (another resource which has become scarce within the social and economic relations of capitalism where there are monopoly providers with built-in vested interests slowing research into renewable sources of energy). The forces of capital stretch all the way through the changing corporate structures of the media, the role of the state, the use of new technology and the cultural forms and meanings the media generates. These forces are contradictory, riddled with surprise twists and turns and meet, to varying degrees and at varying levels of intensity and strength, resistance and counter-forces.

It is this narrative, of a newly unrestrained capitalism, restructuring itself and the world it is embedded into (including our own sense of self and identity), on the one hand, and the practical and theoretical forces of resistance on the other, which this book tries to portray amongst contemporary trends as they are filtered through the media. The key concepts that will be our guide, our compass, derive from Marxism.

Marxism is rather more than a methodology for studying the media. It is a political, social, economic and philosophical critique of capitalism that has been much fought over, contested and condemned ever since a nineteenth-century German bloke with a big beard developed it out of a synthesis of French radical politics, German idealist philosophy and British economic analysis. As a critique it has predictably received a bad, begrudging or caricatured press from those who feel that there is no going beyond our present social and economic system. It has also been severely damaged by the track record of those who have acquired power and proclaimed themselves Marxists of one persuasion or another. Even though this track record had its Marxist critics it was the pro-capitalist bourgeois critics who got the most exposure.

Marxism in the West had its high point in academia back in the 1960s and 1970s, riding on the crest of a wave of political radicalisation throughout the developing and Western world. Today, within the study of culture and media, it is at best often gestured to as part of a history of methods, whose main themes, concerns and approaches have now been surpassed with infinitely more sophisticated tools of analysis. There are signs that this is beginning to change, perhaps because people are recognising that, as Fredric Jameson once noted, 'attempts to "go beyond" Marxism typically end by reinventing older pre-Marxist positions' (Jameson 1988:196). This book is written in the hope that there are people out there studying the media who are increasingly looking for more radical approaches to their subject, searching that is for ways of making sense of the media and culture which really get to the roots of why things are as they are.

Marxism I believe is the best methodology we have to begin to do that. It does not by any means have all the answers and it is in any case a field of dispute between Marxists. Yet as a set of tools it has enormous durability, with the world today looking more recognisably like that described by Marx in *The Communist Manifesto* than it did in 1848, when the *Manifesto* was first penned. This book is not organised as a history of Marxist thought, but is instead more of an intervention into contemporary trends, drawing on and elucidating Marxian concepts in the expectation that they will help us understand media culture in the context of advanced capitalism. I have tried to explain and apply these concepts as lucidly as possible without sacrificing their complexity. The latter is particularly important, as opponents of Marxism are quick to dismiss it as being 'too simple'. In some ways capitalism is incredibly and brutally simple. In others, it is immensely complex and Marx devoted his entire adult life to developing the means to analyse and understand its historic significance for the human race.

In integrating an exposition of key Marxist concepts with an analysis of the media, this book moves, broadly speaking, from a discussion of the contextual determinants at work on media practices and structures, to the more textual concerns of media meanings and finally onto more philosophical issues to do with the nature and fate of consciousness and knowledge under capitalism. In some chapters, a variety of different media are drawn on to illustrate the conceptual issues at hand, but, in most, there is a clear emphasis on grounding the discussion in particular media as case studies. The Internet and digital technology and culture are discussed in Chapters 1 and 2. Hollywood's media–industrial complex dominates Chapter 3. UK television is a frequent point of reference in Chapter 4. Television again features in Chapter 5, with a case study of the international phenomenon known as *Big Brother*. The print media are centre stage in Chapter 6, Hollywood film in Chapter 7 and the documentary in Chapter 8. Nowhere do these chapters intend to offer histories of those different media. Instead, in a reciprocal dynamic, the hope is that I demonstrate the explanatory power of Marxism by analysing contemporary media practices and that, in turn, the media (and the questions they raise) will clarify, sharpen and question Marxian concepts. The various chapters also necessarily engage with and critique alternative non-Marxian and quasi-Marxian positions within the field while simultaneously, where appropriate, using those other positions to illuminate the blind spots within Marxism. Because the methods we choose to understand the world have an impact on how the world changes, the questions of which tools are deployed and how remain unavoidably political. This book is a contribution to putting Marxism squarely back on the agenda for the study of media and culture.

1   Class and Creative Labour

What is capital?
Capital is *stored-up labour*.
                              Marx, *Economic and Philosophical Manuscripts*

The more higher education becomes a qualification for specific labour processes, the more intellectual labour becomes proletarianized, in other words transformed into a commodity.
                              Mandel, *Late Capitalism*

If any one concept could be identified as absolutely central to the Marxist methodology and critique of social formations, then it would be class. Class designates a social and economic position and it always involves an antagonistic relation between classes. It is not the only cause of social division and conflict and is indeed usually complexly interwoven with other factors, from geography to other social identities such as ethnicity or gender. The nature of the relationship between class and other social relations has been the topic of much debate, controversy and argument, as well as conflicts between different political strategies. But, for Marxists, class is fundamental because of its integral links with labour and production, the very basis of social existence and development. This is an unfashionable proposition in today's so-called 'consumer society', a term which conveniently conceals the human labour which makes consumption possible. If you doubt the fundamental character of labour, then just consider how much you were dependent on it in your first waking hour this morning. Assuming that you did more than stare blankly at the ceiling for 60 minutes, your morning's dependence on labour would have begun as soon as you flicked a switch for gas and electricity; as soon as you turned a tap for water; as soon as you reached into the cupboard for your cornflakes and into the fridge for your milk; as soon as you put on the clothes you are wearing while you read this book (assuming you are wearing any). And if you did just stare at the ceiling for 60 minutes, well, someone had to make the ceiling too. All these things depend on the labour power of others, organised under particular social and economic relationships, and, while we may take these things pretty much for granted, without them, life would get brutish and short very quickly. The political and methodological implications of this (growing) social interdependence and reciprocity are nothing short of revolutionary.

The question of creative labour in cultural analysis has usually been discussed within the category of individual authorship, with the stylistic features of cultural artefacts being linked back to the key creative personnel involved in their making. There are ways of doing authorial analysis within a Marxian framework (see McArthur 2000 for example) but my concern here is with the wider social conditions of creative and intellectual labour as a *collective* relationship occupying a contradictory position between capital and the 'traditional' working class. We will need to stage an encounter between Marxist and sociological conceptions of class to explore this contradictory position, while grounding intellectual labour in some of the specific conditions of media production, such as its divisions of labour and the impact of technology.

MAPPING CLASS

Let us begin with an emblematic image – one that as a microcosm provides a map of class relations and an indication of some of the pressures and transformations within class relations in recent times. From there we can begin to crystallise the ambiguities in the class position of creative or cultural labour. The image comes from Ridley Scott's classic science fiction/horror hybrid film, *Alien* (Ridley Scott 1979 GB/US), that inaugurated a remarkable series of films, which have tapped a zeitgeist around questions of the body, gender and reproduction (Penley 1989, Creed 1993, Kuhn 1990). Less remarked upon but just as central to the films and to *Alien* in particular is the question of class.

Conceptions of class are encoded implicitly into popular culture as a kind of common sense, an instantly, spontaneously, almost unconsciously understood code, part of our reservoir of popular wisdom and knowledge that is in general circulation. Barthes calls this knowledge, which media texts draw on and reconfigure within their specific narratives, a *cultural code* (Barthes 1990:20). In *Alien*, the crew of *Nostromo*, a deep space mining ship, have been awakened from suspended animation to respond to a signal from an unknown planet. In one scene, packed with signifiers of class, Parker (Yaphet Kotto, who the year before had starred in Paul Shrader's classic working-class drama, *Blue Collar* (1978 US)) and Brett (Harry Dean

Stanton) demonstrate their reluctance to go and investigate the mysterious signal and seek reassurances from Ripley (Sigourney Weaver) that they will be compensated for this extra work. The location for this scene is down in the bowels of the ship, the domain of Parker and Brett; despite the future setting of the action, this location is all machinery, engineering parts, pipe work and steam shooting out of valves: all classic signifiers of the industrial domain of the *man*ual *working* class. The verbal discourse of Parker and Brett also signifies class location: they make it clear that they want to be remunerated for this extra work – there is clearly no sense on their part of doing something for 'good will'. Their attitude could be said to be representative of a working-class perspective, which realistically assesses their limited career opportunities and the conflicting interests between them and their employers that make notions of 'good will' or 'common benefit' a non-starter. Ripley meanwhile clearly occupies a different class location. She has a pen and clipboard (signifying some sort of supervisory status); it is she who is answering questions rather than asking them; she quotes 'the law' at Parker and Brett (it apparently guarantees them their share of whatever is found): *believing* in the law and being knowledgeable enough about the law to quote it also indicate a different class position, in terms of *education* and *outlook* (both, as everyone intuitively knows, important indicators and determinants of precise class location). Finally, Ripley invokes the class dimensions implicit in the spatial relations of the ship (above/below) when she sarcastically tells Parker and Brett that if they want anything, *she'll* be 'on the bridge', an explicit reference to the division of labour (and the prestige, status and power which go with that division) on the ship. Ripley, then, has all the signifiers of being *middle* class. These are importantly combined with the gender frisson of Ripley's female class power over two men, and in this, as in much else, the film prophetically anticipates the influx of female labour – both middle- and working-class – which would become so marked from the 1980s onwards.

Now, what we have here, so far, is a *partial* map of class relations, but it is this partial map that dominates sociological discussions of class. Generally, mainstream sociology presents class as a series of layers, using occupation, income, education and consumption patterns as key criteria for defining class belonging. Mainstream sociology provides important shadings and nuances to any map of class but it characteristically excludes the really central fact of class as far as Marxism is concerned: *the social (and economic) relations of production*. As a result, there are huge swathes of social experience which mainstream sociology cannot address because the *dominant* pole in its class map, the social and economic force most responsible for the generation of change, is undertheorised and/or invisible. For example, mainstream sociological definitions of class cannot explain why in the same year that Barclays bank ran a 'big bank for a big world' advertising campaign, it was closing smaller branches; why developing world countries pay more money into Western banks than they do on healthcare and education; why a 0.25 per cent tax on financial speculation would raise £250 billion to tackle global poverty and why that tax is unlikely ever to be implemented; or why GM foods are being driven onto the market despite widespread consumer concern over the safety and environmental impact of the technology. Questions about the occupational or educational background of people do not begin to address how class is shaping *these* social phenomena. Consider this mapping of class from a popular A level sociology textbook:

> Recent studies of social class have focussed on the white-collar non-manual middle class and the blue-collar manual working class. These classes are often subdivided into various levels in terms of occupational categories. A typical classification is given below.
>
> Middle Class   Higher professional, managerial and
>   administrative
>   Lower professional, managerial and
>   administrative
>   Routine white-collar and minor supervisory
>
> Working Class   Skilled manual
>   Semi-skilled manual
>   Unskilled manual
>
> (Haralambos 1985:48)

Now it should be clear that the picture of class that the sociologists draw is just as much a *representation* of class as that found in a popular text such as *Alien*. Class is in this sense what Fredric Jameson calls an *ideologeme*, that is, a belief system which can manifest itself primarily as either a concept or doctrine (in a work of sociology for example) or as a narrative in a fictional text. While it is likely to be weighted more towards one or the other of these poles, there is always an element of both components at work since narratives cannot work without underlying abstractions and even the most conceptual work usually tells some sort of story (Jameson 1989:87). We can see that *Alien* draws on an ideologeme of class similar to that described in the standard sociological text, with Ripley locatable as 'routine white-collar/minor supervisory' and Parker and Brett as 'skilled manual'.

However, the striking thing about the sociological map is precisely what is absent from the account. The fine grain attention which sociology pays to the differences within and between the working and middle classes is conducted via a repression of the class force which these stratas have to relate to. What is interesting about *Alien* (and the subsequent films in the series) is that another class force emerges, most spectacularly when one of the crew, Ash, turns out to be a robot who has been programmed by the Company to return the alien to them at the expense of the lives of the crew. This sudden and abrupt foregrounding of the Company as secretly shaping the course of events, draws our attention to that class which often disappears within mainstream sociological discussions of class: the capitalist class. To talk of the capitalist class is to stress their agency as a class; their conscious attempts to organise and shape the world according to their own interests. But capitalists are also in some sense 'personifications of capital' (Mészáros 1995:66) for even they must operate according to and within the parameters set by the 'logic' of capital. This is a structuring principle of life, which, if individual cap-italists did not obey, would soon put them out of business. This logic has two main features: the drive to accumulate profit and competi-tion. In *Alien* we now have a class map in which Ripley, as representative of the middle class, is dramatically relocated *between* the working class on the one hand and capital on the other. The figurative and conceptual blockage in mainstream sociology lies in the fact that the capital side of the sandwich which places the 'middle class' in the middle is unaccounted for. In *Alien* what Ripley and we the audience learn is that, despite her differentiation from the labour of those below her (Parker and Brett), she is viewed by the forces above her (capital) as equally expendable. And this indeed is emblematic of wider socio-structural changes. The extension and penetration of the powers of capital, particularly its restructuring of the production process, have begun to impact on wide layers of the middle class through, for example, casualisation and de-skilling. These processes cut across and come into conflict with the differen-tiations and privileges which capitalism also fosters.

Alien not only provides us with a more complete map of the class structure but it is important to understand that it is a map drawn from a very particular *perspective*: that of the middle class. For Ripley is the film's heroine and it is in her in which it *invests* its hopes for overcoming the threat of the alien and the designs of the Company. One sign of this class perspective is the way the film *withdraws* from the tentative possibilities of a class alliance between Ripley and Parker (who will save her from Ash's murderous designs) by killing Parker off. Thus the film may be understood as a narrative manifestation of the *political unconscious* of the middle class generally and specifically of the cultural workers who occupied key creative positions (principally Scott and writers Dan O'Bannon and Walter Hill) in the making of the film (Heffernan 2000:9).

We now need to explore in more detail the Marxian conception of class as mapped out in Figure 1.1. Moving from left to right we see how labour sells its labour power to capital. Labour power, Marx writes, is 'the aggregate of those mental and physical capabilities existing in a human being, which he [sic] exercises whenever he produces a use-value of any description' (Marx 1983:164). Freely is in inverted commas because although there is no official compulsion to sell your labour power, unless you do or can, labour is condemned to a very impoverished and marginal existence. Thus, what Marx called 'the dull compulsion of economics' coerces labour, which has no other means of survival, to enter into a subordinate relationship with capital. Labour, as Marx ironically notes, is, therefore, free from, 'unemcumbered by, any means of production of [its] own' (Marx 1983:668). Conversely, it is the ownership of the *means of production* (land, equipment, raw materials) that defines capital and allows it ultimately to 'own' or possess for the working day the body which is inseparable from the power to labour. The diagram shows that for part of the working day the labourer is working for herself, insofar as the value, which she generates through her labour, is paid back to her in the form of wages. However, for part of the working day, labour is working free for capital since labour power has the peculiar ability to generate more value than it needs to survive and reproduce itself (clothing, eating, shelter and so on). This is called *surplus value* and it is this value which is embodied in the commodities which labour produces. Like an evil spirit capital then moves from the body of labour whose power to labour it activates, and into the commodity labour has produced only to then leave this material body when it is exchanged so that its use-values can be consumed; at the point of exchange, the spirit of capital flees this material body and enters into money capital which converts the surplus value (embodied in the commodity) into profit. (This analogy between the spirit of capital and ghostly spirits is developed further in Chapter 7.)

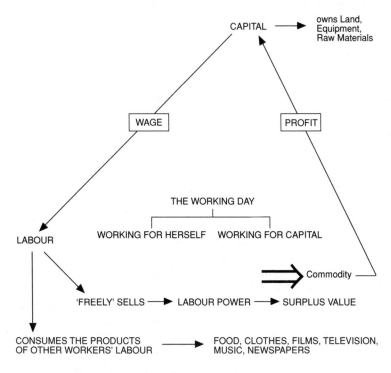

Figure 1.1   The Dichotomous Model of Class Relations

With capital replenished with profit, the personifications of capital will do two things. First, they will siphon off a part of this capital into their own personal consumption. But second – if they wish to remain personifications of capital tomorrow and the day after – they must reinvest that capital in further means of production and in wages to buy more labour power to exploit in order to recommence the whole sordid cycle all over again. Labour meanwhile takes the wages which it has earned and uses them to buy *non-productive property* (consumer goods) which have been produced by other workers. Some of those goods will be media commodities.

The class map tells us that the relationship between capital and labour is *inherently, structurally,* antagonistic. The extraction of surplus value requires capital to be the prime controller of what, where, why, when and how commodities are produced. Thus production is inherently, structurally, a site of *contestation* where labour deploys strategies from the small-scale to the large-scale, from the individual to the collective, which resist and subvert the priorities of capital, and capital deploys a variety of strategies to contain and stifle any challenge to its priorities and logic (Barker 1997). This contestation is called class struggle. A number of commentators who are hostile to Marxism point out that there is very little class struggle going on these days. But it all depends on what you imagine 'struggle' to encompass. At one end of the spectrum there are strikes and barricades in the streets, the icons of insurrection and revolution; but, on the other hand, class struggle can take quite passive and individualised forms such as absenteeism at work, or minor redistributions of wealth. Thus in *A Letter to Brezhnev* (Chris Bernard 1985 GB) good-time girl Theresa emerges from the factory where she spends her time with her hands up the arses of poultry, with a prime turkey specimen for her friend because it is Christmas. On the soundtrack a police siren wails in the distance. This signifier of the law asks us to ponder the meaning of Theresa's theft compared to that larger theft of life, wealth and opportunity that constitutes her working life.

Now, it has often been objected that the dichotomous cleavage between two fundamental classes which Marxism invokes, assumes too high a degree of *internal* coherence and homogeneity for the two classes while at the same time failing to address the important role of the middle class. These objections need to be addressed. Let us begin with Figure 1.2. We have seen that it is commonplace for sociologists to specify differentiations within and between the middle class and the working class. Differentiations such as skilled and semi-skilled within the working class and white collar and lower professional within the middle class are indeed important differentials, but sociology often sees *only* the differentials. Marxists would stress that such differentiations are not absolute, but different facets within the social and economic 'unity' of the class that sells its labour power to survive, and this *includes* the kinds of 'intellectual' labour carried out by the middle class. A classic formulation of this view of wage-labour (one which subsumes the middle class into the category

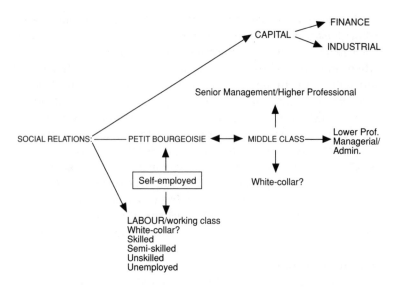

Figure 1.2   Class Relations: Marxian and Sociological Perspectives Synthesised

of *labour*) was made by Marx where he argued that as labour became subordinated to capital and new technology,

> 'the real *functionary* of the total labour process becomes, not the individual labourer, but increasingly a *socially unified labour capacity*, and since the various labour capacities ... participate in very different ways in the immediate process of the formation of commodities ... one working with his hands, the other more with his head, one as a manager, engineer, technologist, another as a supervisor, and a third as a direct manual labourer ... the *functions of labour capacity* are ... directly exploited by capital and *subordinated* to its valorization and to the production process as a whole. If we consider the *total labourer* who makes up this workshop ... it is a matter of complete indifference whether the function of the individual labourer, who represents only a limb of the total labourer, is more or less distant from the immediate labour done by hand. (Quoted in Mandel 1978:195)

One side of the process which capitalism develops is the hierarchical divisions of labour within and between mental and manual labour, and it is these differentiations which sociology characteristically foregrounds. Marx by contrast emphasises the other side of the selfsame process by which capital develops a socially unified labour capacity in which particular roles represent 'only a limb of the total labourer', while all roles are subjected to a generalised exploitation by capital. Another strand to Marx's argument, one which is central to the Marxist critique of capitalism, is that these hierarchies and the exploitation for private profit which they facilitate, cut against the progressive *socialisation* of production. Socialisation of production refers to the way labour becomes increasingly *interdependent*, so that what is done in one part of a production process or one sector of production is reliant on the labour of other workers elsewhere. For Marx, the socialisation of production provides the objective possibility and the moral necessity to transcend the hierarchical and profit-driven structure of capitalist production. But where sociology focuses too much on differentiations within the workforce, thus destroying in theory the possibility of establishing a unity of class interests, Marx certainly goes too far in suggesting that such differentials are a matter of 'complete indifference'. Instead we have to see how the traditional working class and the intellectuals take up differential relations to the same socio-economic force: capital. Insofar as those relations are different, the objective unity of labour capacity can be fragmented and the growth of class consciousness can be checked and stunted; insofar as the differential relations are *all* relations with capital, whose gods are accumulation and competition, labour of different kinds may be said to share fundamental interests.

The ambiguities in the two models of class are represented by the question mark over white-collar labour, which I have placed under both labour and the middle class. Even sociologists have debated to what extent white-collar work has become as routinised and managed from above as any 'working-class' occupation. As we have seen, *Alien* and the fate of Ripley may be taken as indicative of trends towards the proletarianisation of white-collar work. As we shall see, the rise of the middle class means that the working class should be viewed as a particular category of labour rather than labour being subsumed into the working class. Ehrenreich defines the working class as: 'all those people who are not professionals, managers or entrepreneurs; who work for wages rather than salaries; and who spend their working hours variously lifting, bending, driving, monitoring, typing, keyboarding, cleaning, providing physical care for others, loading, unloading, cooking, serving, etc' (1995:40–41). The working class constitutes 60–70 per cent of the American population, she contends, and she notes that they nowhere appear in the media in anything like this proportion. Again we have that sociological distinction between wages and salaries which indicates some important differences (job security, career progression) between the working class and the middle class. But it could also conceal some important lines of continuity.

The petit bourgeoisie (or small capitalists) are defined as the self-employed, small business-person. Their place in the social relations of production is characterised by the fact that they do not sell their labour power to an employer since they are the employer and sometimes in turn employ a small number of people. In terms of family background, educational and cultural capital, the petit bourgeoisie may either come from the middle class or the working class. The latter are often to be found running their own small shops or market stalls, or working in trades (plumbers, electricians, etc.) and services (cleaning for example). They therefore have a *contradictory class location* (but all class locations are contradictory), being culturally working-class but economically small capitalists. The middle-class petit bourgeoisie tend to set up businesses commensurate with their educational capital, which is to say their investment (of time) in acquiring formal educational qualifications (Bourdieu 1996:287); for example, information technology companies, interior designers, alternative therapies and medicines and of course 'independent' media companies. This class is continually under pressure and competition from monopoly capitalism, which exerts enormous power in the market (see Chapter 3). Indeed, one of the most frequent class dramas in Hollywood films takes the shape of the struggle of the petit bourgeoisie to survive in a world dominated by monopoly capitalism (see *You Have Mail* (Nora Ephon 1998 US) and *Antitrust* (Peter Howitt 2001 US) for example).

THE MIDDLE CLASS/INTELLIGENTSIA

I want to now turn to the middle class because it is this class in which we can locate cultural and media workers. In what follows I want to do three things: a) define the middle class in terms of their social relations of production as knowledge workers; b) look at the distribution and function of knowledge workers in the production and reproduction of social life under capitalism; c) explore the political implications of the class location of cultural or knowledge workers and the possibilities of antagonism which may exist between them and capital in the context of technological changes which have placed increased emphasis on knowledge, culture and information.

Knowledge workers

Within the Marxian conception, classes are defined by their social relations of production. One needs to stress *social* because there has been a tendency to abstract one determinant out of the social and privilege it in isolation from the rest: the economic. For Marxism, there can really be only three classes under capitalism. The principal classes are defined by the selling and buying of labour power, done respectively by labour and capital. The third class, the petit bourgeoisie, who do not sell their labour power but own only small-scale facilities, lie at an oblique angle to this principal antagonism. So far, then, the three classes have been defined by their *economic* relations to production. But the point about the economic determinant, it needs to be remembered, is that it provides the principal means through which the *social* control over the labour of others and the social control over one's own labour within the labour process are either lost or gained (Wright 1979:194). What happens then when people must sell their labour power and therefore effectively cede control over the production apparatus *as a whole* to capital, while at the same time retaining some real if limited and variable control over their *own* labour? Such is the position of much of the middle class.

Crucially, the middle class must sell their labour power like anyone else in return for a wage. This wage generally secures a higher remuneration (particularly in the private sector) for their labour power than is secured for most members of 'the working class' and this is not an unimportant differential. However, this is not the most defining differential and it is not always true in any case. A skilled car worker on a production line for models at the upper end of the market can earn as much or more than your university lecturer. The crucial feature of the middle class, which differentiates them from the working class in the social relations of production, is that they are knowledge workers. Their central activity is, as Wright notes, 'the elaboration and dissemination of ideas (rather than simply the use of ideas)' (Wright 1979:192). Gramsci calls this class the intelligentsia for this reason. 'All men are intellectuals', Gramsci argues, 'but not all men have in society the function of intellectuals' (Gramsci 1971:9). Under capitalism, the elaboration and dissemination of ideas become specialised within a particular category of people who monopolise premium modes of knowledge (formally accredited in educational institutions) and augment their advantages with social capital (personal networks, 'knowing the right people') and what Bourdieu calls cultural capital, the socially determined acquisition of competences and preferences which make up cultural tastes and further help to reproduce class differences (Bourdieu 1996). Wright also calls this group intellectuals, preferring to see them less as a *distinct* class than a group torn in a three-way split between labour, capital and the petit bourgeoisie (1979:203).

Two points are worth underlining here. First, that the split between intellectual labour and more manual or technical labour is central to the division of labour within the cultural industries. Second, there is a close relationship between specialising in the elaboration and dissemination of ideas and meanings, and acquiring some relative autonomy and independence, at least at a day-to-day level, in the production process. This is because ideas develop over time as a process, and constant monitoring and interruption threatens to disrupt and break down this developmental *form*. Specialising in the production of ideas also provides leverage because the *content* of those ideas derives from inside the heads of people or (in the case of on-screen stars) in a performance which is inextricably part of their labour power (or labour performance). In either case, the inextricable connection between the value (for capital) and the use-values (for consumers) which they produce and their *own* minds and bodies (a connection which can be severed by capital with more routine and material kinds of labour power) means that creative labour constitutes a problem for capital's command and control structure over it. This is why there persists within much cultural and intellectual production the sort of artisanal modes of production which pre-existed modern capitalism where skilled labour had close control over its own output (Garnham 1990:36–7). Capital's control over intellectual labour is thus somewhat loosened relative to its normal practices at the point of production, but control of reproduction, dissemination and revenues (once the cultural product has actually been made) is fully integrated into advanced capitalist structures of control (Hesmondhalgh 2002). So intellectual labour does not present an insuperable problem and to be sure different media industries develop different ways of shaping and influencing creative, intellectual labour and establishing certain parameters for it. In this way, because intellectuals sell their labour, their real but variable autonomy is under constant threat. As the middle class expands and/or becomes industrialised, as in the case of draftsmen, technicians, engineers, accountants, teachers, nurses and media workers, so their skills and knowledges experience a kind of inflation, where they lose value as they become more prevalent and therefore replaceable, or as those skills are integrated into new technologies (Braverman 1974:407, Wright 1979:210–11). When, for example, the advent of PCs enormously increased the productivity of scriptwriters, this did not lead to them working less time to produce the same amount of product, but instead working harder to produce more product than hither to. Here is scriptwriter Paul Abbott (creator of the working-class BBC TV drama *Clocking Off*, 2000–2001) describing one example of how increasing competition and technological development brought about a partial 'proletarianisation' to the writer's craft:

> In the early 90s, TV schedulers started gearing up for guerrilla warfare. I was a storyline writer on *Coronation Street* when they first went word-processed ('wave Tippex goodbye!'). The stories remained the same, but the speed of output could double. We in the story office imagined this was purely for our benefit. No chance. They were about to increase the number of episodes to Monday, Wednesday and Friday. I have vivid memories of looking at the newly installed computer archive that could, apparently, tell us what colour cardigan Hilda was wearing when Stan died. The guy in charge of 'modernising' us was Jules Burns (now joint MD) who proudly switched on the archive computer with a fanfare, beaming, 'Whadya-think?'[1]

Here we see how the category of the intelligentsia is internally differentiated into a hierachical division of labour. Film and television producers, for example, mediate between creative workers such as writers like Abbott and the senior executives in charge of profit accumulation. This mediation can take place either within the same organisation or between petit bourgeois producers who own their own production companies and the creatives they hire for particular projects and the financial investors in those projects. In this particular example, computer technology is used by management to compile and retrieve archive data, thus facilitating the expanding productivity of writers and loosening the company's reliance on the memories of long-serving scriptwriters.

Distribution and function

Braverman describes the middle groups as embracing 'engineers, technical and scientific cadre, the lower ranks of supervision and management ... marketing, financial and organisational administration ... as well as, outside of capitalist production proper, in hospitals, schools, government administration' (1974:403–4). However, it is worth unpacking this a little and exploring the distribution of knowledge workers and their social functions. Why has the middle class expanded so prodigiously since the time of Marx? John Clarke reminds us of Marx's discussion of the 'circuit of capital'. This involves the processes of production, the circulation of products, their exchange (or purchase) for money and their consumption or practical use. Surplus value cannot be achieved unless this entire circuit is closed. The problem for capital is that this process, as Clarke points out, is complex, involving all sorts of 'gaps, interruptions, blockages, tensions and contradictions' (1991:48–9) which need to be administered. The middle class therefore have emerged and expanded in order to address the problem of co-ordinating (and speeding up) all the factors (human, logistical, technological and cultural) that enable the circuit of capital to be completed.

This idea of co-ordinating the circuit of production does capture something of what much of the middle class do and perhaps describes most of what various fractions of the middle class do, particularly accountants, lawyers, administrators, senior managers, lobbyists and so on. Cultural producers also play a key role here in co-ordinating the circuits between production and consumption, as is the case with advertising, marketing, public relations and market research (Murdock 2000:16).

It has often been suggested that the middle classes are involved in helping to *reproduce* the social relations of production, oiling and co-ordinating the wheels, rather than directly contributing to the production of surplus value proper. This is the gist of the Ehrenreichs' classic study of what they call the Professional Middle Class (PMC) (1979:12). The Marxist economist Ernest Mandel, however, reminds us that Marx 'unequivocally stated that the labour of the research worker and engineer was productive in character' insofar as it is employed to generate surplus value and profit (1978:255). Rather than sharply distinguishing between direct producers and those who reproduce the relations of production, we ought to see them as closely interrelated. The co-ordinators, after all, are essential to the production cycle (which would come apart without them) while the producers (both working-class and middle-class) are helping to reproduce the relations of production by the very act of production

(Noble 1979:131). And what about cultural workers? From the point of view of the impact of their symbolic products, they may be engaged in reproduction (producing ideas and values, otherwise known as ideology, which legitimise the dominant social order); but, viewed from the point of view of production, it is clear that they produce commodities which realise surplus value for media capital, and, indeed, cultural goods as commodities have become increasingly important for capital investments and profits. There is, however, no necessary fit between the economic imperative and cultural values and, indeed, there are good reasons why they often diverge.

Economy, technology and culture

In his important analysis of the social and economic contradictions of the culture industries, Garnham notes that cultural and informational goods are classic public goods because they are not used up and destroyed by consumption (1990:38). They are also public goods in another related sense. Because they are not used up in their consumption, there is an objective basis for cultural goods to acquire their meanings and values and pleasures *because they are shared*. The pleasures and meanings of consuming film or music are evidently part of a collective experience in the way that satisfying biological needs such as eating and having shelter, or using private-based utilities such as your fridge or washing machine are not. Of course collective meanings are attached to even these very functional goods (for example in their design) and even more so in relation to such public commodities as clothes and cars. But this is only to say that culture (questions of status and identity) have become attached to them. With cultural goods whose sole *raison d'être* is cultural expression, the collective dimension of use and consumption is that much more pressing. There is a peculiar tension in this *culturalisation of consumer commodities*, because while they gesture towards collective if also exclusive (taste) groups, they exist as privately owned, sold and bought. Culture wrapped consumption then increasingly relies on socialised meanings in a system of *private* property rights. Struggles over cultural products as social products which cut against their status as private commodities are one issue I want to look at in relation to software engineers. But the contribution of intellectuals to that struggle is also bound up with the *culturalisation of production*. This is the process by which production becomes ever more dependent on the production and dissemination of ideas and information.

What Ernest Mandel defines (perhaps optimistically) as 'late capitalism' is precisely a dependence on computer technologies for generating, storing and distributing information. The entry of data processing machines into the private sphere of the American economy in 1954 (after they were developed by the arms economy) was crucial to the technological revolution that subsequently transformed capitalism (Mandel 1978:194). The high costs involved in research and development, in technological innovation and the merciless nature of competition between firms, in turn make 'ever more exact planning within the late capitalist enterprise' crucial (Mandel 1978:228). The computer, with its capacity for 'the rapid processing of colossal quantities and complexes of data' (Mandel 1978:229), makes planning within the firm possible, while, paradoxically, inter-corporate competition makes it necessary (and in turn makes democratic planning in society as a whole impossible). Planning within the firm entails the self-reflexive management of knowledge and information as a crucial underpinning to the adaptability, innovation and survival of organisations and constitutes a new mode of consciousness amongst bosses and managers (Prusak 1997). Thus, within business management theories, there has been a renewed awakening of the importance of the cultural assets and knowledge resources which all workers have. Communication technology products have magnified the importance of knowledge in sustaining competitive advantage (Tapscott et al. 1998). The relative and variable autonomy of the intellectuals does not rest on the difficulties of standardising knowledge; knowledge can be standardised into machines, as the working class has found to its cost. Crucially, though, the *application of knowledge* (Castells 1996) as a flexible and continually developing resource is, in fact, very difficult to standardise since to do so immediately freezes that knowledge and inhibits its responsiveness to new conditions. To avoid such rigidities, '[n]ew information technologies are not simply tools to be applied but processes to be developed' (Castells 1996:32).

The problem, however, in sustaining and developing the cultural and knowledge resources of the workforce is that, as with cultural products themselves, this requires or more accurately points towards social structures that cut against *actually existing* capitalism. Thus the development and dissemination of knowledge and skills requires, one business management book tells us, 'free communication' and a sense of shared goals. And it goes on, apparently without any sense of irony: 'This attitude, it has been observed, comes through the building of trust between managers and employees. Only trust can make knowledge flow inside the company, generating a shared world of experience' (Roos 1997:127). The notion of a culturalisation of production has been a key theme in those accounts of contemporary capitalism which argue that we are moving towards an Information Society. Very often, the claim that goes with that thesis is that class conflict, associated with the industrial production of 'hard goods', is now a thing of the past. My argument is less comforting for capital. If culture in all its ramifications (as ideas, values, pleasures) is all about the sharing and exchange of meanings, the culturalisation of production is a problematic development, a problematic *mode of development* within a mode of production which imposes strict limits, inequalities and distortions on sharing, on interdependence, on the socialisation of production and consumption.

Capital and the intelligentsia: a case study in antagonism

We have seen that the intellectuals are contradictorily located between capital and labour, as well as the petit bourgeoisie. They are integrated into capital to some extent and differentiated from the working class by their cultural privileges, relative workplace independence and (usually) by remuneration levels. Yet they are not capitalists and their status as labour reasserts itself whenever they are subjected to similar processes of exploitation and proletarianisation as the working class below them. Squeezed between capital and labour they are also constituted by them economically (using their culture as 'capital', yet still they are hired hands) and influenced by them at the level of ideas. But not being fully integrated into either social class they often gravitate towards the petit bourgeoisie, either at the level of ideas (seeking individual solutions to social problems) or literally moving economically in the direction of being their own boss. It is hardly surprising then that the questions of autonomy, independence and the existential meaning of work, have been crucial ones for the intellectuals (Heffernan 2000:39–71). One way in which intellectuals have attempted to explain their social role has been to depoliticise what it means to be elaborators and disseminators of ideas. This involves uncoupling knowledge production from vested social interests, defining professionalism as rising above the social conflict between capital and labour, and instead promoting 'objectivity' and 'rationality' as the very essence of what it is intellectuals do. Nevertheless, it is also true that while the ideology of 'objectivity' has, under the guise of working for all humanity, justified their role to capitalists, it has also inevitably led the intellectuals into conflict with their employers as and when the irrationality and partiality of capital has become too acute to ignore (Ehrenreich and Ehrenreich 1979:22). One kind of mode of antagonism between capital and the intellectuals occurs when the latter seek pragmatic reform of capital to try and make its interests re-converge with more general interests. However, another mode of antagonism separates the intellectuals rather more dramatically from capital as they raise demands which (whether they know it or not) fundamentally conflict with capitalism's *modus operandi*. Here pragmatic reform begins to shade into demands that point to a fundamental divergence between the interests of capital and the rest of humanity.

An excellent example of the different modes of antagonism that can exist between capital and the intelligentsia can be found in the software culture industry. A thriving movement has emerged around the issue of making the code which software is written in accessible to the user. Corporate software increasingly adopted a proprietary model as the Internet expanded. This model keeps the code that makes the program what it is secret. So even if this software is given away free (in terms of price), it is not *free* in terms of expression and use. Without access to the source code it is impossible to modify or customise the software or fix bugs in it as well as illegal to copy and distribute the code to other users. The key reason why access to the code software programs are written in has become a political issue is precisely because of the dual dynamic which has seen the culturalisation of production and the expanding production of cultural goods. The culturalisation of production has placed a massive premium on the knowledge and skills of software engineers. It is very clear to such knowledge workers that they are the key assets that are generating a company's wealth. Yet at the same time they must work within the parameters of corporate strategies and agendas. Thus progress is kept secret; different software engineers in different companies are coming up against similar problems but are unable to discuss them or share solutions because of corporate competition. The 'free' communication of ideas, which business management theorists are advocating that companies explore so that they can plan more effectively, here seeks to transcend the limits of communication as they are trapped *within* the boundaries of the company. Condemned by the logic of capital to perpetually reinvent the wheel, many software engineers working for private companies by day work for more public purposes at night. Alternatively, software developers are setting up Internet co-operatives, such as FreeDevelopers.net with the explicit intention of introducing democratic principles into economic activities and contesting corporate governance.

The issue of access to source codes has a broader social significance precisely because software is a cultural product, not a material product like a VCR or a typewriter, but a means of expression and communication. This is what makes the proprietary model in the case of software contentious and a site of struggle. FreeDevelopers.net, for example, states that

> Our enemy is the proprietary software companies and the managers at the top of those companies. These are the people that disproportionately benefit from perpetuating the system of proprietary developer servitude, which results from hiding the code ... This cabal will fight us furiously and to the end.[2]

However, not everyone in the software development community sees the issue in such antagonistic terms. The movement to open up access to source codes has two wings to it. The Open Source movement represents the more pragmatic wing. Open Source stresses the commercial benefits of sharing the source code. By using the co-operative and distributive power of the Internet, a software program can be tested and cleansed of bugs by the millions of worldwide users far more thoroughly than it can if it is locked away within a company's laboratory. So there is plenty of scope to argue that Open Source is a more rational and efficient means by which to develop software. It is still then perfectly possible for corporations to sell some software that is Open Source but subjected to other restrictions that do not threaten their revenue streams. For example, companies can place restrictions on copying and distributing the code, or modifying it. Or a company can restrict access to the source code to within the company, say to its support service team, thus making its support services more effective in dealing with technical difficulties, but not disseminating the source code to the public users. Open Source thus becomes a marketing and PR tool obscuring the many ways in which the freedom to do what you want with the source code is being controlled.

A more radical approach to the question of source code is adopted by the Free Software Foundation (FSF) set up by Richard Stallman. Stallman has devised a 'copyleft' system, the General Public License (GPL), which guarantees that the source code is kept genuinely free.

The GPL has four components: the freedom to run a program for any purpose; to study how a program works and adapt it to your needs; to redistribute copies; and to modify programs and release them to the public.[3] Generally such activities are 'free' in a financial sense as well, although the FSF does not insist on this. Developers can charge for software they have designed, but under the copyleft system such software will naturally spread around (since it can be copied and redistributed by other purchasers) to users who do not want or cannot afford to pay. Whereas the Open Source model seeks to make capitalism more efficient, the FSF has followed the logic of the argument further: the aim of the FSF is to abolish the proprietary model when it comes to software. As Richard Stallman has argued,

> If ... [people] don't write software, they probably cook. If they cook they probably share recipes. And they probably change recipes. It's natural to share something with other people. But those who want to profit by controlling everyone's activities try to stop us from sharing with each other – because if we can't help each other, we're helpless. We're dependent on them.[4]

But ambiguities persist in the Free Software Movement where many developers, such as at FreeDevelopers.net, see themselves as anti-corporate, not anti-capitalist and certainly not socialist. But this position can only be sustained by refusing to follow the logic of the argument through and by arbitrarily limiting the debate about 'worker control', participation and general social collaboration to software and its developers.

The specificities of cultural practice: film and music

We have seen that under capitalism labour exists to produce surplus value. This is true of *all* labour, irrespective of its type or the human needs it serves. There is then a generality about capital and its relations to labour which any critical theory aspiring to adequately know the world has to match. But this generality, the remorseless generality with which capitalism applies its logic to all and sundry, is also part of the problem which theory/thought has to avoid. If everything under capitalism becomes a commodity, something to be bought and sold, this generalised commodification is only a necessary but not sufficient basis of understanding the different and concrete forms which cultural labour takes under commodity production (Garnham 1990:29). For the generality of capitalism's logic should not blind us to the concrete and particular ways capital and different kinds of labour get articulated together. It is for this reason that we have begun exploring the contradictory position of cultural workers generally. As labour they exist to produce surplus value or are a crucial component in ensuring the production of surplus value by their co-ordination of the circuits of capital. But their very assets require some autonomy, dialogue and temporal duration not easily harnessed to capital's usual mechanisms of top-down control, while the inextricable connection between their use-value to capital and their individual minds and bodies places certain barriers in the way of making them *as* interchangeable and controllable as more routine and material kinds of labour power. The political hip hop punk/rock group Rage Against The Machine cannot simply be replaced by their record label with a more politically docile personnel and product, since the personnel and the product are inextricably connected. Similarly, when the creative personnel of *Cold Feet*, ITV's successful late 1990s drama about middle-class angst, decided that they did not want to make a fifth series for fear that their labour would become stale and standardised, ITV, who were desperate to exploit this cultural product further, could not simply draft in new writers, actors and so forth and recreate the series because it was the labour power and performance power of the cultural workers making the series which made it what it was and gave it its distinctive identity.[5]

Nevertheless, this difference in creative/intellectual labour has not been all bad news for capital. It has meant the expansion of a class fraction that has differentiated itself from the working class and has happily exchanged a privileged position in return for acquiescence to the broad agenda and goals set by capital. Although in a contradictory class position, the intellectuals have only sporadically occupied *oppositional* positions. For just because cultural labour has some inherent resistances towards its own rationalisation and disempowerment that does not mean that capital has not tried (and very successfully in many ways) to work its usual logic. The industrialisation of culture that saw the separation of conception and execution from the majority of the workforce (Braverman 1974) and the concentration of conception into the hands of a controlling managerial elite was very effectively implemented in the Hollywood film studios. The shooting script functioned as blueprint for the film and a means by which producers could keep daily control over the production process, measuring the rushes against the plan (Bordwell,

Staiger and Thompson 1988:135–7). This division of labour and hierarchical control, coupled with standardised production procedures led Adorno and Horkheimer to argue that the culture industry destroys all authentic individuality, leaving only a pseudo-individuality, 'mass produced like Yale locks, whose only difference can be measured in fractions of millimeters' (1977:374). This strikes a chord today when we look at boy and girl bands manufactured and co-ordinated from above. Indeed this manufacturing process itself became a television programme in the case of *Popstars* (ITV 2001) where performers auditioned for the group that was to eventually roll off the production line as (the inevitably short-lived) Hear'Say.

From a macro point of view, the constraining social, organisational and economic determinants can look all-powerful, yet these power relations still have to be negotiated at a more micro day-to-day level, which reintroduces the question of human agency (Negus 1997:69). As Vincent Porter notes, a director's choice of camera angle or the particular nuance elicited from a performer could alter the meanings of the film in subtle but significant ways (1983:181). Hesmondhalgh also stresses the 'unusual degree of autonomy' which creative cultural workers enjoy (2002:55). Yet 'autonomy' is difficult to measure, especially given the human propensity to internalise the institutional norms and expectations which structure our actions. Bourdieu calls this process the development of a habitus, which he defines as 'necessity internalized and converted into a disposition that generates meaningful practices and meaning-giving perceptions' (1996:170). The story of Hollywood is littered with directors who have tried to squeeze a little more than a nuance of difference out of a film and push the boundaries of institutionalised norms and have found themselves rewarded with redundancy for their efforts.

In 1957 Universal Studios took over the editing of Orson Welles' last Hollywood film, *Touch of Evil* (Orson Welles 1958 US). As film editor Walter Murch observed, Welles' film

> Committed perhaps the worst sin in the Hollywood book; it was a decade or so ahead of its time. Somehow, the executives had been expecting a conventional B picture, and they were upset and confused by the film's innovative editing and camera work, its use of real locations, its unorthodox use of sound and, thematically, the boldness of its reversals of stereotypes and routine acceptance of human degradation.[6]

Welles subsequently wrote a 58-page memo detailing the differences between his vision for the film and the final studio cut product. As Murch makes clear, the studio's final cut sought to reintegrate the formal and thematic differences which Welles had crafted, back into a more standardised product.

Experiences such as Welles' are not confined to the particular organisational forms of the classical studio era however. More recently, Richard Stanley, the British writer and director of cult horror films, suddenly experienced the powerlessness of wage labour when he was sacked from making the US film *The Island of Dr Moreau* (it was eventually directed by John Frankenheimer and released in 1996). This sort of thing is not supposed to happen according to Information Society guru Robert Reich: 'The idea merchants ... exert at least as much authority, and have as much control over the final product, as do the executives back at headquarters' (1991:102). Stanley had written the script which had attracted Marlon Brando and Val Kilmer. New Line were the film's financiers. However, when Stanley fell out with Kilmer, widely reported on this and other film sets to be an ego out of control, it was Stanley who was sacrificed. The dynamics of power between different cultural workers and capital and the very cynical process by which challenging ideas can be remodelled into something bland and uncontentious are nicely described by Stanley to the writer David Hughes:

But surely it was Stanley – or his script – that had first attracted somebody of Kilmer's calibre? 'It doesn't matter. The script is just a lure. They don't actually want or need a script to shoot the movie – they need it to draw the talent. Once the talent's on board, the script gets thrown over your shoulder and it's time to do something completely different ... In my script, Prendick was a sort of civil rights lawyer working for the UN, who has just come from trying to negotiate a peace settlement in somewhere like Bougainville in the South Pacific, when a limited nuclear exchange breaks out in the rest of the world.' This premise, not part of the original novel, was the cornerstone of Stanley's update. 'The beast people became the cradle of civilisation, and were potentially what was going to come next in the evolution of the species. Moreau was diligently working on a replacement species for Man.' In Stanley's draft, Prendick takes on the role of law-giver when Moreau dies, and has to sort things out for the beast people. 'It was going to turn into a kind of piss-take on Yugoslavia or Somalia, where the man from the UN did extremely badly and succeeded in messing things up even worse for the people he was trying to protect. That is all completely gone ... It's now the slave bunch liberated by the outsider, who leads the rebellion – the same old pro-democracy liberal American message which creeps into everything if Americans are given half a chance.'[7]

As I write this in early October 2001, American and British forces are bombing Afghanistan; *their* Doctor Moreau this time is not Saddam Hussein as in the Gulf War (1991) or Slobodan Milosevic (as in Kosovo), but Osama bin Laden. Public support for their action (such as it is) depends fundamentally on Western politicians and institutions being able to say that there is a qualitative moral difference between their actions and those of their foes. And this in turn requires suppressing the similarities, alliances and complicities between them and their foes just as the continuities between Moreau and Prendick were suppressed in Stanley's script. In this context then, we can perhaps see that Stanley's experiences are part of a continuum of cultural struggles which have enormous implications for public debate (or lack of it) and for the diversity (or narrowness) and sceptical (or credulous) quality of the cultural imagination.

The industrial nature of film and television production has allowed capital to monopolise it in ways which are quite distinct and it has also cemented a division of labour in which working-class access to these arms of cultural production has been, relatively speaking, largely restricted to the technical and manual components of the labour process. The middle class meanwhile have dominated the creative side and provided the key mediating agency in the cultural process as well the political unconscious irradiating through the finished cultural product (even if in dialogue with capital and labour). This domination of capital and the intelligentsia is relative and distinct when compared to the music industry. There did exist, for example, in American cinema a small black independent cinema during the decades of the Hollywood studio system, but it was incomparably marginalised in its cultural influence compared with black music. It was not until briefly in the 1970s, around 'blaxploitation' films, and in a more sustained and more authentically black manner in the late 1980s that black talent on-screen, and in creative positions behind it, really broke through.

It is because of the specific qualities of music, its production and consumption that it could act as a conduit for black talent and creativity in a way which the film industry has only very recently begun to aspire to, if not match. In an ocular culture, black film-making was bound to remain specifically tied to black representation, black 'issues' and black audiences. But part of the impact of black music, both on other cultural producers and audiences, has been its ability to cross the racial divisions of America. The mode of consumption in public places, bars and cafes, mixes music with other activities, giving it a social reach that outstrips the more dedicated activity of film consumption. Furthermore, while film (until the advent of video) could only be consumed in the public spaces of the theatre, the domestic consumption of music meant that one actually bought the product, on vinyl and then tape, rather than just the experience of the product (as with film) in specialised venues. This vastly expanded the retail outlets and distribution possibilities of music, making it much harder to establish white-owned monopoly positions within the industry. Domestic consumption also meant that music was interwoven into everyday life far more powerfully than film. Dr Dre, hardcore hip hop artist and formerly of the band Niggaz With Attitude, remembers how he would 'put on a record at my mother's card parties, and people would scream out or get up and dance. I just loved stirring people up.'[8] Music has thus been integral to American black working-class life in a way that film has not. In addition, the same piece of music tends to be consumed multiple times, while a film, more narrative-based and less amenable to being combined with other activities simultaneously, tends to be subjected to far fewer reiterated acts of consumption by the same person. These cultural skills and knowledges then could be acquired outside formal education, and, what is more, the relative cheapness of musical cultural production (when compared to the capital intensive nature of the film industry) has opened the medium up to black talent and particularly black working-class talent.

Hip hop has been one manifestation of this, with varying cultural politics, from the social realism of Grandmaster Flash in the early 1980s, to the black nationalism of East Coast rappers such as Public Enemy, to the controversies around so-called 'hardcore' hip hop, or gangsta rap, such as the music of the West Coast band Niggaz With Attitude whose 1988 debut album, *Straight Outta Compton*, featured songs like 'Fuck tha police', and went double platinum (2 million sales).[9] Even less likely to appear in a Hollywood film are the sort of sentiments articulated by Marxist hip hop band The Coup. On the album *Party Music* (2001), singer Boots Riley tells his baby daughter something of the power structures of the world she is growing up in:

> The World ain't no fairy tale
> And it's run by some rich white scary males
> To make it simple for you
> Let's call them the bosses
> They take your money while
> The people take the losses
> Sold black folks from Africa to work for free
> And we still barely get paid enough to eat.
>
> (© The Coup/75ARK, 2001)

Black cultural production in music (although unfortunately not its Marxian strand) did contribute in the early 1990s to a small expansion of black films, such as *New Jack City* (Mario Van Peebles 1991 US), *Straight Out of Brooklyn* (Matty Rich 1991 US), and *Boyz N the Hood* (John Singleton 1991 US) although these films are by no means unproblematic (McCarthy 2000). But for all the reasons listed above, black musicians have been able to turn themselves into producers, highly successful petit bourgeois businessmen (they usually are men) with their own record labels. In one stroke this helps to secure their own positions, making them less dependent on corporate support, while also crucially helping to *reproduce* the next wave and generation of black music by opening up access to new talent. Yet if hip hop has been the product of the ghetto, and hip hop artists have been 'organic intellectuals' (Gramsci's term for knowledge workers who emerge out of and retain a direct link to the social and productive life of a class), success catapults black musicians out of the class and culture which informs their music, turning them in a way into 'traditional intellectuals' (Gramsci's term for intellectuals who over time, through the division of labour or the ascendance of new class forces, lose touch with the ongoing dynamics of social and economic life). This trajectory produces class specific tensions and ambivalences in their work and their relations to their public. The trajectory of success raises fundamental questions for the musicians involved. Some, like the members of The Coup, choose in various ways to resist class assimilation, others, like Sean 'Puff Daddy' Combs, now found hobnobbing with the white social elite,[10] welcome their social trajectory more uncritically.

THE ABSTRACTION OF LABOUR

I want to end this chapter by turning to a more 'philosophical' discourse in order to understand what it is about human labour that makes it so central to us as human beings. And I also want to examine what happens to this central human activity under capitalism. This will in turn help us understand the special quality and role of cultural labour and the particular problems posed for capital to set cultural labour in motion profitably. The crucial concept here is that of *abstraction*. The ordinary, dictionary definition of the word abstract refers to *thought* which has lost contact with material objects and examples; thought which is not concrete, thought which lacks detail and attention to particulars, to light and shade, to variety. However, for Marx, under capitalism, it is *material reality itself* which exhibits the most powerful abstraction. It is material reality that has lost contact with the concrete and the particular.

The concrete and the particular that concerns Marx are about labour. For Marx, labour is not just an activity; it is an essential part of what it is to be human (what Marx calls our species-being). Labour is production without which there would be no human progress, no human societies, and no culture. Through labour, human beings transform the natural and social world around them, thus, simultaneously, transforming themselves. It is in the 'Nature-imposed condition of human existence' (Marx 1983:179) to be part of nature while at the same time transforming it and opening up the vistas of human history. This is why, as Marx notes, although the 'bee puts to shame many an architect in the construction of her cells ... what distinguishes the worst architect from the best of bees is this, that the architect raises his structure in imagination before he erects it in reality' (1983:174). Thus humanity escapes the cycle of nature and blind instinct. In labour, human beings make choices and decisions; human labour is of its essence practical creativity. In escaping the blind dictates of nature, even as it continues to depend on nature for the resources of life and living, human labour demonstrates the conscious control and transformation of our world. Thus, 'the exercise of labour power, labour, is the worker's own life-activity, the manifestation of his life' (Marx 1973:49). Yet, under capitalism, labour yields control to capital (selling its labour power), to the personifications of capital. The practical effect of this is that the worker's own 'life-activity' is put at the disposal of others who arrange it and control it in ways that maximise profitability. Life for the worker now begins outside their 'life-activity', consuming the products and services of other workers engaged in similarly life-denying activities.

For Marx it is the material process of labour that has become abstract. The activity of labour has lost touch with the concrete particularity of labour. For capital, labour power is a source of appropriated surplus value which, via the circulation of capital as commodities and money, will be turned into profit. Everything about the labour process and the products it produces must be subordinated to this aim. What is abstract then is the very real dominance of the profit motive. The profit motive is rather like the monster in *The Blob* (Chuck Russell 1988 US), absorbing everything it touches into its own homogeneous structure. Such 'blobification' – the reduction of everything to the same goal – is intimately connected with the domination of money, of financial calculations, of quantitative assessment criteria which overwhelm qualitative ones, and these economic priorities are a manifestation of the social domination of capital and its personifications.

To explore a little more the idea that it is the particularity of labour which is made abstract under capitalism we need to understand Marx's concept of *value*. The substance of value is the capacity of labour power to produce social wealth; value is congealed in the products of human labour. Value is thus a very abstract *concept*. But, it is important to note that it is only a concept. Marx noted that Aristotle had groped towards a concept of value in ancient Greece. Aristotle saw that the value of one commodity could be made *equivalent* in quantitative proportion to another commodity. Thus for example: 5 beds = 1 house (clearly this was before the housing market spiralled out of control). Such a comparison implies some *equality* between them, some *measure* of comparison. But, asks Aristotle, how can 'such unlike things ... be commensurable?' (Marx 1983:65). His answer is that it is merely a convention, 'a makeshift for practical purposes'. Marx's answer is that they are commensurate because they are both products of labour. Aristotle could not, Marx argued, formulate the concept of value because Aristotle lived in a society which required slave labour, which is to say a society where labour was manifestly not commensurate or equal.

To say that what a bed and a house share is that they are both examples of human labour is of course an example of abstract thought. The particularities of making a bed, working with particular materials in particular ways for particular human needs, and making a house, are lost from view. Still, there is no harm necessarily done, it is merely a way of making certain generalisations as to the pervasiveness of human labour stored up in the world we make around us. But what happens when the world around us is actually organised *as if* there really is, in *practice*, no difference between different kinds of labour, their products and the needs and uses they satisfy? What happens is that you get people like Michael Green, Chairman of Carlton Communications. More than two thousand years after Aristotle puzzled over the very *thought* of making 'unlike' things commensurable, Green reveals that he is very happy to abolish the unlikeness of things and make them commensurable *in practice*: 'I think of television as a manufacturing process' he once said. 'What is the difference between a television programme and this lighter?' (Tracey 1998:12). As Marx argued, under capitalism, 'the abstraction of the category "labour", "labour in general" ... the starting point of modern political economy, becomes realised in practice' (1973: 49). Under capitalism, all the concrete different types of labour that constitute the productive life of society become 'practically abstract labour' (Murray 2000). The substance of value (social wealth derived from labour) is made abstract. Labour is materialised into products (a general condition of human labour throughout history) but materialised according to an abstract and systemic logic of profit accumulation (a logic specific to capitalism). This does not, however, produce an 'equality of exploitation' for reasons that I will spell out at the conclusion of this chapter.

For Marx then, socialism involves the emancipation of labour from the abstract tyranny of capital. For Marx material production would have to be quantitatively transformed (massively shortening the working day) and qualitatively transformed, which is to say that there is great scope for making material production a far greater realm of participation and satisfaction than it currently is. But still, material production would remain tied to the realm of necessity insofar as the requirements to sustain life according to a historically acceptable level remained. Thus Marx associated genuinely free labour with cultural play and production. It is here, once material needs have been satisfied, that the greatest scope for realising what Marx called the 'development of human potentiality for its own sake' resides (1980:166).

This chapter has set two models of class in contention with one another and criticised the sociological model from a Marxist perspective. Mainstream sociology's repression of the capitalist class and the dynamics of accumulation is profoundly problematic, but I have also allowed that the sociological attention to the differential distribution of assets raises certain questions for the Marxist model of class. In particular I drew attention to the question of the middle class (and their 'knowledge assets'), or, as I have preferred to call them, following Gramsci, the intelligentsia. We have seen that their position in the class structure is contradictory, buffeted by and trying to differentiate themselves from capital on the one side and labour on the other. They play a central role in co-ordinating production, in developing new techniques of production and applications, and in generating values, beliefs, knowledge and public discourses and representations of the world we live in. We have seen that within media production the question of autonomy for the intelligentsia versus the question of controlling and rationalising the intelligentsia for capital is a crucial dynamic.

The accumulation logic of capital can be grasped by its abstract indifference to the particularity of human labour (and human needs). One of the key implications of making labour abstract, commensurate and equivalent is that individual members of the labour force become equivalent and interchangeable, thus weakening their bargaining power *vis-à-vis* capital and making them easily replaceable. The interchangeability of labourers is a key feature of abstraction. But insofar as the cultural worker is not easily or as easily interchangeable with other cultural workers, this sets up certain problems for capital's command and control structure over creative labour.

The abstract quality of capitalism's accumulation logic does not produce an equality of exploitation, that is all labour being exploited to an equal degree and in equal ways. This is for three reasons. First, the endless search for competitive advantage means that capitalism seizes on any social or natural differentials that can be built on to increase profit margins. Second, the resistance to capital's imperatives are uneven. Third, despite capital's abstract indifference to the materiality of human life, in practice it *has to* respond to and work through the differentials which the particularities of material practices produce. This can work to its advantage when, for example, the differential qualities of knowledge workers allow them to suppress their identities as wage-labourers. But it also opens up differential prospects and spaces for resistance to the logic of capital. So, for example, we have seen that the distinct materiality of the cultural practices of film and music offers different possibilities and limitations for black and working-class cultural producers. The proposal that capitalism is a practical abstraction of the real concrete materiality of social practices is an important theme in this book. If by abstraction we mean a systematic indifference to the details and particularities of material life, than capitalism is a kind of dematerialising materialism, an idea that we will return to especially in Chapter 7, on commodity fetishism. But, throughout this book, this dematerialising or abstract materialism behoves a critical theory like Marxism to walk a tightrope, constantly seeking to grasp the sheer *generality* of capital's accumulation/competition dynamic while remaining attentive to the concrete materiality of practices where difference and resistance are to be found.

2 Mode of Production: Technology and New Media

> Historical systems ... are just that – historical. They come into existence and eventually go out of existence, the consequence of internal processes in which the exacerbation of the internal contradictions leads to a structural crisis. Structural crises are massive, not momentary. They take time to play themselves out. Historical capitalism entered into its structural crisis in the early twentieth century and will probably see its demise as a historical system sometime in the next century.
>
> Wallerstein, *Historical Capitalism*

> [C]apital ... is an essential relationship for the development of the productive forces of society. It only ceases to be so when the development of these productive forces themselves meets a barrier in capital itself.
>
> Marx, *Grundrisse*

> If a record company has spent millions to develop and control the works of musicians, banking on their value as consumer goods ... company officials might be shocked to discover what they hope to sell and control has become pure information, flowing freely around the globe.
>
> Alderman, *Sonic Boom*

In this chapter I want to explore the Marxian concept of mode of production, both illustrating it through examples of the new media economy, culture and technology and *vice versa*, offering the concept of mode of production as an explanatory tool in understanding the new media. As a category, the mode of production is composed of two concepts that amount to the *master couplet* of Marxian theory. These two concepts are: forces of production and relations of production. Together these two concepts compose the mode of production. We are already familiar with some aspects of the relations of production from Chapter 1. We have seen that under capital the key social relations are forged around an antagonistic axis of labour and capital, with the intelligentsia, that crucial group involved in the production and dissemination of ideas, occupying a contradictory position between capital and labour and the subsidiary petit bourgeoisie. In this chapter, we will explore how these social relations interact and come into contradiction with the forces of production. Productive forces include machinery (fixed capital), human labour power, knowledge and skills articulated to industry and even the energies of nature as they are tapped by human labour. Productive forces are always configured within social (and cultural) relations and in turning this master couplet to analytical use, we shall see how important it is to stress the contradictory ways in which forces and relations relate to each other. The struggle between classes in effect is a fight carried out over the uses to which the forces of production are put. Here our focus is on the struggles around the communicative forces of production, themselves an important subset of the productive forces generally. The central communicative productive force that concerns us in this chapter is new digital media technology.

The dot.com crash of 2000–01 had the merit of exploding the theory, widely touted within business circles, that information technology now provided capitalism with a new economic paradigm: namely that it was no longer subject to the economic cycle. Such technotopias are merely the most evident example of a widespread technological determinism that penetrates well beyond the gurus and ideologists of the business world and into social and cultural theory as well. By new media I mean digital microprocessed information, that is data that has been turned into 'bits', electronic bursts generated by switches (the 1s and 0s of computer language). The prime carrier of the digital media is the Internet, which links computers, and the World Wide Web, the software that enables easy navigation (through hyperlinks) and interface from one part of the Net to another. All the debates around the new media essentially turn on the extent to which this technology integrates into, alters and/or comes into friction with the social relations of capital.

The juxtaposition of an 'old' time-worn concept such as mode of production with the cutting-edge developments within media technology is therefore deliberate and strategic. It is my contention that the mode of production is a far richer conceptual ensemble than either critics of Marxism or sometimes Marxists themselves have allowed and that it has considerable explanatory potential when translated into the sphere of culture and communication. To explore the contradictory relations between new media technology and capital I will draw on Marx's discussion of automated machinery (fixed capital) in the *Grundrisse* ('Outlines'). We will also need to combat all forms of technological determinism, a species of which exists within the Marxian tradition as well as outside it. In order to link new media technology with the fundamental dynamics of capitalism, I will make use of the potential within Manuel Castells' concept, *mode of development*, by anchoring it (in a way that Castells does not) within the mode of production. The argument throughout will be focussed on the Internet and will conclude with a case study of Napster, the music file-swapping web site that fell foul of the copyright laws and the music industry's attack-dog trade association, the Recording Industry Association of America (RIAA).

TECHNOLOGICAL DETERMINISM AND THE NEW MEDIA CRASH

The concept of the mode of production, if properly conceived, can be used as a critical weapon against the rampant discourses of technological determinism that accelerated capital-driven change is generating. Technological determinism can be hard to spot however. It comes not only from the political right, but from the left as well and it can be optimistic or pessimistic. The common feature of technological determinism is that it levers technology, its development, implementation and effects out of the social relations in which they are embedded, thus a) marginalising or removing the social relations from analysis, and b) ascribing powers and characteristics to technology which are the result of social relations between people, rather than properties intrinsic to things.

The 1990s saw an example of technological determinism feeding into the economics of the new media and telecommunications sector. In this decade there was an explosion of corporate activity, interest and investment in telecommunications and the Internet. The new media appeared to be driving a cornucopia of opportunities in new technologies, transforming business structures and their relations to their customers, while boosting productivity and innovation. City analysts, boardroom executives, senior politicians and academic apologists for capital, started to excitedly talk about a 'new paradigm' in which technology escaped the hitherto iron law of capitalism: its propensity for cyclical development, where economic expansion is at some point followed by economic contraction. There was much talk of the so-called 'weightless economy', meaning e-commerce, and, later, m-commerce (mobile phones), liberating itself from the slow, lumbering world of traditional manufacturing and its periodic contractions.

In *The Economic and Philosophical Manuscripts*, Marx writes of how bourgeois economic analysis cannot grasp the tendencies of capitalist development as arising from its inner dynamics and structural pre-dispositions, preferring instead to conceive its development as down to 'external and apparently accidental circumstances' (1972:106). There was nothing accidental or contingent in the rise and stock market fall of the new media. It is one of the juiciest ironies – mitigated only by the fact that the people who really paid when the inevitable bust came were the workers – that the techno-bubble and technobabble of the new paradigm rendezvoused with a disavowed reality at the start of the twenty-first century. This confirmed that the *fundamental* dynamics of capital remained remarkably similar to its earlier eighteenth, nineteenth and twentieth-century incarna-tions. The crash was not restricted to the fledgling dot.com companies, whose emergence had had a wide if shallow impact on popular culture. Semiconductors (microchips) glutted the market and manufacturing contracted. There was also the humbling of giant telecommunications corporations in Europe such as British Telecom, France Télécom and Deutsche Telekom, while mobile phone companies like Vodaphone saw their profits slump. Marconi, meanwhile, was more than humbled; having only recently converted itself from an arms manufacturer to an IT company, Marconi saw its share price slide precipitously from £12 a share to an embarrassing 29 pence by late 2001.[1]

Even while the ideologists of capital were formulating their theories of the new paradigm, the telecommunication corporations were entering the market in *exactly* the manner in which capitalism always lays the basis for future sorrows. Marx dryly observed how capitalism is subject to a periodic 'epidemic that, in all earlier epochs, would have seemed an absurdity – the epidemic of overproduction' (1985:86). Overproduction is the classic feature of the boom/bust cycle, as each company pours investment and resources into a sector in anticipation of capturing a segment of the market for the medium term and making profits in the shorter term. 'It was as if 20 players each thought they would grab a 30 per cent market share' one com-mentator ruefully remarked.[2] '*The financial crisis*', Michael Aglietta observes of the capitalist boom/bust cycle, '*begins with a business euphoria*' (1979:358, original emphasis). Thus accumulated surplus capital rushed to capture a commanding position within the new technology markets and, as is characteristic of a feverish speculative period, rushed to turn liquid capital into fixed capital (Harvey 1984:303–4).

It soon became clear, however, that the scale of the investments was running ahead of the capacity of the innovative technologies to effectively deliver the new services. In particular, broadband Internet services, which were to carry the vast information traffic at speed, encountered a series of false starts. The dot.com crash replayed a feature typical of many, although not all, crashes. As the turnover time of capital, the time between investment and returns, extends, so the average rate of profit which investment capital expects from the venture starts to look vulnerable and investors begin to nervously wonder whether their capital would be making more profits elsewhere.

Most devastatingly of all, the technotopia prophesised by industry gurus and the investments that had been made on the basis of their profit predictions were simply way in advance of consumer demand. The regulation of the relationship between production and consumption has been the foundation of capitalism since the early decades of the twentieth century (Aglietta 1979:158–61). With consumer tastes fragmenting and rapidly changing in recent years, new information technologies within the production process were hailed as a means of recalibrating the relations between production and consumption. Yet the industry's view of consumer demand is that it is infinitely expandable, manipulable and changeable. The division between production and consumption and the competitive pressures driving capital mean that the technotopians are often unable to engage with 'real user perspectives' (Dijk 1999:75). The already established media are embedded in the everyday culture, habits, routines and emotional attachments that cannot be erased simply by the needs and profit targets of capital. All those prophecies and anxieties for example about the death of the book, or the convergence of television and the PC, merely took what was technologically possible and mistook it for what was culturally desired. The technotopia of capital works by reducing everything to a homogeneous, smooth, interchangeable space and not engaging with the cultural and contextual meanings and embedded social relations which the media operate in. Debord claims that 'alienated consumption becomes for the masses a duty supplementary to alienated production' (1983:42). However, in the first wave of the new media, the corporate exhortations went sufficiently unheard: the online customer base did not materialise in line with predictions, the mobile phone market was saturated and consumers were unwilling to move so quickly onto the Third Generation Internet access replacements the industry had already lined up.

This resistance it is true also has non-cultural dimensions. There is also an economic component to consumer resistance to the infinite expansion of needs. As workers, consumers have their wages squeezed by capital looking to extract maximum profit from their labour, but while this is rational from the point of view of the individual unit of capital, it means, for capital as a whole, workers as consumers have limited disposable income. This means that every now and again productive investment of accumulated surplus capital will outstrip demand that cannot absorb all the consumer goods that the workers themselves are producing for capital. This contraction of demand for consumer goods (what Marx called Department II of the economy) in turn impacts on demand for the means of production goods between different units of capital in the production process (what Marx called Department I).

Finally, it is worth noting that none of these four contradictions arise directly from the axis of antagonism between capital and labour. The first three contradictions (surplus capital, inter-capitalist competition, overextended turnover time) are all internal to the operations of capital, while the fourth contradiction emerges between capital and consumption. Yet, at the same time, the division between capital and labour, the removal from the direct producers of ownership and control over the means of production, the logic of accumulation for the sake of accumulation, generate a structure or mode of production from which these contradictions necessarily arise and, as we have seen, converged around the new media industry in 2000–01.

The story of the rise and dramatic fall of the communications industry in this period starkly reveals the problems of a technological discourse – one not without important exacerbating effects on the economic cycle – conceiving technology outside or above or transcending fundamental social (and cultural) relations of production and consumption. It was not inevitable or preordained that *this* dot.com/new media explosion would lead to a crash. There was, and is, only the systemic, structural and reiterated predilection within the capital system that makes crashes inevitable – but when and where, under what precise configuration of circumstances, cannot be predicted. None of this is to underestimate the transformations which communications and new media will probably make in the long term, but it is to underline that whatever impact they have will take place *within* some of the fundamental dynamics of capital, rather than reworking those dynamics in radically new ways.

MODES OF PRODUCTION AND DEVELOPMENT

If then, at an economic level, the new technology paradigm failed to transcend the capitalist economic cycle, what are the implications of new technology at a broader social and cultural level? New technology is undoubtedly new and it will not do simply to deflate the boosters' exaggerated pretensions. How can we assess the continuities and differences *within* a mode of production that is oriented towards the perpetual transformation of technological forces and social relations, as capitalism is? A useful concept here might be Manuel Castells' notion of a mode of development. If we can get the category mode of development to 'sit inside' the category mode of production, it might provide us with another tool for refining our sense of the impact of new media technology. A mode of development is characterised by particular 'technical relations of production' (Castells 1996:16) which give production its concrete qualities and imply (which is not to say that they cause in any unilinear manner) certain social and cultural relations. Castells' distinction between two modes of development, industrialism and informationalism, fits into debates concerning Fordism and post-Fordism which we will explore in more detail in the following chapter. For now it is enough to note that under informationalism productivity 'lies in the technology of knowledge generation, information processing, and symbolic communication' (Castells 1996:17). Castells is aware that knowledge has always been an important element in the production process, but he argues that with informationalism it is 'the action of knowledge upon knowledge itself' (1996:17) which becomes central to productivity. Thus it could be argued that under industrialism knowledge was instrumentally applied to the production of goods, while under informationalism the production of goods is increasingly mediated by 'the action of knowledge upon knowledge itself'. We might clarify this by arguing that informationalism develops a general culturalisation of the production process, where the forces of communication become absolutely pivotal to the development of the productive forces generally. Hence, for example, a new business management discourse concerning the knowledge resources of the company and the importance of communication within it as vital for retaining competitive edge by making efficiency gains, refining products and responding to rapidly shifting market trends (Thrift 1999). Castells does not associate informationalism with the emergence of a service sector at the expense of manufacturing. It is not so much a question of what people are making but how they are making it. Nevertheless, we might also note that the increasing importance of culture, communication, the exchange of ideas, feedback systems, data analysis and so forth, in the production process, is also inevitably linked with the increasing amount of capital being directed into cultural production as consumer goods, particularly digital media.

However, the difficulty with Castells' own deployment of the concept, mode of development and his term 'informationalism' is that he does not sufficiently and consistently ground it in the capitalist mode of production. Thus at times his mode of development sounds suspiciously like a new mode of production which has transcended the antagonistic contradictions of capitalism.

> Industrialism is orientated toward economic growth, that is toward maximising output, informationalism is orientated towards technological development, that is toward higher levels of complexity in information processing ... it is the pursuit of knowledge and information that characterises the technological function under informationalism. (Castells 1996:17)

Note how industrialism is associated with accumulation for the sake of accumulation ('economic growth' and 'maximising output') and therefore the structural tendency towards over accumulation, while informationalism is associated with an ever richer complexity of information generation, as if that information processing exists outside the imperatives of accumulation. Echoes of the 'new paradigm' thesis are evident in Castells' claim that the application of information processing to the technology of information produces, 'a virtuous circle [that] should lead to greater productivity and efficiency, given the right conditions of equally dramatic organisational and institutional change' (1996:67). 'Organisational' and 'institutional' change suggests alterations in company (and regulatory) structures rather than broader and more radical social transformations. It implies that technology, as a component of the forces of production, need no longer be in contradiction with the social relations of production and may indeed resolve their propensity to crisis. Crisis is here reduced to a technical problem of information management rather than social antagonisms.

If we want to retain the essential contradiction between the forces and relations of production, we will need to anchor the concept of the mode of development much more firmly within the mode of production. We will need to see informationalism as reconfiguring and in some respects exacerbating contradictions within the mode of production. What I would like to do here then is draw on aspects of Marx's discussion in the *Grundrisse* of fixed capital, its development into automatic machinery and its relations with necessary labour time, to think through the *cultural* contradictions which information technology and digital media are raising to new levels.

Machinery as an instrument of labour that works to produce surplus value is of course a particular mode of existence of capital; it is capital objectified into physical and 'intellectual organs' (Marx 1973:154). Once integrated into the capitalist production process, fixed capital undergoes a series of 'metamorphoses' culminating in 'an automatic system of machinery' (Marx 1973:154). Marx, as usual, reads this particular development of automatic machinery dialectically (that is as a two-sided contradictory process). It is both a further enslavement of the labourer while also providing the material conditions for labour's emancipation. On the downside, Marx contrasts the development of automatic machinery with the worker's relationship with the tool. The latter required some independent initiative from the worker and some specialised, monopolisable skills (Harvey 1984:109). With machinery, the workers' skills are sucked out of them and transferred to the machine which instead becomes the 'virtuoso', while the worker is reduced 'to a mere abstraction', an attendant to machinery whose activities regulate and determine the worker on all sides (Marx 1973:155). However, Marx also spies progress on the underside of these new conditions of alienation.

> [A]s ... industry develops, the creation of real wealth depends less on labour time and on the quantity of labour utilized than on the power of mechanical agents which are set in motion during labour time. The powerful effectiveness of these agents, in its turn, bears no relation to the immediate labour time that their production costs. It depends rather on the general state of science and on technological progress, or the application of this science to production. (Marx 1973:164)

The transformation of the instruments of labour into machinery increases productivity thus lowering necessary labour time. But under capitalism this does not lead to a corresponding decrease in the amount of work people are doing but instead it leads to increases in surplus labour time (the time the worker is producing value over and above what they get in the wage packet). Of course, at an economic level, this benefits capital at least in the short term. However, it also opens up a *cultural* crisis as the disproportion between labour expended and wealth or profit generated for capital becomes a gaping chasm. While economic value may be increased by the technological reduction of necessary labour time (see Figure 2.1), the cultural values necessary to legitimise value relations of exchange are eroded. Thus everyone is well aware that music CDs cost a few pence to make, but that they sell for around £15. The music industry is widely held in contempt, by both musicians and consumers, as a result. Napster's success taps into a latent reservoir of resentment at such profiteering. This discrepancy between the economic value of new technology and its cultural value derives from the way culture has the particular quality of prefiguring and anticipating potentialities within the new economic arrangements which have yet to be realised, as Walter Benjamin argued (1999a:4–5). To give another example connected with our case study, digitalisation abolishes at a stroke vast swathes of the necessary labour involved in reproduction, distribution and retail. The conversion of resources to binary digits is a profound challenge to the whole concept of scarcity on which capitalist political economy depends. Again this also has cultural, not just economic, implications. In his prophetic essay 'The work of art in the age of mechanical reproduction' written in 1935–36, Benjamin argued that the key feature of the new means of communication (photography and film in particular) as productive forces is their reproducibility. This has revolutionary implications for traditional notions of art and for cultural production generally. While the manual reproduction of art was known as a forgery, thus ensuring that 'the original preserved all its authority' (Benjamin 1999b:214), the *technical* means of reproduction calls art, origins and traditional notions of originality into crisis. Reproduction 'detaches the reproduced object from the domain of tradition' (Benjamin 1999b:215), a process that led Benjamin to his famous prognostication: 'that which withers in the age of mechanical reproduction is the aura of the work of art' (1999b:215). Formerly the work of art was cocooned in a socially constructed 'aura' of hierarchy, deference, servility, awe, respect and, within particular traditions, fixed meanings policed by authority and centralised institutional control. Now reproducibility takes the work of art out of exclusive zones of production and consumption, allowing 'the original to meet the beholder halfway, be it in the form of a photograph or a phonograph' (Benjamin 1999b:214). Reproducibility is a product of and helps facilitate the presence of the masses in cultural consumption in a new historically unique manner. This, as we shall see, is central to the threat which Napster posed for the music industry.

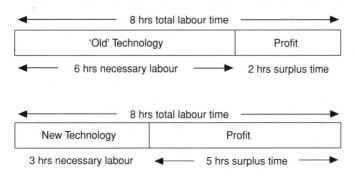

Figure 2.1   Necessary Labour and Cultural Legitamacy

The increased productivity of machinery which leads to the decrease in necessary labour time is also closely connected with the *socialisation of production* – a central site of contradiction between the forces and relations of production. Although the machine has the appearance of being (and really is) 'the property of capital', it also embodies 'the general productive power of society's intelligence' (Marx 1973:156–7). Fixed capital is thus an index of a growing social interdependence and collective contribution to increases in productive powers and hence in turn the extension of social ties. For Marx there is a close connection between the level of the forces of production and the growth or stagnation of sociality. Within the feudal mode of production, the lack of social interaction among peasants outside extremely parochial limits, exacerbated by poor communication, is intricately tied to the low level of the productive forces (Marx 1984:108–9). The revolutionary transformations of the productive forces which capital's social relations develop, in turn extend and thicken our modes of sociality, which come into contradiction with social relations based on the private, competitive and

UNIVERSITY OF WOLVERHAMPTON

Harrison Learning Centre

ITEMS ISSUED:

Customer ID: 7605409578

Title: Marxism and media studies : key concepts
and contemporary trends
ID: 7623113480
Due: 16/04/2010 23:59

Total items: 1
23/03/2010 15:20
Issued: 3
Overdue: 0

Thank you for using Self Service.
Please keep your receipt.

Overdue books are fined at 40p per day for
1 week loans, 10p per day for long loans.

hierarchical ownership of the means of production. New media technology is the perfect medium in which this contradiction gets worked through. The networking logic of the Internet and the World Wide Web are the product of the cumulative development of the forces of production generally and the forces of communication specifically (telephone lines, transistors, mathematics) not an accidental property of a discrete technology. This is so not only at a hardware level, but, also, indeed more so, at the cultural level of the media which are all about communication, the exchange of ideas and co-operation, values which can only be reconciled with capital if that exchange has an exchange value or if it takes place within the parameters of the company, sealed off from potential competitors. The whole development of new media technology and specifically the technology of the Internet cuts against the social relations of capital, as the Open Source movement discussed in the previous chapter testifies. Of course, the connectivity of the Internet is not just an abstract question of technology and social relations, but has been decisively inflected (or mediated) by place, particularly the 1960s libertarianism of West Coast America, where Silicon Valley is based (Castells contrasts the interactive properties of the Internet's forerunner, the ARPANET, with the more hierarchical, ordered French computer system, Minitel (1996:342–57)).

One of the features of fixed capital is that it represents capital 'firmly tied to its existence as a particular use-value' (Marx 1973:157). But of course once it is tied to use-values, there is no guarantee that the actual uses to which the machine is deployed in the service of capitalism will not be contested, will not be inflected in new directions that loosen fixed capital to capital in general, either economically or ideologically, and will not be used to produce new machines that further cut against value relations and the cultural values which sustain value relations (such as copyright). Marx explicitly acknowledges the possibility of a contestation around the use-values of fixed capital:

> If capital only adequately displays its nature as use value within the production process in the form of machinery ... this never means that this use value (machinery by itself) *is* capital, or that machinery can be regarded as synonymous with capital ... it does not follow that its subordination to the social relations of capitalism is the most suitable and final social production relationship for the utilization of machinery. (1973:158)

The productive forces generally as well as fixed capital specifically thus have a latent surplus that goes beyond the intentions behind their initial development or the relations of a particular field of production into which they are embedded. Again the Internet is a classic example. It began life as a US military project designed to decentralise communications networks so that in the event of a nuclear attack there would be no one 'command centre' which could be knocked out. Compare this aim of decentralisation and the dominant social forces initiating this technological infrastructure with the use of the Internet by the Zapatista movement in the south of Mexico. The Zapatistas famously used the Internet to articulate the social demands of the indigenous Indians and stimulate the imagination and solidarity of people around the world. Indeed the Zapatista uprising on New Year's Eve 1994 might never have inspired the recent anti-capitalist movements had it not been for the global-ising communication powers of the Internet that magnified the impact of a small band of insurgents in a remote corner of the world a hundred fold (Downing et al. 2001:217–34).

THE RELATIONS BETWEEN FORCES AND RELATIONS

The contradiction between the forces and relations of production is central to the Marxist critique of capitalism. As we have seen, over-production is one facet of that contradiction. Within the Marxian conception, the forces of production are constantly calling into question the viability and suitability of the social relations of production, not only at an economic level, but also at a social, cultural and ethical level. One crucial facet of the contradiction between the forces and relations of production is the contradiction between the *potential* and the *actual* uses of new technologies (of communication). As Marx noted,

> The productive forces at the disposal of society no longer tend to further the development of the conditions of bourgeois property; on the contrary, they have become too powerful for these conditions, by which they are fettered, and so soon as they overcome these fetters, they bring disorder into the whole of bourgeois society, endanger the existence of bourgeois property. (1985:86)

Now, clearly the Internet and digital communication generally will massively extend the social and cultural range of capitalism, offering new platforms for the sale of commodities, as Schiller has argued (1999), rather than be used to extend participation in cultural resources. It is not quite as straightforward as Marx here suggests. There has been no definitive sense in which the productive forces 'no longer tend to further the development of the conditions of bourgeois property'. Equally clearly, however, the Internet constitutes an economic and political problem for bourgeois property relations and, viewed from this angle, those social relations are, in Marx's key term, *fetters* on the development of the forces of production. Take, for example, how the Internet as a communicative production force potentially outflanks, or at least acts as a counterweight to, the state's management of news in a crisis. It is clear that the media *could* make use of the increased possibilities for the production and dissemination of information by people 'on the ground', in the heart of a crisis, as a means of diversifying their sources and becoming less reliant on the state. Jon Snow, Channel 4's ITN-produced news anchorman, argued that this is precisely what did happen when the foot and mouth disaster struck cattle in the UK in 2001. There is, however, a problem. Snow argued that against the Ministry of Agriculture, Food and Fisheries' (MAFF) 'self interested manipulation of figures', Channel Four had direct access to

> information from the 'field' ... by direct communications from people affected by the consequences of the disease. These are not the propagandist circulars from the Soil Association or other pressure groups, but person to person emails ... The sheer weight of these messages has outstripped any spinning Maff or anyone else could manage. So that 'towney' hacks ... found themselves sucked into an understanding of a rural disaster not seen in our lifetime. There's the hotel owner in Borrowdale; the pig breeder in Wiltshire; the aristocratic sheep owner in the Borders ...[3]

Thus it is that the forces of communicative production, which open up major possibilities and questions for diversifying the gathering of information and the overcoming of the divisions of class and geography, are here resolved very comfortably within the dominant social relations as a means by which such eminently 'respectable' sources as the rural bourgeoisie can put their side of the story. Yet today the Internet is also the site of sources of information and analysis outside the taken-for-granted assumptions which underpin the dominant news organisations. So Schiller's timely historical and empirical account of 'digital capitalism' from a traditional political economy perspective downplays how cultural change, cultural dynamics, cultural contestation and cultural contradictions are driving as well as problematising technological and economic developments. As a result, there is a somewhat functionalist tenor to his argument.

Without some sense then of the productive forces butting up against the social relations of production, the objective conditions for class struggle disappear and, instead, class struggle is replaced with class domination. Kroker, for example, ridicules the pro-technotopias of the media and business class. However, while he acknowledges that 'every technology releases opposing possibilities towards emancipation and domination' (1996:171) the productive forces have no real weight within his discussion of digital technology and thus he quickly succumbs to a nightmarish Orwellian scenario in which the productive forces are seamlessly integrated into class domination: '[V]irtuality without ethics is a primal scene of social suicide: a site of mass cryogenics where bodies are quick-frozen for future re-sequencing by the archived data networks' (1996:169). A similar problem is evident in Brian Winston's model of technological development. Refreshingly sceptical of the hyperbole surrounding the information revolution, Winston insists that, beneath the blizzard of innovation, Western capitalism 'has displayed, despite enormous changes in detail, fundamental continuity' (1998:2). Winston stresses how potentially disruptive technologies are embedded into existing social institutions (1998:11). He calls this 'the "law" of the suppression of radical potential'. He argues that the modern corporation is the 'major factor impacting on a whole range of technological developments' (1998:51). However, by restricting his focus to the development of media technologies and their initial bedding down into established institutions, the subsequent cultural impact, dissemination and potentialities, the productive surplus of such technologies *vis-à-vis* their social relations is underplayed and their integration into the social relations without contradiction assured.

The issue of whether the forces or relations of production have primacy in explaining social change has been a continuing theme in Marxian debates. Rigby asserts, for example, that Marx, at least in some of his work, fell into a 'productive force determinism' whereby the development of the forces of production remodels and develops the social relations in accordance with their productive potential (1998:106). For instance, Marx argues that at a certain stage (but what stage?) in the development of the means of feudal production 'the feudal relations of property became no longer compatible with the already developed productive forces; they became fetters. They had to be burst asunder; they were burst asunder' (1985:85). In fact there is no 'had to' about it. There was nothing inevitable about the rise of capitalism from the 'womb' of feudalism, just as there is nothing inevitable about capitalism 'giving birth' to communism. Clearly, though, Marxists can comfort themselves with this sort of narrative: capitalism has developed the forces of production; the social relations of production are demonstrably fetters on their further development, at least in the interests of the majority, so those social relations must be burst asunder.

As Rigby notes, however, the forces of production do not have some immanent tendency to develop in a unilinear manner throughout history. Instead, the forces of production have stagnated for long periods of history and have regressed in others as well as developed. China had the technological wherewithal to 'go capitalist' by the late Middle Ages, but failed to and so was condemned to near stagnation for 400 years in which time the West massively outstripped it in the development of productive forces. How can this be explained if there is an immanent tendency for the forces of production to develop? (Rigby 1998:123). It can in fact only be explained by reintroducing the social relations of production (and therefore the question of human agency) as the primary determinant in accounting for why and how the forces of production develop (or not) in particular directions at particular times and in particular places. It is precisely the class struggle at the heart of the social relations of production which productive force determinism marginalises in favour of some abstract transhistorical ontology of human desire for 'progress'. Cohen, for example, argues that because intelligent and rational human beings want to reduce scarcity, they tend to select productive relations best suited to developing productive forces (1978:150–60). This assumes that reducing scarcity is a socialised and institutionalised aim and that human agents are free to 'select' the appropriate relations required to further develop the forces of production. Yet the crushing of Napster to protect copyright hardly suggests the free selection of relations of production best suited to diminishing scarcity.

Rigby offers a devastating critique of productive force determinism, charging it with being teleological, functionalist and empirically unsupportable. Yet he ends up annulling the productive forces of any reciprocal determining effect on the social relations. We need to distinguish between productive force determinism, which, as we have seen, is problematic, and giving some determinism to the productive forces. The development of the productive forces generally, and the forces of communication specifically, establish an important component of the objective circumstances in which the class struggle is played out. As we have seen, the objective conditions for particular struggles in new fields of cultural practice are shaped by the development of communicative forces in terms of production, reproducibility, miniaturisation, convergence, storage and dissemination. The development of 16mm film stock in the 1930s offered new possibilities for left film-makers to produce and distribute (mainly) documentary material outside the established chains of production, distribution and exhibition (Hogenkamp 1986). The development of video, and now the Internet, extends and reconfigures these struggles of communication and meaning in the public sphere (Wayne 1997). We have also seen that the development of the forces of communication is both an index and a contributor to the general growth in the socialisation of production which butts up against private ownership of the means of production. Finally, we have seen that productive forces have an objective potential that is surplus to their immediate use-values. The productive forces are thus best understood as nothing more than the outcomes of the social relations of production, outcomes which have an objective material form and weight (and therefore reciprocal impact) and that 'disclose' the social conditions under which they are made and used (Harvey 1984:100).

THE NAPSTER FILE

Most discussions concerning the potential of the Internet to construct a new reinvigorated and dialogic sphere of public communication tend to focus on news and information content. I want instead to extend the issues which I have been discussing using the master couplet of the forces and relations of production, and the mode of development, to the sphere of entertainment, pleasure and leisure, the sphere most often defined as non-political, in order to demonstrate that, on the contrary, the technological developments of the new media politicise everything, as Benjamin has argued (1999b). For the anti-capitalist culture which crystallised into political opposition in the late 1990s, has at least some of its roots in the kind of informal anti-corporate culture fostered by the file-swapping services provided by Napster (the most popular) and others (such as Kazaa, Music City and Grockster). As we have seen, Marx argued that the technological development of the productive forces slowly weakens the grip which scarcity exerts on humanity. The transformation of the physical world of atoms into a digital world of bits massively boosts the elasticity of information resources both quantitively and over space. This extended possibility of music outside the exchange relations of capitalism is part of the same political continuum that sees the growing demands for the cancellation of Third World debt and the ethical necessity to feed the hungry in a world of food mountains.

The global music industry is dominated by the Big Five record labels: Warner, Universal, Bertelsmann, Sony and EMI. Between them they account for $14 billion in yearly revenue in the US market alone (Alderman 2001:4). These labels are themselves vertically and horizontally integrated, multimedia industries with interests in film, television, print media, electronic hardware and so forth. They own smaller brand labels such as Geffen, Atlantic and Virgin (owned respectively by Universal, Warner and EMI) as semi-autonomous subsidiaries. A major contradiction for the music industry between intellectual property rights and the connectivity of the Internet was opened up by two technological developments in the 1990s. First, there was the development of MP3, a digital file format that allowed audio content to be transmitted over the Internet. Described by one commentator as 'possibly the acronym of doom for the record industry',[4] MP3 only in fact became dangerous once it was hooked up to a new software that could effectively connect music fans. This software was developed by a 19-year-old American, Shawn Fanning, who founded Napster and wrote its peer-to-peer (or P2P) program. It is worth noting that the origins of Napster lay not in the research and development laboratories of large corporations (who had no motive to develop file-swapping software) but in the shared and generalised knowledge concerning digital media in circulation amongst people working in their spare time. Thus the PC, MP3 and P2P are all examples of 'the general productive power of society's intelligence' which Marx spied in automated fixed capital (Marx 1973:156–7). A film like *Antitrust* (Peter Howitt 2001 US) provides a dramatically fanciful but in some ways socially acute diagnosis of the tensions between this generalised social knowledge and corporate needs to maintain competitive edge. In the film, the software corporation NURV, run by Gary Winston (Tim Robbins, playing a Bill

Gates double), sets up web cameras in the bedrooms of hundreds of young crack software engineers, in order to steal their ideas.

Fanning is a bit like the young idealistic computer genius of *Antitrust*. His immediate motivation for developing the file-swapping program lay in response to the problems a friend of his was having in connecting with the MP3 files he wanted.

> The importance of the community potential of the project to Fanning cannot be stressed enough. Fanning had learnt more in his life from talking to people than he has from traditional academic means. Put simply, he loved the idea that users would be able to chat to each other about, and share information about, their favourite types of music. (Merriden 2001:4)

Fanning's uncle, a businessman, was then able to raise money from venture capitalists right at the peak of the dot.com boom, despite the fact that it was evident from the beginning that Napster had serious copyright hurdles to get over. The peer-to-peer system which Napster developed worked like this. Members (and membership was free) simply downloaded Napster's program to their own computer and designated which music files they wanted to share. Napster's servers did not store the files (and it was hoped by Napster that this would save them from litigation) but instead merely recorded who had which MP3 files. Thus the Napster program acted as matchmaker, connecting a user's computer with another user who had the desired music track on their computer. Launched in June 1999, Napster soon had 500,000 people swapping files on a nightly basis (Alderman 2001:108) and an estimated Napster 'community' of 32 million (Merriden 2001:15). Some have quoted figures as high as 80 million at the peak of its popularity.

Developments such as the Internet are often cast in terms of an individualisation and personalisation of media consumption. But, while this does describe some facets of the P2P technology and the file-swapping culture it spawned, P2P also links individual data banks up into a massive public network accessible to all. From this perspective, P2P is a remarkable extension of communal property. There is a major difference between the Internet, MP3 and P2P technology and earlier forms of reproducibility such as video cassette recorders. Hollywood tried unsuccessfully to use the US courts to block Sony's development of the Betamax VCR and Napster's lawyers attempted to draw a parallel between their technology and the earlier one. But the digital technology is incomparably more dangerous to corporate profits because not only does it amount to a giant copying system but it is also a virtually cost-free *distribution* system. The film industry, for example, thinks that 1 million illegal film files are being downloaded a day. The abolition of scarcity in distribution and retail is crucial because as more and more productive cultural capacity has come onto the market as consumer goods or relatively inexpensive professional fixed capital (video cameras, digital editing, desktop publishing) so the control of distribution networks and retailers has proved essential for monopoly capitalism (see Chapter 3 for more).

In December 1999, six months after Napster's phenomenally successful launch, the Recording Industry Association of America (RIAA) served its copyright infringement lawsuit. Shortly afterwards, the heavy metal band Metallica and rap artist Dr Dre warned of litigation when they found fans of their music trading MP3 files of their work. The action by Metallica and Dr Dre attempted to give a human face to the corporate machine defending its interests. The prospect of fabulously wealthy stars of the music world leaking some returns on their work was too much for many media commentators who appeared to agree with Dick Brass, vice-president of technological development at Microsoft, that P2P and other advances in reproducibility threatened 'human progress and prosperity'.[5] One world-weary hack rediscovered his ethics and, having tested out the Napster technology and downloaded Elvis Presley's 'Jailhouse Rock' onto his PC, deleted the file because (hand on heart) 'it simply did not seem fair to Elvis's estate or his record company to enjoy his music without paying something for it'.[6] Is there a socialist ethic being contravened here? The fact that software engineers in the Open Source movement are prepared to forgo permanent private control over their work relativises somewhat the apparently immutable state of affairs which decrees that singers and bands who make modest if enjoyable contributions to human affairs should enjoy proprietary rights in perpetuity and, as a result, lead lives unimaginably distant in wealth and opportunities from the fans who made them rich. The artistic community was in fact split. Dave Grohl of the Foo Fighters came out and declared that Napster should exist and, in a reference to the move towards subscription-based membership, declared that Napster should be 'free to everyone'.[7] The problem with the argument that file swapping hurts the artist is that the artists most affected look least like they're starving in a garret somewhere. If reproducibility is eroding the possibility of endless remuneration for a one-off piece of cultural labour, then artists can always go out and do what most musicians outside the musical aristocracy do: touring and gigging. The biggest threat from the industry's point of view is the way albums yet to be released are finding their way onto the Internet. But, once again, it is hard to get too worked up about this. The 'leakage' is caused by the amount of promotional material being sent to radio stations, TV music channels and club DJs. In other words, the artists and bands that already dominate the marketplace are having their profile pushed by the record companies to maximise profits, a process that homogenises the diversity of music on offer.

The successful court action by the RIAA, which forced Napster to pay royalties and therefore set up a (unsuccessful) subscription-based service, may be seen as an exemplary case of what Winston calls the 'law' of the suppression of radical potential. Yet at the same time the technology of MP3 and P2P cannot be put back into the bottle. Its emergence and development are ample evidence of the 'surplus' generated by the productive forces that come into friction with the dominant social relations. As one report noted,

> Even more music and video files are being swapped online since the court-ordered closure of the file-swapping site Napster – casting a gloomy light over the record labels' hopes of reining in internet-based music piracy and replacing it with their own substantive service.[8]

The problem for the industry is that systems such as Gnutella are purer forms of P2P. They lack a central controlling system which matches files between desktop computers, the very mechanism which made Napster, in the eyes of the court, 'responsible' for copyright infringement and therefore vulnerable to lawsuits. These purer forms of P2P are mobilising the resource 'at the edge of the Intenet', the PC, which has until now been 'the far-flung outpost of the Internet empire' (Merriden 2001:127). Here the forces of communication offer a utopian prefiguration of alternative social arrangements, namely mediations without either 'state'-like structures (central servers) or the market (exchange without value).

In the meantime, the major labels have launched subscription-based online music sites. Music Net is backed by EMI, AOL Time Warner and Bertelsmann while Press Play is backed by Sony Music and Vivendi (owners of Universal). Such services will have all sorts of encrypted limitations in terms of reproducing the music and eventually highly refined price differentiations providing access to greater or lesser services. *Business Week* was not alone in wondering whether 'folks will now pay for what they once got for free'.[9] Yet this is a very typical process whereby capitalism turns what was once held in various forms of common ownership, into a commodity. It began in England with the enclosure of the common land under the Tudors. Graham Murdock finds an 'electric affinity' between the land enclosures and the struggles of resistance which they sparked and the contestations around the developing mass media from the nineteenth century onwards (2001). The Internet is only the latest site in the struggle to retain a 'digital commons' as the forces of commodification descend upon it.

In conclusion then we have seen that, properly reconstructed, the category of mode of production and its master couplet of the forces and social relations of production still provide the fulcrum to any critical interrogation of the new media 'revolution' and a means to combat widespread technological determinism. Despite claims to the contrary, there is no new paradigm by which the economics of capitalism transcends its absolutely fundamental tendency towards overproduction and hence crisis. Properly anchored within the mode of production, Castells' concept of the mode of development can help us understand how the contradictions of the mode of production get reconfigured within specific new technologies and media practices. I drew on Marx's discussion of the development of automated machinery to explore the cultural implications of the contradiction between decreasing necessary labour time and increasing surplus labour time. The increase in economic value which this buys capital in the short term is won at the cost of eroding the cultural values (adherence to copyright law for example) which value relations require. I suggested that two such disparate phenomena as the popularity of Napster and the emergence of the anti-capitalist movement were connected in this respect (irrespective of the subjective politics of file swappers). We saw that the socialisation of production (and consumption) which automated fixed capital measures and develops is a central feature of new information technology. Knowledge as a productive force and consumption as the production of knowledge come to have ever more extensive roots in a widening social base. This is incompatible with social relations based on the private, hierarchical and competitive relations of capital, as debates within the Open Source community and the massive extension of communal property via MP3 and P2P demonstrate. We also saw that Marx laid the basis for thinking through the contradiction between actual and potential (or surplus) uses of fixed capital. In a sense, the development of automated fixed capital constitutes a kind of *cultural overproduction* (a cultural crisis to match the economic crisis of overproduction), in which the potential uses have to be continually squeezed back in and made compatible with the narrow social priorities of capital's relations of production. The forces of production are thus the site and the stake of the class struggle.

3   Powers of Capital: Hollywood's Media–Industrial Complex

[I]n the latter stages of monopoly or postindustrial capitalism not only the multiplicity of small business units, but also distribution and ultimately the last free-floating elements of the older commercial and cultural universe, are now assimilated into a single all absorbing mechanism. Now, when the entire business system with its projections in government ... depends for its very existence on the automatic sale of products ... marketing psychology obliges it to complete its conquest of the world by reaching down into the last private zones of individual life, in order to awaken the artificial needs around which the system evolves.

Jameson, *Marxism and Form*

Flexible specialisation is a strategy of permanent innovation: accommodation to ceaseless change, rather than an effort to control it. This strategy is based on flexible multi-use equipment, skilled workers, and the creation, through politics, of an industrial community that restricts the forms of competition to those favouring innovation ... the spread of flexible specialisation amounts to a revival of craft forms of production.

Piore and Sabel, *The Second Industrial Divide*

Capital steadily accrued gigantic powers in the course of the twentieth century, but especially in the last quarter it underwent major changes in its corporate structures and saw considerable expansion of its activities. The largest of the multinational corporations now generate revenues in excess of the gross domestic product of medium sized national economies. Transnational agencies such as the World Trade Organization and the International Monetary Fund remorselessly promote and facilitate the interests of Big Capital around the world. Privatisation and deregulation have become the watchwords of governments, whatever their political colours, everywhere. Public systems of communication have been privatised or had private capital investment and competition with private capital increasingly determine their choices. The nation-state and governments have been extensively penetrated by the agenda, policies and personnel of the corporations. The interlocking relations between political elites and business elites have seen a decisive tilt in the class struggle in favour of capital with an accompanying penetration of the profit motive or commodification into hitherto uncharted areas and/or the intensification of the logic of accumulation to new levels in areas long under the sway of capital's dominion. This is the macro-context in which we must understand contemporary developments within the media–industrial complex in this chapter and media policy in Chapter 4.

Rather than providing a detailed narrative of the recent manoeuvrings and changing fortunes of individual moguls and corporate protagonists, this chapter focuses on the methodological tools which can be used to analyse the contemporary media landscape. These methodological tools will be drawn from two paradigms which are in some respects conflicting. The argument that capitalism is characterised by a tendency towards monopoly is central to the political economy approach to the media characterised by such writers as Schiller (1989), Herman and Chomksy (1994), Wasko (1994), Bagdikian (1997), Herman and McChesney (1997) Schiller (1999), Golding and Murdock (2000) and Wilkin (2001). However, capitalism's tendency towards monopoly is also contradictorily combined with new corporate structures and market strategies that give a looser, decentralised, more flexible, diverse and competitive *appearance-form* to advanced capitalism than one necessarily gets from the monopoly capitalism paradigm. These changes are closely tied up with the new technological forces of production and communication which we examined in the previous chapter under the terms informationalism and mode of development. Here we will situate these categories within the context of debates concerning two modes of development: Fordism (industrialism) and post-Fordism (informationalism). If in the previous chapter I integrated the category mode of development into mode of production, in this chapter, a similar integration is replayed between the post-Fordist paradigm and the monopoly capitalism paradigm. These paradigms seem in many ways to contradict each other. I will argue that the post-Fordist paradigm needs to be integrated into a monopoly capitalism paradigm in order to understand the dialectic between monopoly and competition, concentration and fragmentation, cultural domination and cultural diversity, within advanced capitalism as corporations of ever growing scale seek to plug into ever more diverse and volatile markets around the world. At the same time, we shall see that the post-Fordist argument that the *concentration and centralisation of capital* has been corrected or reversed by new organisational structures and technologies is untenable. Theorists who invest in such post-Fordist scenarios are offering the fantastic proposition of a capitalism without the social and economic downsides of competition, a capitalism where competition only leads to technological and cultural innovation and where competition can be coupled with the new caring, sharing, 'network sociality' of post-Fordism; and all this depends on a capitalism without monopoly. This is not a scenario that has 'legs' as commissioning editors in television like to say. My analysis will be grounded in a case study of Disney and I will then go on to discuss the implications of the new corporate structures for the public sphere, the realm of symbolic exchange in which communication, identity and meanings are forged.

MONOPOLY AND COMPETITION

Monopoly and competition constitute 'a paired reality of historical capitalism' (Wallerstein 1989:34); like squabbling conjoined twins, they are both inseparable and conflicting. Competition is a pervasive logic of capital, setting worker against worker, industrial sector against industrial sector, region against region, capital against capital. One can no more squeeze competition out of the capitalist system than you can squeeze air out of a knotted balloon. Competition is the means by which the 'discipline' of accumulation exerts itself as a structural coercive force on all. As Herman and Chomsky note, 'If ... managers fail to pursue actions that favour shareholder returns, institutional investors will be inclined to sell the stock (depressing its price) or to listen sympathetically to outsiders contemplating takeovers' (1994:11). However, because 'competition' is the favoured language of the enemy, it is often assumed that the word has only 'rosy' implications (innovation, lower prices) while Marxists often imply that it in any case diminishes as 'pure' market exchanges are replaced by conglomerates. But, as David Harvey has argued, within monopoly capitalism, competition is *internalised* within the corporation and this in turn ratchets up competition (for profits) between corporations (1984:141–8).

There is a distinction then to be made between market competition between actors independent of one another (the unrecoverable nineteenth-century model anachronistically championed by today's free marketeers) and corporate competition as a generalised logic of capital operating irrespective of the numbers, size, interdependence and power of actors in the market. Although pro-capitalist economists and politicians espouse competition as a great boon to consumers, ensuring choice and product diversity, monopoly capitalists themselves are not hugely keen on it. Because market competition drives down profit margins there is an ineluctable pressure to diminish the number of competitors operating in the market, by takeovers and mergers and by raising barriers of entry to a market. Thus competition generates a tendency towards its opposite: monopoly, *but without ever erasing competition from the system*. A strict monopoly, where one company is in control of an entire market is rare, at least outside state-owned monopolies. An oligopoly is the more typical situation, where a handful of very large companies dominate a market.

The tendency of capitalism towards such skews of market power is a severe embarrassment to apologists of this economic system. Such people tend not to lie awake at night worrying about social inequalities, such as, for example, that 1 per cent of the wealth of the 200 richest people in the world could fund free access to primary education for every child in the world.[1] Yet economic inequalities between suppliers are more troubling for the authentic free marketeer for this suggests flaws in the idealised model of 'free competition'. Promoters of capitalism generally do not sing the praises of monopolistic tendencies and indeed they do their best to shut their eyes to those tendencies even when the empirical evidence would appear to be tweaking them by the nose. Thus Hoskins, McFadyen and Finn, in surveying Hollywood's domination of the film industry, come to a rather odd conclusion: '[I]f creativity and cultural goals are paramount, the opportunities remaining within this American-dominated system for independent producers around the world may be both artistically and commercially attractive' (1997:67). Between 1997 and 2000 Hollywood's domination of the UK box office was never less than 60 per cent and was 83 per cent in 1998. If one includes US co-productions with non-UK companies (often German or French) the figures are even higher. UK/US film productions meanwhile included films like *Chicken Run* (Peter Lord and Nick Park 2000 GB), *Snatch* (Guy Ritchie 2000 GB), *Kevin and Perry Go Large* (Ed Bye 2000 UK), *Star Wars Episode I: The Phantom Menace* (George Lucas 1999 US), *Notting Hill* (Roger Michell 1999 US/GB), *The World is Not Enough* (Michael Apted 1999 GB) and *Shakespeare in Love* (John Madden 1998 US). This left around 4 per cent of UK box office revenue for British films and around 4 per cent for the rest of the world between 1997 and 2000. The exception was 1997 where the percentage for UK films rose to over 8 per cent courtesy of *Bean* (Mel Smith 1998 GB), made by the UK company Working Title and distributed by its parent company, PolyGram Films (now bust).[2] Far from being artistically and commercially attractive, the cultural goal, for example, of making British films which address the complexities of life in Britain appears to be squeezed to the very margins of existence and survival.

The pro-capitalist economic philosopher Milton Friedman similarly deals with the tendency towards monopoly by fervently wishing it away:

> The most important fact about enterprise monopoly is its relative unimportance from the point of view of the economy as a whole. There are some four million separate operating enterprises in the United States; some four hundred thousand new ones are born each year; a somewhat smaller number die each year. (1982:120)

Quite typically for capital's advocates, what is lost from view here is that, amongst these millions of economic enterprises, there is a hierarchy, an economic inequality (just as capitalism breeds social inequality), and that a small number of companies in each industrial sector will dominate the rest overwhelmingly. In the United States, by the middle of the twentieth century, around 500 major corporations (that's someway short of several million) produced *half* of the nation's industrial output and owned *three quarters* of the nation's industrial assets. General Motors alone was responsible for 3 per cent of America's gross domestic product (Reich 1991:46).

The tendency towards monopoly can be effectively measured over time. Since the mid-1980s, the 50 biggest media corporations have shrunk to around nine or ten (Bagdikian 1997:xiii). Time Warner is generally regarded as 'the daddy', after its $106 billion merger with AOL. Disney, Viacom, News Corporation, Sony, TCI/AT&T and General Electric would also qualify as tier one media corporations. Two European companies also make the list. The German company Bertelsmann, a publishing and music giant, and the French company Vivendi which climbed into the top tier in 2001 by purchasing Seagram, the Canadian drinks company which owned Universal music and movies, for $34 billion. (Vivendi has subsequently run into debt trouble as a result.) Competition still exists within this oligopolistic structure, but it does not operate in the way capitalist economists think, that is there is minimal or only temporary price competition and product diversity. Instead, there is competition for market share, which can be achieved through heavy advertising campaigns or mergers and takeovers. Competition to raise profits meanwhile can be achieved by cutting costs, concentrating on wealthy consumers and taking minimal cultural and political risks with output. To these negative effects of competition we can add that the theoretical upside of competition is blocked by networks of joint ventures and the buying of shares in other companies (Herman and McChesney 1997:56). Thus John Malone, former owner of the cable company TCI (which he sold to telecommunications giant AT&T for $54 billion), now heads Liberty Media which, at the time of writing, holds a 25 per cent stake in Telewest, the UK cable company, 19 per cent of Rupert Murdoch's News Corporation as well smaller holdings in AOL, Vivendi and Motorola. The power and reach of such corporations is something we will return to later, but for now we have to take a detour via debates concerning the periodisation of capitalist modes of development, namely Fordism and post-Fordism.

TWO PHASES OF MONOPOLY CAPITALISM

In the late 1980s and early 1990s, a number of commentators within the post-Fordist tradition, argued that capitalism's tendency towards monopoly had been effectively reversed by changes in corporate structures and practices, by new technologies, by changes in cultural markets and by global market exchanges. The post-Fordist paradigm is not a homogeneous one. There are different strands and traditions within it. The Regulation School associated with writers like Aglietta (1979), Lipietz (1987) and Jessop (1997) are broadly Marxist in orientation. They explore how a system built around potentially explosive social antagonisms can be regulated so that accumulation can take place, relatively smoothly, according to a set of institutional and normative patterns (Amin 1997:8). The Marxist geographer David Harvey (not generally regarded as a member of the Regulation School) defined post-Fordism in terms of flexible accumulation which circumvented the rigidities of Fordism in the labour processes, in labour markets, products and in responding to changing patterns of consumer behaviour (1990:147). The keyword 'accumulation' emphasises the continuity of post-Fordism with exploitative, antagonistic social relations. This is rather different from another strand of post-Fordist analysis called flexible specialisation theory, which is much more liberal in its politics, and has had a rather more popular impact, appropriated by policy makers and converging in some texts with orthodox free market bourgeois economic analysis. Piore and Sabel's *The Second Industrial Divide*, first published in the mid-1980s, was an early influential proponent of this paradigm. They situate flexible specialisation, which requires skilled workers able to shift within and across whole families of goods, within a nineteenth- and early-twentieth-century tradition of craft production which was marginalised by the rise of mass production (narrowly (de)skilled workers operating single-purpose tools) and all but snuffed out in Europe under the American model in the post Second World War 'modernisation' drive (1984).

Yet in one area this tradition has had little impact, and that is with the institutional and economic analysis of the media itself. The reason for this is fairly obvious. Flexible specialisation theory tends to argue or imply that the trends towards monopoly capitalism have been or are being reversed. Political economy approaches counter such arguments with detailed historical and empirical accounts of the media–industrial complex. For example, Janet Wasko's analysis of Hollywood provides abundant evidence of this kind which calls into question what she calls the 'myths' of the information age, namely that it has brought more competition and product diversity (1994:249–52). Yet a historical and empirical critique, while absolutely necessary, is not the same as a *theoretical* engagement with the post-Fordist paradigm. For the post-Fordist paradigm does at least have the merit of identifying changes in the *structure* of corporate capitalism's organisational modes which we do in fact need to integrate into our account, since these have important effects on the production of cultural goods and the strategies developed to resolve contradictions involved in the commodification of culture. But we need to integrate such an account into the monopoly capitalism paradigm.

FORDISM AND POST-FORDISM

The key dynamic then of the capitalist mode of production in the age of monopoly capitalism is the tendency towards the *concentration* and *centralisation* of *capital* (what we might call the Three Cs Thesis). Concentration of capital refers to the amassing of capital accumu-lated via the exploitation of labour. We can see the concentration of capital at work in the increasing quantity of capital invested in the production process. Thus the average cost of film production keeps rising in real terms and this does act as a barrier of entry for competitors. Yet, paradoxically, the generation of capital also has a decentralising potential insofar as quantities of amassed capital can be spread around, split off into new ventures and companies and spread over a wider net of family members within the capitalist class. However, this decentralising potential interacts with and is subordinate to the *centralisation* of capital, its amassing into a small number of hugely powerful units of capital due to the detrimental effect which competition has on profit margins. Historically, this centralisation of capital took place in both the industrial and banking sectors, which, as each grows in size, become increasingly intermeshed with one another, thus further locking production into the accumulation imperative.

Now we can graft onto the concentration and centralisation of capital, which are inextricably linked with the capitalist *mode of production*, structures and practices associated with Fordism and post-Fordism which are contingent – in their precise manifestation – on specific historical circumstance, and which constitute, therefore, different modes of development. To take Fordism first, we find that the concentration of capital at a given level of technological development of the productive forces opens the way for mass production. Large pools of workers assembled within giant firms were able to win relatively good wages that in turn facilitated the purchasing power to buy the mass of goods which were being produced. (The approach was pioneered by car manufacturer Henry Ford – hence Fordism.) The articulation between production and consumption helped diminish – but did not resolve – capitalism's cyclical economy (Aglietta 1979:117). The companies themselves were able to utilise their size to achieve economies of scale and they sought to control every aspect of the production process from raw materials to finished product at the point of purchase. Thus developed the vertically integrated corporation, which in the Hollywood film industry meant that the five 'majors' controlled film production, distribution networks and exhibition circuits by the 1920s. Vertical integration is not a contingent feature of monopoly capitalism since it is the means by which monopolistic tendencies are achieved, but the in which vertical integration manifested itself under urned out, contingent to historical circumstances,

Within the Fordist corporation there was a separation between ownership and day-to-day control, which saw the growth of layers of managers and the expansion of the intelligentsia generally. Such an expansion is not a contingent but rather a necessary fact of life for an increasingly complex system of production which needs co-ordination and, in the contemporary jargon of edu-speak, 'problem solving'. However, the organisational structures within which the intelligentsia work are contingent on particular historical circum-stances. Below the intelligentsia, working within a strictly hierarchical system were/are the working class, subjected to various procedures of 'scientific management' (Taylorism), which controlled minutely their every move. Although corporations vied for international markets, the 'locus of economic activity' was the nation-state (Webster 1995:140). This in turn meant an increasing interlocking between capital and the nation-state, something that was reinforced by the role of the state in economic planning during two world wars. Those wars and the experience of planning laid the basis for the 'Fordist' pact between capital and organised labour that was cemented after 1945 in the social-democratic consensus of Western Europe (Jessop 1991:136–7) and the United States whose economic and military power underpinned the internationalisation of the Fordist system after 1945 (Piore and Sabel 1984:133–64, Harvey 1990:141).

What seems clear now is that although this first phase of monopoly capitalism diminished competition within national markets and helped contain the more chaotic effects of anarcho-free market capitalism, the growing concentration and centralisation of capital was intensifying international competition as capital sought ever new markets and means to raise accumulation levels. For profit levels stagnated and declined in the United States from the mid-1960s (Piore and Sabel 1984:165–87, Reich 1991:75–6, Harvey 1990:137), as national markets in standardised goods were saturated and international competition intensified (Piore and Sabel 1984:184, Jessop 1997:259). The latter factor was greatly enhanced by the efficiency (and therefore cheapness) and sophistication of global transport and communications networks, which kept the corpora-tion in touch with its increasingly dispersed operation. At the same time, cultural and political changes meant that consumer markets were becoming progressively differentiated and thus the old Fordist production line of standardised goods made in long runs by de-skilled workers became increasingly problematic. Post-Fordism by contrast has been associated with microprocessor technology which made possible the swift adaption and reprogramming of machine tools that allowed for more specialised, differentiated and plural products intended to have a short shelf life (Aglietta 1979:125, Reich 1991:82–3, Amin 1997:15).

In order to turn this intensely global competitive environment to its advantage, capital had to decant from the social-democratic consensus of nation-states with which it had been interlocked in the post-war period. Hence politically the rise of neo-liberalism to legitimise the new situation: 'neo' because it could be seen as a continuation of an earlier phase of *laissez-faire*, free market capitalism which existed before the rise of 'Fordism'; and 'liberal' in an economic sense that any controls, constraints and regulations on capital were said to constitute a violation of freedom (Friedman 1982:120). Rustin argues that the 'social gains of the subordinate classes' and the expansion of a relatively de-commodified public sector in the post-war period were 'threats to capital accumulation and authority' that had to be rolled back in order to rescue profit margins (1989:308–9). With the 1973 oil price rises, energy costs began to bite deep into profit margins and the bourgeoisie were compelled to develop new production structures and new ways of stimulating and responding to consumer markets (Harvey 1990:145).

Aglietta similarly stressed the role of class struggle in determining both the crisis of Fordism (e.g. worker resistance to the production line) and its potential, temporary solutions (1979:162–5). He called his early diagnosis of these trends neo-Fordism in order to indicate the continuities between the two phases and resist the sort of simplistic binary opposition between Fordism and post-Fordism which subsequently became rather widespread. Crucially, the new corporate structures associated with post-Fordism, and around which there has been much confusion, are not in fact that new. Cowling identifies three organisational forms for corporate capitalism that have been operational during the twentieth century. The U-form is a single *unitary* hierarchical structure encompassing all the different elements necessary for the production of commodities and realisation of capital (the purchase and use of said commodities). The H-form is that of a *holding* company which is comprised of an unco-ordinated group of companies falling under a single financial entity. As the U-form of corporation (the one most associated with Fordism) got larger through mergers, takeovers and other monopoly capitalist trends, so its cumbersome hierarchies and centralised control became increasingly inefficient. As the H-form of organisation got larger so it became increasingly sprawling and uncoordinated (Cowling 1982:83). If the U-form was too centralised, the H-form was too decentralised. The organisational solution to this problem turned out to be the M-form. This was the *multi-divisional* structure in which responsibility for the different facets of production and selling was decentralised, while higher-level management retained control of overall strategic decision-making and ultimate sanction on its various divisions by controlling capital allocation (Cowling 1982:84). Aglietta also argues that the problems of internal corporate structure were resolved by the divisional structure, which created 'profit centres' in relation to the particular category of commodity that divisions were responsible for (1979:257). However, the divisional structure was not new, but had been pioneered by Dupont and General Motors back in the 1920s. As Harvey argues: 'this decentralized structure is so organized that each division (whether it be a product line or a territory) can be held financially accountable' (1984:148). What was new was that it became the *dominant* corporate structure which was then combined with two other long-established but now increasingly central aspects of advanced capitalism: inter-corporate relations organised around *subsidiaries* and *subcontractors* and a renewed and expansive role for advertising (branding).

The organisational structures that came to dominate saw the totality of production broken up and 'outsourced' to other companies, whether subcontractors or subsidiaries. To be sure, subcontracting has long been a feature of capitalism, and Marx himself discussed it (Harvey 1984:140) but there is today a quantitative increase in subsidiary and subcontractor relations which provide an essential decentralising ('competitive') counterpoint to centralisation and a new plurality of units of capital operating in the market place. Reich sees the emergence of a 'web' of semi-autonomous subsidiaries and independent subcontractors working on various components of production (conception, design, production itself, packaging, distribution, marketing) that are parcelled out to different companies (1991:100). Sabel likewise points to 'the reorganisation of large, multinational firms. Product lines are being concentrated in single operating units which have increased authority to organise their own sales, subcontracting, and even research' (1997:103). The claim of *autonomy* is something we will question later, but it is worth noting that it underpinned hugely optimistic hopes that capitalism could now be reconciled with cultural difference, innovation, creativity for workers, collaboration and even greater democracy at work (Piore and Sabel 1984:115, Hall and Jacques 1989:15).

But let us for the moment look at the apparent new plurality of capital's operating units which appeared to have reversed the tendency towards monopoly. Lash and Urry write of the end of 'organised capitalism' (1987:2) and, in contrast to the centralisation of capital, discover a new 'deconcentration' of capital (1987:5). Yet this deconcentration of capital turns out on closer inspection to refer not so much to concentration of ownership, with which it is confused, but such contingent features as a shift away from large plant sizes towards smaller plant sizes and the *geographical* relocation of capital around the world (often to developing countries where labour supply is cheap) as opposed to its regional concentration under Fordism. Neither plant size nor geographical dispersal is incompatible with a continuing centralisation of capital.

Another popular term within flexible specialisation theory, very similar to 'deconcentration', is 'vertical disintegration'. Christopherson and Storper (1986) and Storper (1997), for example, argue that the Hollywood film industry could be taken as a model of the shift to post-Fordism. The stability of the market which Hollywood's Fordist structures had cultivated and depended on was disrupted by two shocks: the antitrust action by the US Supreme Court (1948) which forced the studios to sell their interests in the cinema chains, and the rise of television in the 1950s. In response, the old studio system of in-house production was now parcelled out to independent producers, as well as 'intermediate inputs' (Storper 1997:211–12) such as editing, lighting, sound and film processing and special effects companies. Compare the end credit titles of an old studio film with those of a film made in the last 25 years and you will see very visibly the new corporate structures at work.

The large pools of technical and creative talent which the old studios used to have on long-term contracts were now fragmented into these smaller units, or operated freelance or under agents and were brought together for each individual film.Yet it is highly misleading to apply the term vertical disintegration to the production sector alone when questions of market dominance are assessed by the vertical links *across* production, distribution and exchange. Distribution in particular remains the key strategic point of control within the film industry, linking products to audiences (Askoy and Robbins 1992:7). As we have already seen, Hollywood continues to dominate the UK box office in terms comparable with its domination of global film markets. And, while Hollywood withdrew from direct control of exhibition after antitrust rulings in the late 1940s, this contingent political environment changed with the rise of neo-liberalism in the 1980s. Accordingly, Hollywood majors have moved back into exhibition with a large global multiplex expansion programme.

While Hollywood used to be a single- or dual-sector cultural industry (making films and then films and television), it is today at the centre of multi-sector and integrated cultural industries. Film is the pre-eminent media content/commodity driving sales at the box office, on television and through a host of 'synergies', videos, books, comics, music soundtracks, computer games, theme parks and merchandise (Askoy and Robins 1992:17). To understand the present structure of media corporations, then, we need to deploy at least four terms: vertical integration – the linkages between raw materials to point of sale – which still persists; horizontal integration which refers to ownership of different companies within the same sector of the industry, such as numerous film production companies or newspaper titles; cross-media integration which refers to the tying together within one parent company of different types of media and media-related materials, thus generating synergies; and finally cross-industry integration, where media companies are part of corporations with substantial non-media holdings. Thus US television network NBC is owned by General Electric (GE), which is one of the biggest companies in the world. GE has interests in heavy industry, financial services, medicine and domestic electric appliances.

DISNEY: A CASE STUDY OF INTEGRATION

Let us take a more thoroughly media-centred corporation such as Disney as an example of how these new corporate structures work. By the early 1980s, Disney had declined into a marginal Hollywood corporation which lacked sufficient integration and was still governed by a business ethos hanging over from the days of Walt Disney (who died in 1967). In a sign of how the pressures of accumulation have intensified, this ethos, which put restrictions on how aggressively the corporation could exploit its commercial assets and brands, now looked to be endangering Disney's survival as an independent company. The arrival of Michael Eisner as a new chief executive officer in 1984 and the new management team he built up were to transform Disney into one of the world's most powerful media corporations. One of the first decisions Eisner took was to increase the prices at Disney's theme parks which generated the revenue to expand film and television production (Grover 1997:73).

In 1996 Eisner made Disney's largest acquisition under his leadership when they bought Capital Cities, the parent company for the ABC television and radio network, for $19 billion. Cross-media integration would ensure that Disney's films and television programmes were guaranteed airtime. ABC also owned the hugely popular ESPN cable sport channels. ESPN were gaining a foothold in international markets such as Asia and Latin America, and Disney realised that they could promote themselves in markets which they had hitherto not penetrated very successfully, off the back of the sports channels (Grover 1997:285). ABC also had interests in European, Japanese and Chinese audio-visual markets. Not only could ABC provide airtime for Disney products, ABC programmes could also cross-promote them. Disney has been accused of reducing ABC news programmes at times to a publicity arm of the parent company. One newspaper report notes that

> shortly before Disney's 'real' animal kingdom opened in Florida, ABC's Good Morning America broadcast a fawning interview with Disney Chairman Michael Eisner. 'The last time somebody created a river and a park and a world ... it was ... found in the Book of Genesis' viewers were informed in an extraordinary display of sycophancy.[3]

In recent years, film production has been carefully crafted to take account of national and regional cultures, sucking up stories from around the world and returning them to global markets at strategic moments in an effort to make Disney culturally look like not just an American corporation, but a world corporation. The late 1960s and 1970s saw increasing resistance from Latin America to the cultural imperialism and racism of North America. Disney, perhaps because of the inevitable pedagogic issues raised by its key target audience (children), were (and are) a favourite target (Dorfman and Mattelart 1991). Thus *Pocahontas* (Mike Gabriel 1995 US), which offers a 'postmodern refurbishment' to 'familiar stereotypes' of indigenous South Americans (Sardar 2002:193) chimed in with Disney's renewed attention to Latin American markets in the run up to the ABC/ESPN deal. *Beauty and the Beast* (Gary Trousdale 1991 US), derived from a French fairy tale, was released in 1992, the year that Disneyland Paris (then known as Euro-Disney) opened. The winter release in Europe helped shore up attendances when traditionally theme parks close after the summer months. Further synergies between the theme park and Disney's film production were exploited with the animated version of Victor Hugo's *The Hunchback of Notre Dame* (Gary Trousdale 1996 US). After recording losses for the first few years, the release of this second French-sourced tale coincided with the beginnings of a revival of economic fortunes for the theme park. By 1995, the French made up half of the admissions to the park, which was busy 'Frenchifying' itself with attractions such as the Jules Verne Space Mountain ride.[4] *Mulan* (Barry Cook 1998 US) on the other hand, based on a nationalist Chinese legend, was conceived after senior Disney executives returned from a three-week research trip to China, the largest potential media market in the world.[5]

By 2001 Disney's interests were divided between television and cable channels (38 per cent), parks and resorts (28 per cent), studio entertainment (films, television, video) which accounts for 24 per cent, and consumer products, including merchandising and licensing of Disney products, the Disney stores and publishing, which account for 10 per cent.[6] Clearly the potential for synergies with such cross-media/entertainment holdings is enormous and one which Disney regularly exploits. In addition to cross-media integration, there is horizontal integration. For example, Disney has several production studios which each specialise in material for different audiences. These are segmented according to age and tastes. Walt Disney Pictures produce children's films, such as the *The Lion King* (Roger Allers 1994 US) and *101 Dalmatians* (Stephen Herrek 1996 US), that in turn provide the iconographic material for the theme parks and merchandise. They also subcontract animated feature film production out to Pixar who have been responsible for the more innovative animation films such as *Toy Story* (John Lasseter 1995 US), *Toy Story 2* (John Lasseter 1999 US) and *Monsters, Inc.* (Pete Docter 2001 US). Touchstone Pictures on the other hand make films with big budgets and/or big box office stars, such as *The Sixth Sense* (M. Night Shyamalan 1999 US) starring Bruce Willis, *Enemy of the State* (Tony Scott 1999 US) starring Will Smith and Gene Hackman, *Gone in Sixty Seconds* (Dominic Sena 2000 US) starring Nicholas Cage and Angelina Jolie and the spectacle-led *Pearl Harbor* (Michael Bay 2001 US) starring Ben Affleck. Miramax Films, however, which Disney bought in 1993 for $80 million, cater to a more 'art-house' audience, or at least smaller budget films for adult cinema-goers. Miramax have strong connections with the European film industry and are responsible for

Shakespeare in Love (John Madden 1998 US), *Life is Beautiful* (Roberto Benigni 1999 It), *The Talented Mr Ripley* (Anthony Minghella 1999 US), *Chocolate* (Lasse Hallström 2000 US), *Malena* (Giuseppe Tornatore 2000 It) and *Bridget Jones's Diary* (Sharon Maguire 2001 GB), as well as independent American films such as *All the Pretty Horses* (Billy Bob Thornton 2000 US) and *Gangs of New York* (Martin Scorsese 2002 US). However, Disney also tap into the important teen-movie market through Dimension Films, a genre division of Miramax. Dimension specialises in horror movies such as *The Faculty* (Roberto Rodriguez 1998 US), *Halloween: H20* (Steve Miner 1998 US), *Scary Movie* (Keenen Ivory Wayans 2000 US) and *Hellraiser V: Inferno* (Scott Derrickson 2000 US).

Each of these studios does appear to be 'semi-autonomous' at the level of branding, with each one targeting a segmented global audience. Miramax, set up by Harvey and Bob Weinstein, were able, post 'merger', to draw on Disney's capital base to fund projects while retaining control of marketing and distribution (Wyatt 1998:84). At the same time, there is vertical integration, with these different studios working through Buena Vista International (BVI) which operates a powerful global distribution network to ensure that all Disney films get access to large audiences. BVI regularly makes more than $1 billion from overseas film box-office receipts alone.[7] BVI is also responsible for cross-promotion with other companies to the mutual benefit of both. Tie-ins reached new levels with Disney's *Monsters, Inc.*, which was advertised in the UK in conjunction with McDonald's, Nestlé, Powergen (monsters on the weather report), Robinson's drinks and even Fairy soap powder. Such cross-promotion, together with the large marketing campaign devoted to the film, gives a blockbuster colossal profile in the market place with the effect that it squeezes material underpinned by vastly lesser resources to the margins of public consciousness.

The importance of control of distribution capacity cannot be stressed enough and is the key reason why telecommunications companies like AT&T and content providers like TCI, have been meshing together (Golding and Murdock 2000:80). The advantages of such alliances are illustrated by Disney's problems in lacking new technology distribution capacity. Disney bought the cable channel Fox Family, which reaches 82 million homes, from News International for $5 billion, and rebranded it as the ABC Family channel.[8] However, the cable channel is content not distribution capacity, and Disney came into conflict with the satellite broadcaster, Echo Star, which carries the channel. Of course, in the Chinese boxes that are corporate capitalism, Echo Star is in turn owned by Vivendi who bought it for $1.5 billion.[9] Echo Star/Vivendi argued that the change of control of the children's channel entitled it to renegotiate the contract with Disney.[10] Such conflicts and haggling are part of corporate life, but it is clear that there is a big incentive for a parent company to be essentially buying and selling with itself by owning as many links in the commodity chain as possible (Wallerstein 1989:29).

As we have seen, for writers like Reich and Sabel, the new web-like structures which corporations have adopted have led to a diffusion of power, stressing the autonomy which subsidiaries have within the parent company. For example, large publishing houses have created 'imprints', small publishing houses within the structure of the parent firm, which have responsibility for acquiring and publishing their own books (Reich 1991:92). Yet this autonomy is not substantive, but exists more at the level of brand image. Instead of drawing all the company's operations into a single homogeneous brand identity, the new dispersed, divisional structure allows multiple brands to operate under one umbrella, thus sensitising the company to differentiated audiences. But we should not confuse brand autonomy with real substantive autonomy. Todays structures of subsidiary and subcontractor capitalism operate a kind of decentralised accumulation. In the old Fordist corporation modelled on the U-form structure, a pyramid structure of hierarchical power controlled all operations: in a sense, the power was external to a particular sector operating within the parent firm and had the clear appearance of coercion due to the firm's many layers of management. Now, in the post-Fordist structure, the logic of accumulation which goes with operating within a global corporation is inscribed within the (very) relatively, or formally autonomous subsidiary or subcontractor. Each unit becomes a profit centre. If that is not the case, if a unit within the company is not sufficiently attuned to global corporate strategy, then direct central control can be exerted by the parent company at will.

Thus in 2001/2 Disney found itself buffeted by the downturn in advertising revenue for its ABC television network and poor ratings against competitors CBS and NBC. Revenues in the broadcasting division dropped by $566 million, which sounds a lot until you realise that the revenues were still $5.7 billion, down from $6.2 billion the previous year.[11] The *Financial Times* reported that: 'Mr Eisner said in an interview that he expected improvement at the ABC network this year, following a recent management shake-up at the unit.'[12] It soon became clear what that 'improvement' could mean in terms of programming. The veteran current affairs anchorman Ted Koppel was to have his 20-year-old programme, *Nightline*, displaced from prime time and replaced with celebrity chat show host David Letterman fronting his programme, the *Late Show*, running on CBS. Letterman's show generates more than twice the advertising revenue of *Nightline*; however, this is *not* a reflection of the relative popularity of the two shows with *audiences*. Koppel's serious news programme has an average of 5.6 million viewers, while Letterman's *Late Show*, ostensibly a more 'popular culture' show, averages 4.7 million.[13] However – and this is a key point which explodes the myth that popular culture is, in any straightforward sense, necessarily 'popular' – the average watching age of Letterman's show is 46, while Koppel's is 50, and that age difference makes all the difference as far as *advertisers* are concerned. Eventually the move fell through because Letterman received even more generous terms from CBS. As far as questions of autonomy of a division within the parent company are concerned, this episode is also instructive insofar as the changes were negotiated above the head of David Westin, ABC's president, who was described as 'ashen' after the announcement.[14] This is why monopoly and competition are inextricably connected. The multi-divisional, subsidiary and subcontracting network of inter-corporate relations *extends* the law of value (the need to push profit rates ever upwards) *within* the firm and therefore between firms.

THE PUBLIC SPHERE

So far I have concentrated on understanding corporate media structures and locating them within the wider context of an evolving capitalist mode of production and development, giving some indication of the enormous economic resources and power they have accrued. Now we need to think about the implications that those corporate structures have for the 'public sphere'. The term needs some explanation. It is especially associated with the communications philosopher Jurgen Habermas. In his philosophical history of the public sphere, Habermas noted that in medieval times there was no sphere of debate and dialogue which was not unambiguously tied to the narrow interests of powerful private persons, namely the aristocracy. 'Publicness was the "aura of feudal authority"' (Habermas

1996:8) embodied in lordly codes of conduct, dress and rhetoric. With the rise of capitalism, however, and the technology of printing which it fostered, a public sphere independent of the state gradually emerged. In Britain by the 1730s, 'the press was for the first time established as a genuinely critical organ of a public engaged in critical political debate' (Habermas 1996:60). For example, it was at this time that the first attempts were made to publish parliamentary debates in the teeth of opposition from Parliament. This is a good indication of what the public sphere exists to provide: information about the activities of those in positions of power so that the effects those people and activities have on ordinary citizens can be understood and then responded to. The media themselves, then in the hands of small-scale private capitalists, were not, by and large, part of the 'old' power structure dominated by powerful agricultural capitalists and their class allies the merchants and a still embryonic class of manu-facturers (Thompson 1978:252–3).

The key role of this new public sphere was, Habermas argued, 'the subjection of domination to reason' (1996:117) so that power was no longer simply coercively imposed and arbitrary, but was subject to consent and reasoned use. This was the potential at any rate. The story of the media and the rise and fall of the public sphere has been framed within a narrative of dialectical reversal by Habermas and others (Curran and Seaton 1997). In its early phase, private property was 'the *precondition* for rational-critical debate' (Habermas 1996:164), but then, with the consolidation of the private media into large-scale business, the means of public communication were integrated into the new power structures of a mature capitalist society (1996:188). Thus Habermas writes of the *refeudalisation* (1996:195) of the public sphere, as it becomes once more the expression of private power pursuing its own interests.

In a society characterised by unequal concentrations of social, economic and political power, it is hardly surprising that the principles that might underpin a genuine public sphere, such as transparency, participation, debate, diversity, information, criticism and the capacity to turn knowledge into effective action, are rarely if ever substantially met. The lack of such cultural entitlements then exacerbates inequalities in a vicious circle that can breed violence, desperation and a threat to human security (Wilkin 2001). We now need to turn to a more detailed account of why and how the decidedly unfree free market cannot provide the conditions for a healthy public sphere. The basis of this critique has been summarised by Herman and Chomsky who have identified a number of 'filters' which allow 'the government and dominant private interests' (1994:2) to construct agendas within the media, suited to their goals. Their account has been criticised for being a little too 'instrumental' and presenting an overly integrated system without contradictions (Golding and Murdock 2000:73–4). Certainly we cannot say that critical media material never gets through. However, it does so *despite* the system, or via its contradictions, rather than because the system positively embodies public service principles. We also have to recognise that the discussion in this chapter takes place on a particular *scale of determination*, namely the economic and institutional structures of the media. But to read Eleanor Byrne and Martin McQuillan's deconstruction of Disney/Pixar's *Toy Story* (John Lasseter 1995 US) as an allegory of 'two competing myths of American militarism (the cowboy/sheriff Woody ... and the astronaut/Space Ranger Buzz Lightyear ...) coming to terms with their place in the New World Order' (1999:126), making 'humanitarian' interventions to rescue toys from the psychotic 'bad' boy Eric next door who does not respect his commodity/toys, is to be reminded that the making of meaning circulates through other political, social, cultural and historical scales of determination. The media–industry economics and institutions are one, albeit important, scale of determination, but we will have diminished the complexity of meaning making if we forget that this scale is also in a complex set of articulated relations with these other scales.

PROFIT ORIENTATION

The recent fate of UK commercial television indicates how the ratcheting up of the profit motive hollows out the public sphere. Like other public services, public service television is rapidly withering on the vine. The conditions for its institutional crises have been more or less deliberately fostered, its culture has been delegitimised, its regulatory regimes transformed, competition increased, and penetration by transnational capital facilitated. A pivotal moment was the 1990 Broadcasting Act. The Act prised ITV companies away from the public service principles within which they had hitherto been working. The ITV franchises were to be auctioned off, initially to the highest bidder, although 'quality' considerations were squeezed back in at the last, while ITV's old regulatory body was replaced with a new 'light' touch Independent

Television Commission (ITC). Here Conservative Party policy was also modified under the pressure of criticism and the ITC ended up asserting public service principles rather more robustly than was initially envisaged. However, as with other industries, the ITC, as a regulatory regime, is holding on to the tail of the tiger. The new ITV, competing now with Channel 4 and Five over advertising revenue, is massively more driven by the economic logic of the profit motive than the old ITV. A wave of mergers and takeovers has been allowed to proceed as ITV gears up to compete in the global market or become fat enough to be swallowed up by some larger European or American media leviathan.

In a more profit-orientated system, the minimum level of 'acceptable' ratings is raised. Suddenly a rating of 6 or 7 million viewers becomes unsustainable. News and current affairs programmes inevitably suffer in this environment. Thus ITV's attempt to shift *News at Ten* out of its traditional slot to make way for Hollywood movies and cop shows (only to partially reinstate it after a prolonged outcry and pressure from the ITC) is entirely predictable. ITN also slashed the value of its contract with ITV from £45 million to £36 million in order to see off a rival bid from a BSkyB consortium. The 'benefits' of such competition led to a round of job cuts particularly in its foreign bureaus. At the same time ITV also pressed ITN for more consumer, entertainment and leisure items in a bid to boost ratings and advertising revenues.[15]

Children's programming is another area that has felt the cold blast of commercialism. A Broadcasting Standards Commission report found that, by the late 1990s, children's television was increasingly dominated by imported American cartoons, many of which are geared around selling merchandise. Factual and drama programmes have conversely declined. It is not that animation is intrinsically impoverished, it can be highly inventive, nor is it that American imports are to be condemned as cultural imperialism. They often speak to their audience in a popular vernacular refreshingly different from the white middle-class characters that dominate British-produced children's programming. The key point though is that the force driving children's television programming is the unaccountable, systemic and autonomous logic of the market which will narrow choice and standardise product over the long run. Thus, while in 1981 9 per cent of the BBC's children's programming consisted of cartoons, by 1996 it was 35 per cent. Over the same period, ITV's reliance on cartoons moved from 9 per cent to 40 per cent.[16] As

Herman and McChesney note, 'in every nation there are powerful forces pressing the case for full integration into the global media market' (1997:50).

OFFICIAL SOURCES AND CONTACTS

As the media are transformed into large-scale corporations they increasingly interlock with the state in a symbiotic relationship of mutual benefit. Both formally and informally, the media and the state establish channels of communication with one another with the result that politics becomes defined as what goes on in Washington or Westminster. An extraordinarily narrow range of sources for news and comment becomes established and recycled in the close links between media, state and other corporations. Since the state itself has an enormous range of information and public relations resources at its disposal, it can dominate much of the agenda on any item. Far from challenging this, the media rely on such resources for regular output of data. The media also rely on politicians in particular for comment and so interviews have tacit ground rules concerning what can and cannot be asked and how far a point may be pressed. Print journalists are often so close to their political sources that they are virtually mouthpieces for their views. The reliance on established and mainstream political representatives means that when there is a virtual consensus between government and opposition on any issue of the day, as there is on practically every issue within America and the UK, then whole swathes of public opinion are routinely ignored and alternative policy choices remain unexplored. In those instances where media workers challenge rather than act as conduits for powerful state or corporate interests, they can be stifled and sacked. When Jane Akre and Steve Wilson, two journalists working for a US television station in Florida, investigated the biotechnology company Monsanto over its use of a hormone linked to colon cancer, their programme was never broadcast. The television station was owned by Rupert Murdoch's Fox TV, which kept the journalists rewriting the script for a year before firing them (Cohen 1999:138–40). There is evidently greater commonality and reciprocal sympathy between a multinational media corporation and a multinational biotechnology company, than between a multinational media corporation and its audiences.

ADVERTISING

Much of the media is dependent on advertising revenue and this is one of the most powerful and systemic pressures shaping media content. 'With advertising, the free market does not yield a neutral system in which final buyer choice decides. The advertisers' choices influence media prosperity and survival' (Herman and Chomsky 1994:14). Newspapers are the classic example of this. The final buyer choice is only one link in a longer commodity chain of which the most important for the newspaper and television industries is the purchase of media space or time by advertisers in order to get access to media consumers. The price of the newspaper, for example, does not cover the costs of its production, a simple economic fact that bonds the industry very effectively to the advertisers. As production costs escalate, the choices of the advertisers concerning who they advertise with have over a long historical period massively narrowed the range of voices that can access the public sphere and the constituencies who can be represented within it. One of the weaknesses of Habermas' account of the early capitalist public sphere is his overwhelming and exclusive focus on the *bourgeois* public sphere. There was, however, a working-class public sphere fostered by the early-nineteenth-century print media. At that time radical papers could cover their production costs by the cover price alone once they achieved a certain circulation figure (Curran and Seaton 1997:16). However, with the rising cost of new technology, raw materials and distribution, the industry became more reliant on advertising. Thus the preferences of advertisers to spend their money on papers with a more socially mixed readership that included the affluent middle classes became increasingly decisive. The radical press, which were the voice of the working class and addressed to the working class, went under as advertisers were consistently less attracted to such material. This is not a matter of ancient history. In the UK, the 1960s saw working-class papers such as the *Daily Herald, News Chronicle* and *Sunday Citizen* fail or be absorbed into establishment systems despite huge circulations (Herman and Chomsky 1994:15). In 1980, the *Evening News*, the London daily paper, was subsumed into the *Evening Standard*. From that time on, the *Standard*, a very right-wing paper ferociously hostile to trade unions, has dominated the daily print news agenda of the capital city. Yet the *Evening News* outsold the *Standard* by 500,000 to 400,000 copies at its death in 1980. But because the *News* was orientated to a more working-class readership it generated lower advertising income than the *Standard*, which was orientated to a more affluent middle-class readership.[17] Once again, the choices of the advertisers weighed more heavily in the market place than those of the buying public.

The advertisers also shape the media content of those media which they use to carry their messages. Both directly, by lobbying newspaper editors and television schedulers, and indirectly, by choosing to not advertise around certain media content, advertisers powerfully shape the media agenda. Their principal interest is in finding media environments that will not be detrimental to the feel-good, aspirational messages that they want to attach to the advertised products (Wayne 2000:209–14). Media content which criticises business, which investigates corporate culpability in environmental issues, Third World activities, safety for workers, or even tough-minded consumer affairs programmes are unwelcome as far as advertisers are concerned (Herman and Chomsky 1994:17). Of course, this is not to say that you cannot find such media content in the media, but there are economic limits as to how much media material perceived as detrimental to the advertisers can be accommodated.

CONFLICTING INTERESTS

Shorn of its comforting allusion to a dispersal of power, the metaphor of a web to describe the economy of advanced capitalism is frighteningly appropriate. So sprawling now are the interests of media corporations in hundreds, sometimes thousands, of subsidiaries and subcontractors in all markets around the world, that it is hardly surprising when the interests of profit margins conflict with the promotion of critical reasoning. The public implications of private economic activities constitute the rift in social affairs which the contemporary media cannot heal precisely because their 'publicness' is itself a product of massive private economic interests. General Electric (GE) owns the US television network NBC. How autonomous can NBC news be from the interests of its parent company? Throughout its history, this manufacturer of power plants, nuclear reactors, nuclear missiles, jet engines and so forth has been periodically in the news for corporate fraud of one kind or another (Bagdikian 1997: 209). It is very reliant in its heavy manufacturing sectors on government contracts, opening the prospect that the news becomes a point of leverage with governments, increasing or decreasing in favourable coverage as and when necessary. Thus economic power becomes political power (Meier and Trappel 1998:39).

Like other corporations, General Electric is especially keen to enter the potentially huge Chinese market. Jeff Immelt, General Electric's chief executive officer, has said that 'China's hosting of the 2008 Olympics ... is going to show the world that China is a far cleaner place to do business than a lot of people imagine.'[18] Indeed. Other people 'imagine' that China has an appalling human and civil rights record and no independent trade unions. But Immelt exudes that boardroom machismo so typical of such individuals cosseted from real hardship. 'It's a hard-nosed commercial culture and GE likes it', he says.

China entered the World Trade Organization (WTO) a little over a decade after the Chinese authorities gunned down and crushed with tanks the 1989 pro-democracy movement centred in Tiananmen Square. They were helped in this (entry into the WTO, not the gunning down of protestors) by media moguls such as Disney's Michael Eisner (Disney are building a theme park in Hong Kong) and News International's Rupert Murdoch, both of whom lobbied the US Congress to 'normalise' trade relations with China.[19] Along with AOL Time Warner, Murdoch's Asian Star TV company has been broadcasting from Hong Kong to hotels, government offices and the Chinese elite in the rich Guangdong province. This is all part of a long-term process by which the Chinese market (with a staggering 1.25 billion people) will be gradually opened up to Western capitalism. In 1993 Murdoch gave a speech extolling how a 'free' (that is capitalist) media would strike terror into the hearts of dictatorships everywhere. Murdoch has since taken such a tough line with dictatorships that he threw the BBC World Service TV off his Asian Star TV satellite because the BBC's reporting had upset the Chinese authorities, while his publishing company, HarperCollins, withdrew from publishing a book by Chris Patten after he had infuriated the Chinese authorities by introducing more democracy into Hong Kong before its handover to the Chinese in 1997. News International's defence of freedom does not stop there. In March 2001, Murdoch's son, James, Star TV's chairman, denounced the banned religious group the Falun Gong, many of whose members are languishing in jail (and dying when not languishing). He also lambasted the Western media for their overly negative portrayal of China.[20] One has to wonder how free the many channels of news and information under Murdoch's control can be in their reporting of China and other areas where business interests are at stake. With GE, AOL Time Warner, Disney and others manoeuvring to get access to this market, the spaces for critical coverage are rapidly diminishing.

This chapter has argued that capitalism's tendency towards the concentration and centralisation of capital (the Three Cs Thesis), mapped out by the monopoly capitalism paradigm, is still very much central to its economic logic. However, the precise social and organisational forms through which the mode of production's accumulation process continues have developed in response to changing historical circumstances. These changes in the mode of development (the shift or, perhaps better, overlap between Fordism and post-Fordism) have in turn impacted on the cultural products produced by the media–industrial complex. These new organisational forms give capitalism the appearance of plurality and diversity that is belied by the centralisation of power and capital actually taking place. While media corporations have adapted to and promoted more segmented and differentiated markets with the help of subsidiaries and subcontractors, the cultural goods they produce are part of a pervasive decentralised accumulation logic that has as its corollary the centralisation of media corporate capital. Ultimately, then, the way we can integrate the monopoly capitalist paradigm and the post-Fordist paradigm is by deploying the crucial Marxist distinction between *appearance-forms* (fragmentation, diversity, plurality, autonomy, etc.) which flexible specialisation theory has explored and *real relations* (concentration and centralisation of capital and control) which have been the terrain of most political economy of the media. Within Marxist theory, appearance-forms are not mere illusions: they are, as we have seen, generated up out of the real relations themselves. The M-form corporate structure with its profit centres emerges as the dominant corporate response to the problems caused by the centralisation and diversification of (media) capital within a global market in which the one corporation requires brand flexibility to tap into segmented markets. The implications of continuing monopolistic trends for the public sphere and therefore debate, dialogue, genuine freedom of expression, diversity, education, reason and finally democracy, have profound implications for public policy. To understand the current trends within public media policy, we need to now turn to the question of the state and its contradictory relations with capital.

4   The State: Regulating the Impossible

> The state is the product and the manifestation of the *irreconcilability* of class contradictions.
>
> Lenin, *The State and Revolution*

> The modern state is brought into being in its specific historical modality above all in order to be able to exercise *comprehensive control* over the unruly centrifugal forces emanating from the separate productive units of capital as an antagonistically structured social reproductive system.
>
> Mészáros, *Beyond Capital*

The normative goal of Marxism is to diminish and eventually abolish the power of the state in the affairs of women and men. From this goal derives Marxism's analysis and critique of the state under capitalism. Together with the powers of capital, the state constitutes one of the most important power complexes in society and yet within much cultural theory the role this apparatus of control and intervention has in influencing cultural production and consumption is often neglected. In media studies, the question of the state emerges most clearly around discussions of media policy and the legal regulations and institutional regulators that affect the activities of media companies and producers. Yet most discussions of concrete policy issues and debates take place without any explicit general theory of the state, even those informed by or congruent with a Marxist theory of the state. This is particularly problematic because it opens the way for critical accounts of the state to be assimilated into liberal theories of the state. It is essential therefore to distinguish between Marxist and liberal theories of the state and this in turn requires an explicit theoretical framework. The liberal conception of the state has it managing the competing legitimate claims of different groups in society, balancing them so that all interests are served and that no one bloc or group predominates over the others (Miliband 1987:4–5). The Marxian view is different, but without an explicit theory of the state the sophisticated Marxian analysis – which rejects seeing the state as a mere puppet of capital – may on the surface *appear* to be not so very different from a critical liberal account of the state and

87

its relations with a variety of social interests (see for example Goodwin 1999). It is important then to stress that where liberal theory sees legitimate claims, the Marxian view sees antagonistic and incompatible interests; where the liberal view sees competition, the Marxian view sees an asymmetrical field of power relations; and where the liberal view sees the state as a rational mechanism for resolving disputes, the Marxian view sees the state as a microcosm of the contradictions tearing at the heart of society, standing not outside or above them, but incorporating them into its own structures and strategies.

We need to understand then what is specific about the *capitalist* state if we are to understand how the liberal democratic capitalist state has operated in the past and what recent changes it has undergone in its *modus operandi*. The specificity of the capitalist state lies in its formal, institutional separation between the political and the economic realms, a separation that achieves its highest stage of legitimacy in the liberal democratic state. It is the paradoxes and complexities of this separation between the political and the economic that constitutes a central theme of this chapter. As we shall see, what makes this separation particularly difficult for theory is that it is both a real separation which has to be grasped if the complexities of the state are to be understood, and yet, at one and the same time, it is a separation that has to be bridged theoretically because in practice it is continually breached by the selfsame social relations which wrench the political and economic realms apart in the first place: namely capitalism and the capitalist state. There is a further level of complexity insofar as there are a great many variations of capitalist states and liberal democratic capitalist states as each one is grounded in a plurality of *national* circumstances, with different social, political and cultural histories and configurations. To theorise the state then necessarily requires a degree of abstraction, but this will be illustrated by as many concrete examples as I can squeeze in. We shall explore the changing role of the state in the context of some of the changes in corporate structures discussed in the previous chapter and we shall also look at the problematic relations between the state and the nation which globalisation has initiated.

BEING 'REALISTIC': CONTEMPORARY MEDIA POLICY TRENDS

The new media landscape dates back to the early 1980s when a political shift to neo-liberal market economics interlocked with new satellite and cable technology, to allow private capital extensive entry to a field once dominated by public service broadcasters, whether funded through the state or, where they existed, as in the UK, strongly regulated commercial providers such as ITV (McQuail 1998b:109). There was a 'paradigmatic shift' (Humphreys 1996:160) in the way states right across Europe, and indeed other parts of the world, such as India and Japan, thought about broadcasting in particular and media policy in general. Obviously, policies in this period were not uniform, although there was some broad co-ordination at a European level, but the trends were clear: public service broadcasting (and other public) monopolies were broken up and numerous private commercial operators entered the field; public service obligations for the commercial sector were scaled down; consumer sovereignty was exalted; broadcasting was re-evaluated primarily as an industry, a commodity out of which money could be made and the key question for policy became how to ensure 'competitiveness' in the industry (Meier and Trappel 1998:40). As the industrial and economic dimensions of broadcasting have become paramount within media policy, so there has been a consequent marginalisation of cultural and political questions which European states once took to be axiomatic. There was a period, particularly post-1945, when the state could embody a critique of the free market: its ability to sustain diversity and quality, its marginalisation of any material which fell below certain thresholds of profitability, its regional polarisations, its exclusion of those who could not afford to pay for services, its control by influential private proprietors, all this once constituted the common sense of the state apparatus and its personnel. Yet despite the trends towards privatisation, commercialisation, media concentration and internationalisation (McQuail 1998a:1) the question of cultural politics remains stubbornly, if subordinately, on the agenda; the anxieties generated by the commodification of culture refuse to go away and the complete dissolution of cultural values by exchange value (the reduction of everything to quantitative/financial measurement) is as impossible as free market capitalism dispensing with the state.

The United Nations Educational, Science and Cultural Organization (UNESCO) argue that: 'The question is not *whether* governments should adopt cultural policies, but *how* they should do so more effectively.'[1] Cultural goods are unlike other goods in that they very clearly foreground the socialisation of the mode of production and consumption. Cultural goods 'break through' the model of private appropriation (for consumers and producers) to the extent that they are evidently immersed in and facilitate the communication and exchange of meaning(s) in a way that a VCR, a fridge or a car, does not. This is the basis on which all sorts of agents, including fascists, liberals and leftists, will appeal to the state (although not usually using the same language and rationale), arguing that with culture we are dealing with more than cans of baked beans. Culture, even when it is overwhelmingly produced by capital and through the market, is not, in such discourses, reducible merely to economics and profit margins, but involves such unquantifiable questions as identity, consciousness, history, memory, perception, aspirations, information and education. Thus a liberal humanist like David Puttnam will make the case for the pedagogic role of film, despite its immersion in the profit motive (Puttnam 1997:357). And the case has historically and institutionally been made even stronger in relation to radio and television.

The political balance of forces between capital and labour, as mediated by the state, is the fundamental context in which to understand the current marginality of cultural/political questions within media policy making. For reasons that we will come to, this is the bigger picture that is often screened out of media policy debates. An altered arrangement in the balance of forces – a not inconceivable possibility – would in turn push cultural and political questions further to the centre of policy making concerns. It was after all the political context in which broadcasting first emerged and matured that decisively shaped its subsequent public trajectory. To stress the political as a mediation of the socio-economic cuts against those arguments which suggest that broadcasting emerged as a public medium due to technological determinism. Unlike the print media, radio required a spectrum of the airwaves to be broadcast and, since this was limited, state involvement, it has been argued, grew from if not technological necessity, then the pressure of technological considerations. Briggs writes of the 'alarm at the "chaos of the ether" in the United States' where the 'multiplicity of radio stations and the scarcity of wavelengths led to interference and overlapping' (1961:64). Briggs, however, also notes that behind the technical considerations there was a more fundamental 'division of outlook' (1961:65). Yet the technical argument remains a popular explanation because it provides an apparently non-political explanation for the erasing of public service broadcasting today, since, with the development of cable, satellite and digital provision, spectrum scarcity no longer exists, and so, ergo, neither does the rationale for public service broadcasting (Goodwin 1999:131).

The argument that the roots of public service broadcasting are largely, or even partially, technological, confuses two different kinds of state involvement. State licensing of the legal right to broadcast is certainly necessary where scarcity exists, but state funding/ownership is a rather different matter. It is perfectly possible for the state to hand out licences to commercial operators, as of course happened in the United States with the setting up of the Federal Radio Commission in 1927. Had broadcasting developed as an institutional operation at the same time as cinema, at the turn of the twentieth century, it almost certainly would have been dominated by commercial forces in Europe. The European political context by the 1920s, however, was very different. This was the period in which monopoly capitalism was establishing itself as an irreversible trend; it was the period in which organised labour was making powerful claims against the chaotic and cyclical nature of capitalism. And thus it was also the period in which the state became more involved in regulating and indeed owning large-scale industries in an attempt to bring some stability to national economies. This was the *end* of 'an age in which the fundamental attitude of the government and the economists was ... the less it could manage to intervene in the economy, the better' (Hobsbawm 1968:190). Thus in the UK the railways were amalgamated in 1921, the electricity supply concentrated and partly nationalised in 1926, the same year that radio broadcasting was established as a public monopoly; 1927 saw the first substantive intervention into the film industry, designed to encourage the growth of two vertically integrated film companies (Chanan 1983:57), a monopolisation of iron and steel was state sponsored in 1932, London Transport was unified as a public system in 1933 and a national coal cartel was organised in 1936. Public service broadcasting developed (and today has declined) as a result of *political choices*.

We are today evidently in a different political context, one that has had a corresponding effect on media policy analysis. Media policy analysis has become notably pragmatic, 'long on "realism" ... and rather short on idealism, fundamental criticism and visions of a communication future which does more than service the global market' (McQuail 1997:43). The evacuation of cultural politics from media policy analysis, faithfully imitates the state's own strategic withdrawal from this arena and its subsequent colonisation by an apparently 'non-political' economic logic which gives consumers what they want and not what state appointed elites think they need. Or so the argument goes. Collins and Murroni can be taken as one example of media policy advocacy that has, in some respects, diminished ambitions. However, their 'realist' project is actually rather contradictory. They want a liberalised market but they also want a regulatory regime that can sustain competition (1996:9). The problem, however, is that their desired liberalised market comes out of one political context (the present one) but their desire for a regulatory regime with sufficient teeth to protect cultural goals evokes another political context, one past or future.

At this point it might be useful to distinguish between two types of unrealistic policy analysis. The first type of analysis might be considered unrealistic within a given set of political conditions that are *external* to the assessment itself. There is nothing wrong with this; indeed, it is rather essential. Collins and Murroni's call for fairly tough regulation (as we shall see) falls into this category, but this is disguised by their largely pro-market noises concerning the need for liberalisation. The second type of assessment or analysis may be considered unrealistic because of *internal* contradictions within the discourse. In principle, the first type of assessment might become 'realistic' within a changed political context. The second type of assessment may conversely appear on the surface to be more realistic because it chimes in with the *dominant* political trends at a given moment, but may be in substantive terms less realistic than the first kind of 'unrealism' because of internal conceptual dislocations and inadequacies. Collins and Murroni's analysis of media policy also seems to me to fall into this latter category. Mixed in with some uncritical acceptance of the myths of market efficiency, there are in fact various acknowledgements that the market is flawed. They note that the market excludes consumers, that there is a tendency towards monopoly (1996:9) and that, being risk averse, the market standardises goods over time (1996:63). But these observations are treated discretely and are never synthesised into a coherent theoretical framework. Thus each problem appears to be open to some administrative, regulatory or technological correction. There is no sense that these problems, such as the relationship between competition and monopoly, are being generated from the irrepressible contradictions of capitalism. There is, and this is characteristic of bourgeois political economy and philosophy, a real fissure in their thinking between *is* and *ought*, fact and value, between how the market actually operates and how they would like it to operate. This fissure is precisely what the state in general and regulation in particular seek to resolve and heal.

The problem, however, is that their concrete policy proposals sound unrealistic in the first sense (dislocated from external political conditions) because the liberalisation they desire and the regulation they need to suture the contradiction between is and ought come out of two very different political contexts. For example, in order to protect diversity, they are concerned that editorial and journalistic independence be codified into a system of 'Rights' and draw on suggestions made in the 1977 Royal Commission on the Press (Collins and Murroni 1996:73–4). These include the right to reject material provided by central management; the right to determine the contents of the paper (within the bounds of reasonable economic consideration and established policy); the right to carry out investigative journalism and criticise the paper's own group or other parts of the same corporate organisation. Characteristically, Collins and Murroni give no discussion of the structural pressures on editorial and journalistic independence (see Chapter 3). Since these are systemic and intensifying within a converging, diversifying and internationalising media market, any substantial consideration of them would undermine their pro-market zeal. So, were the Rights which the Commission proposed (in a different political context) actually enforced, it would bring the state into some considerable conflict with private property. The absence in Collins and Murroni's account of the context of political and economic power makes their hopes of reconciling liberalisation and effective regulation seem very unrealistic. Regulation, in terms of social and cultural obligations, is precisely what liberalisation seeks to avoid.

Another example of the pragmatic orientation of policy analysis can be found in Tony Bennett's call for a 'revisionary programme' within cultural studies, one which severs its connection with 'oppositional formulations' (1997:42) and gets on with the task of 'training cultural technicians' (1997:53). Both cultural studies and the graduates it turns out would then distance themselves from the social movements which it had hitherto some, although as Bennett rightly notes, contradictory relationship with, and instead enter 'the fields of social administration and management in which the social and political demands of different constituencies are translated into practicable administrative options' (Bennett 1997:57). The language is deliberately prosaic and hardly intended to set the pulse racing. But in trying to orientate cultural studies to some limited 'practical effects' (1997:55) Bennett is making two assumptions. First, he assumes a universality to the liberal democratic capitalist state which does not exist. This programme would hardly make sense, for example, to the students of Otpor, the Serbian student union that took on the authoritarian regime of Slobodan Milosevic in the 1990s. If this example seems a trifle exotic for Western European/American readers, then, second, Bennett's call for a prosaic cultural politics not only assumes a universality to the liberal democratic capitalist state which does not exist, it also imputes to it a crisis-free stability that is equally questionable. One only has to think about the lamentable role of the American media in informing their public on America's foreign policy interventions and the absence of debate about how to respond to the terrorist attacks on the World Trade Center to realise that severing cultural studies from social movements and committing oneself to working within 'practicable administrative options' could involve a tremendous ethical and political cost.

THEORISING THE STATE

In the previous chapter we saw that the changing corporate structures of capital give the system the *appearance-form* of plurality and diversity. So too with the capitalist state, we enter a world of paradoxes and facades in which the state appears to be an impersonal mechanism of public authority set apart from the socio-economic realm (Holloway and Picciotto 1991:113). As with the corporate structures themselves, this appearance-form is no mere illusion; it has real institutional grounding. Yet at the same time – and this is the point of making a distinction between appearance-forms and real relations – there is something partial, incomplete, one-sided and insubstantial in this reality. In penetrating those appearance-forms we inevitably move beyond social democratic theory that stresses the autonomy of the state. But, in our excitement at reconnecting the state to the real relations of capital that lie beneath the appearance-forms of state autonomy, we must be careful not to fall into the opposite 'vulgar' Marxist error of assuming a simple *identity* between the state and monopoly capitalism (Clarke 1991:3). Conversely, in penetrating these appearance-forms, we also move beyond the neo-liberal fantasy of markets and economic actors operating as if *they* were autonomous from politics and the state.

In thinking about how the state operates in relation to capital and other social classes it is useful to distinguish between its twin operational imperatives: accumulation and legitimation (Habermas 1976:96). Table 4.1 maps out these activities. To take the question of economic accumulation first, one of the most important activities that the national state is involved in during the present conjuncture is international trade negotiations, which establish the legal and regulatory framework for free market capitalism. The most important forum for such negotiations is the World Trade Organization, which in 1997 formulated the General Agreement on Trade in Services (GATS). This included a particular provision committing nation-states to opening up and deregulating telecommunications markets. As a Brussels-based director for the American telephone and cable giant AT&T admitted: 'First among those to benefit from this new environment are operators with international ambitions. Those operators with the greatest financial clout, technical sophistication and diversity of offerings can now expand into markets globally.'[2] One has to distinguish then between the state's withdrawal from social and cultural obligations, which it once guaranteed, and the *extensive involvement* of the state in providing the ground rules for international intra-capitalist competition by harmonising laws and regulations between nations and setting international objectives.

Table 4.1   Twin Operations of the State

Accumulation	i.	International Trade Negotiations
	ii.	Domestic Policy
	iii.	Regulatory Bodies
Legitimation		Consent: Social and Cultural Obligations
		Coercion: Censorship

Accumulation also requires the state to formulate and implement national media and cultural policy and set up the regulatory bodies to oversee the day-to-day operation of media industries (particularly broadcasting and film, the press have their own self-regulatory body). But the state's activities in co-ordinating and administrating accumulation cannot take place without the continual legitimation of the capitalist system. Legitimation has two modes: consent and coercion. Through the mode of consent, famously first explored within the Marxian tradition by Antonio Gramsci, the state registers and accommodates those interests and needs which the subordinate classes have organised and mobilised around and which can be channelled into the parameters of capitalism. The winning of the consent of the subordinate classes to the rule of the dominant class, what Gramsci calls hegemony, thus requires the latter to make strategic concessions to the former, to make sacrifices which nevertheless do not 'touch the essential ... the decisive function exercised by the leading group in the decisive nucleus of economic activity' (Gramsci 1971:161).

In the field of media and cultural policy, this is evident where accumulation strategies are tempered by social and cultural obligations that would not be catered for by the market. Such concessions are achieved through direct cultural subsidy (public service broadcasting for example) and/or regulatory supervision (the Arts Council, the Film Council, OFCOM, etc.). It is clear that the current period is characterised by a diminution in the amount of concessions the state calculates it needs to extract from capital in order to facilitate its reproduction. Consent is not just a registering of interests and needs from 'below', it also involves the state 'talking back', through the media, through its own agencies, through its management and interpretation of data, and in this way framing the debate and setting the agenda. Thus the withdrawal of the state from protecting social and cultural obligations has paradoxically involved extensive state propaganda designed to persuade and cajole populations into accepting the 'benefits' of flexible, deregulated labour and consumer markets.

The state also works to sustain the legitimacy of the system through more coercive means, whereby the legal apparatus can be mobilised to check and contain threats to the state or corporations. There are a panoply of laws around national security, defamation and copyright that either the state or corporations or rich individuals can mobilise to restrict media expression. UK libel laws are particularly constricting since they place the onus on the defendant to prove that the charge is true (Petley 1999:145). Legitimate areas of concern or suspicion can become no-go areas for the media unless they have cast iron evidence prior to publication. Thus, for example, the *Ecologist*, the flagship radical green magazine (funded by millionaire Teddy Goldsmith), had a special issue criticising the genetic engineering company Monsanto pulped by their own printers who were afraid that they may be sued by the company.[3] The police federation used the threat of libel to try and censor and suppress screenings of the film *Injustice* (Ken Fero and Tariq Mehmood 2001 GB), which investigated cases of black people dying in police custody. At various screenings around the UK, police solicitors faxed the cinema shortly before the event warning of litigation and forcing managers to put the cinema's assets before free expression.[4] Driven underground, the film-makers began shifting screenings at the last minute to alternative venues (squats, cafes, halls, etc.) in an extraordinary return to the kind of guerrilla cinema once associated with Third World dictatorships (Wayne 2001:56–60).

Finally the state can resort to direct physical force – indeed, for many writers, the state's monopolisation of what is regarded as legitimate force is one of its defining features. During the war in Afghanistan following the 11 September destruction of the World Trade Center towers, American pilots 'accidentally' bombed the Kabul offices of Al Jazeera, the Arab television station that had come to prominence after it broadcast videotape footage of Osama bin Laden. This was regarded as something of a propaganda coup for bin Laden and the US were clearly disturbed by his access to Arab public opinion. Meanwhile, back home, the US White House press secretary, Ari Fleischer, denounced Bill Maher, the host of ABC's satire *Politically Incorrect*, after he questioned whether it is, strictly speaking, 'cowardly' to stay in a plane while you are ploughing it into a building. Fleisher in turn warned that all Americans had to 'watch what they say and watch what they do'. Disney/ABC subsequently declined to renew Maher's contract.

THE POLITICAL AND THE ECONOMIC

In all earlier modes of production, the dominant socio-economic class also personally dominated the state apparatus. What is novel and historically unique about capitalism is that it is the first mode of production to wrench the political and economic realms apart. This separation profoundly marks mainstream media analysis which often discusses industry economics abstracted from political power and institutions while the politics of media policy making is often discussed abstracted from socio-economic relations. Such crippling compartmentalisation in consciousness has its social roots in the institutional separation of political and economic power. The CEOs of Time Warner, Vivendi, and Bertelsmann, and so forth, do not sit in their respective national legislative assemblies or cabinet executives alongside their capitalist competitors. This is not to say that businesspeople do not become politicians. Mike Davis has described US President George W. Bush and his cabinet of millionaires as 'virtually an executive committee of the energy and defence industries'.[5] The colonisation of the executive by capital suggests that, like fish, the liberal democratic capitalist state rots from the head down. Prior to

11 September 2001, Bush's close connection with multinational corporations was definitely generating a problem of legitimacy. It is a problem that also dogs the Italian Prime Minister, Silvio Berlusconi, re-elected for a second time in 2001. As a media mogul, Berlusconi owns the holding company Fininvest which has controlling stakes in film production, publishing, and television networks. Of the latter, Berlusconi owns the three largest private broadcasters in Italy. As Prime Minister he also has powers of patronage over appointments to the Italian state broadcaster RAI, thus effectively giving him control and/or influence over 95 per cent of the television media. Within Europe, Berlusconi is an exceptional case, and the taint of illegitimacy this gives to his government makes it permanently crisis-prone. But even within his government Berlusconi is the exception, surrounded by conventional (if very right-wing and even 'post'-fascist) politicians on whom he depends. The ideological crisis of the Berlusconi government shows how a scenario in which the CEOs participated directly in government would haemorrhage political legitimacy for the liberal capitalist state. This legitimacy is the bread and butter of media reporting in the West, which rarely explores the network of ties and relations between the activities of elected functionaries and capital. But the thought of CEOs sitting in cabinet together as representatives of their companies is in any case an impossible scenario for good socio-economic reasons. The representatives of the corporations would be unable to provide the necessary cohesion and direction for capital in general since they would serve only their own particular corporate interests.

Marx described capitalists as a band of hostile brothers, and this *intra-class* competition within the capitalist class is one very powerful reason why capitalists need the state. One role that the state performs here is to provide the legal framework within which competition can take place and to provide the mechanisms of adjudication when the legalities are broken. Thus, for example, in 2002 the French company Canal Plus filed allegations against NDS, a company controlled by Rupert Murdoch's News Corporation. The charge is that NDS used a laboratory in Israel to crack the codes of the television smart cards produced by Canal Plus and used for subscription television by Murdoch *competitors*. Canal Plus allege that the codes were then publicised by a web site that received NDS funding, thus creating a black market in the smart cards and a black hole in the finances of companies, such as Murdoch competitor ITV Digital, which used them. It is clear at any rate from other examples of business practices that have come to light in the courts that, without the state, capitalism would rapidly descend into commercial warlordism.

Thus Mészáros defines the state as providing 'the totalising political command structure of capital' (1995:49) as it tries to effect some control and cohesion over the otherwise disruptive 'unruly centrifugal forces emanating from the separate productive units of capital' (1995:50). Intra-class competition means that the state has some independence from *particular* agents of capital, but this independence is paradoxically a condition of its integration into the parameters of capital in general. For once the state is constituted as a separate political realm it becomes the target, the point of convergence, on which all the competing 'unruly' units of capital seek to exercise their influence. A minister flies to a foreign country and, if it is a high-profile visit, the media will no doubt cover it. But what will remain invisible or at best only obliquely referenced in the television and newspaper reports is the phalanx of businessmen (they usually are men) also on the plane with the minister, and whose commercial interests in our foreign country the good minister seeks to extend. The minister's independence from any one personification of capital on that plane is the very condition for his or her subordination to the role of sales agent for capital in general.

The state then works on behalf of capital *in general*, but we have to be careful here because it would be quite wrong to imply that capital itself has a general interest. If it did then the task of the state would be a great deal simpler than in fact it is. Although one could propose that capital has a general interest in a very broad sense, namely securing the conditions of capital accumulation, when it comes to formulating and implementing concrete policies and specific strategies, there is no general interest of capital, only a host of competing interests. Thus, while the state works on behalf of capital in general, this work can be very conflictual precisely because capital has no general interest in most concrete circumstances (leaving aside possible revolutionary threats to the entire edifice). For example, the Conservative Party's 1988 White Paper on broadcasting concerned itself with restructuring ITV as a more market-orientated network. To this end, the White Paper proposed that the franchises (the licences) to broadcast be auctioned off to the highest bidder, a move that signalled that the 'quality' of the provision, the cultural value of the output, was of absolutely no interest to the government whatsoever. This proposal was 'bitterly contested' (Goodwin 1999:138). The companies *already* operating as broadcasters joined forces with trade unions, consumer groups, and so on, against the plan. 'The critics pointed out that newcomers eager to cash in on the promised boom, would overprice their bids and then be left with insufficient cash to make their programmes' (Mattelart 1991:102). In this instance, the competition between the incumbent capitalists and prospective newcomers helped weaken the capitalist bloc and, in the event, 'quality' considerations were introduced into the bidding process, thus allowing the incumbents an advantage since they could point to their track record in producing cultural value and not just economic value.

It is also important to grasp that the state is not a homogeneous unity counterpoised against the fractured competing units of capital. The state apparatus is itself internally fractured, with different sections and components of it having traditional ties, leanings and alliances with competing and conflicting interests in wider society. This internal differentiation of the state is not to be conceived in liberal democratic terms as some kind of balance of powers. For these different arms and compartments of the state are characterised by an asymmetry of power skewed towards minority interests outside the state. This is very evident in the European Union (EU) bureau-cratic apparatus. The European Commission, which is responsible for initiating EU policy, is composed of different organs, such as Directorate General III which took the lead in formulating the free market deregulation of television in the 1980s, while the weaker Directorate General X, historically linked to the older public service broadcasters, became a vehicle for some mild counter-pressure (Humphreys 1996:269). The most recent success of this counter-pressure was the 1997 amendment to the 1989 free market directive 'Television Without Frontiers'. The amendment stipulated that

> Member states remain free to apply to broadcasters under their jurisdiction more detailed or stricter rules ... concerning the achievement of language policy goals, protection of the public interest in terms of television's role as a provider of information, education, culture and entertainment.[6]

Here we see a minor comeback for policy with cultural as opposed to merely economic ambitions. The reason for this resurfacing of cultural criteria points to another feature of the state that we need to take on board. States do not exist in isolation but as part of an *interstate system* which has two essential features: it is a hierarchical system with some states much more powerful than others and it is a system made up of a patchwork of alliances and competition between states (just like companies). The size of the state's nation in which it sits and the concentration and centralisation of capital within the nation – which forms the basis of tax receipts for the state's operations – are crucial in determining the place of the state in the pecking order of power and influence. As members of a competitive alliance of unequal nation-states, it became clear to the European elites during the late 1980s and 1990s, that their free market audio-visual policies could lead to the television market being flooded with American imports, which commercial broadcasters could purchase more cheaply than making their own (European) programmes. American producers could sell programmes at bargain-basement prices because, as with the film industry, they had already covered their costs by selling to their own huge market. For some capitalist operations within Europe and for some states, such as Germany and the UK, this is hardly a problem. For the smaller television producers within Europe, for some states, such as France, and for the public service broadcasters, the prospect of such 'cultural dumping', as it is known, represents a threat around which there has been some continuing struggle. There was, for example, the inclusion of quotas within the Television Without Frontiers directive, which was a French inspired measure to keep a lid on the amount of American television that European broadcasters could import. The quotas, which stipulated a 50 per cent limit, were fatally weakened by a clause that allowed broadcasters to stick to them 'where practicable'. The 1997 amendment is just another staging post in this ongoing struggle.

The fact that the intra-capitalist competition which the state regulates is not only that of its 'own' capital units, but also between its own capital units and international competitors within a hierarchical interstate system, is one of the most important social fault-lines determining media and cultural policy. If the relations between capital and the 'traditional' working class set the general ground tone for policy, the fault-line between the national intelligentsia and the international bourgeoisie (and their national 'comprador' capital allies such as cinema exhibitors) is the more immediate class relation determining media policy. The intelligentsia are a highly differentiated grouping, occupying the state apparatus, overlapping with capital as small (petit bourgeois) producers, for example, and, as cultural workers, overlapping with wage-labour. The different compositions of cultural capital amongst the intelligentsia, for example, whether they are orientated towards mass markets or more art house audiences, are also a key differential. But both mass- and art-orientated film-makers and producers have been responsible for a long tradition of pressure within nations dominated by Hollywood (which is most of the world film market) for 'their' state to protect them from complete commercial annihilation by Hollywood and even aid them through various measures such as tax breaks, quotas, subsidies, and institutional promotion and direction of the domestic industry (Moran 1996). The state is then torn between the economic and cultural claims which such lobbying makes concerning the importance of domestic film production, and the fact that policy action that conflicts with American business interests could easily provoke the anger and power of the United States state. Within the UK the most recent outcome of these pressures, tensions and compromises has been the establishment of the Film Council, funded by National Lottery money and tasked with the aim of providing a coherent policy approach for both the commercial and more independent wings of the cinema. This includes direct subsidy to film production, distribution and marketing as well as training and educational initiatives. However, neither the Film Council nor the British state will touch the domination of the crucial distribu- tion networks by North American capital, since they are protected by the US almost as vigorously as oil pipelines.

Within Europe there are two programmes for promoting audio- visual culture. The MEDIA programme was pushed by the French through the European Commission. MEDIA I ran between 1990 and 1995, MEDIA II between 1996 and 2000 and the MEDIA Plus programme runs between 2001 and 2005. The emphasis of the programme is on training professionals, developing projects and companies, distributing and promoting film and television work and providing support for film festivals. It has, however, very modest budgets which limit its work and reflect that 'its sponsoring direc- torate general', DGX, is 'not a notably strong voice in the Commission's bureaucratic hierarchy' (Humphreys 1996:281). The other programme, Eurimages, was set up by the French – again reflecting the particular traditions of prioritising culture which that state has had historically – through the Council of Europe in 1988. It too has very modest budgets, evidence of the struggle between and subordinate position of cultural policy in relation to industrially- oriented policy. Within the new political framework, such state interventions may be designated as neo-corporatist (Jessop 1997:268). They are corporatist as in the old Fordist/Keynesian period when states attempted to forge a consensus between different social agents, but they are 'neo' insofar as the centre of political gravity has shifted and intervention takes place on the neo-liberal basis of encouraging international competitiveness, making markets work and ironing out historical inequalities in the playing field. Eurimages offers direct subsidies for European film-makers, encouraging co-operation across national borders by funding co-productions between two or more states who are paid-up members of the fund. Eurimages now has two schemes, one stressing the circulation potential of the proposed film (this is the economic scheme) and one that stresses its 'cultural' potential. Here the 'artistic and cultural value' of the project is paramount.[7] Yet, in a sign of the paucity of thinking around cultural policy and its subordination to economic and industrial policy, there is no explanation of what 'cultural value' might actually mean. This is particularly disappointing given that UNESCO, for example, has developed some liberal humanist criteria for thinking about cultural goals. Here at least the value of cultural pluralism will be addressed, the need to combat discrimination, the need to widen access to cultural production, especially for women, the role of culture in fostering empowerment and citizenship, and so forth. None of this is flagged in the Eurimages scheme, let alone more radical visions of cultural value, which might, for example, sharpen the liberal concept of cultural 'conversations' into the role of culture in meditating on anxieties and social conflicts that may get little airing within official news media or political discourses. This is something which of course mainstream popular culture does all the time, albeit often obliquely and wrapped up in the guise of 'mere' entertainment. A radical cultural policy aimed at tapping into such ruminative powers would seek to draw out this often implicit social commentary and articulate it in socially progressive directions.

LIMITS OF THE STATE

The separation of the political and the economic realms is then both appearance and reality. If as an appearance it fosters exaggerated claims as to the autonomy of the state, as a reality, it exerts real limits on what the state can actually control and do. This is worth pointing out since the power of the state has been exaggerated by Keynesian reformists who hope that the state can resolve the contradictions of capital, while the expansion of the state into the economic sphere is sometimes thought to be synonymous with socialism. For Marx, however, the state was part of the problem not the long-term solution. The idea that the penetration of the state, from 'outside' and 'above' the productive life of society, can correct the inequalities of the system or amounts to socialism is quite foreign to Marx's project. For Marx, socialism is characterised by a more emancipatory project in which control is taken back from 'within' the productive life of society and from 'below'. Where the extension of the powers of the state is a response to popular pressure from below for the guarantee of certain entitlements, or where it offers provision that would otherwise wither on the vine, then this represents some progress over pure market relations and ought to be critically defended. I say critically because it cannot be forgotten that such modes of social control are being routed through an elite hierarchical structure that is in any case continually in danger of being outflanked by capital. For Marx, the real life of the bourgeoisie is to be found in the intra-capitalist competition over the antagonistic extraction of surplus value from the direct producers (and the realisation of surplus value as profit by the further exploitation of consumers), and not in the legal regulation and administration of this process (the realm of the state) indispensable as that is.

Insofar as the state tries to have a co-ordinating and cohesive role through policy decisions, it aspires to some form of sociality. This is the view of the state in bourgeois philosophy, running from Hegel's image of civil servants and state bureaucrats as a universal class, all the way through to Tony Bennett's call for cultural technicians to translate the demands of the 'different constituencies' of society into 'practical administrative options'. The problem for the state is that its sociality is, as Marx described it, *post festum* ('after the feast'). At the heart of the productive life of society there are fundamental social antagonisms and conflicts, and yet the role of the state is conceived as somehow coming along, 'after the feast' of production, and reconciling and resolving these contradictions. The state, as a *post festum* mode of intervention, is thus external to true sociality, grafted on from the outside, its remedial actions continually failing to stick (Mészáros 1995:475–6).

Thus one of the problems for competition policy is that the bar is continually being raised as to what constitutes acceptable levels of media concentration as policy is outpaced by the real movements and activities of capital's expansionary dynamic. After the UK

Broadcasting Act of 1990, which set up a newly competitive ITV, there was further deregulation by the Conservative government in 1993 to allow the large regional companies to merge and combine (Humphreys 1996:217). In 2002, New Labour's White Paper prepared the ground for the two survivors of this process of consolidation, Carlton and Granada, to merge into a single company. These developments point to another feature of the contradiction between national and international markets. While states may like to preserve some minimum degree of competition within their domestic markets in order to foster (market regulated) innovation, reduce their dependence on any one company and keep consumer rights organisations at bay, the logic of *internationalisation* inexorably diminishes diversity as companies seek the economies of scale necessary to compete in foreign markets or stave off being gobbled up by foreign competitors. The goal of competitive plurality that the state sets is continually being shredded by the tendency towards monopoly. The terrestrial digital platform, ITV Digital, for example, was designed to be a counter to Murdoch's BSkyB. However, when ITV Digital paid too much for rights to screen football, it was placed into administration by the courts. In admitting defeat it had followed the same path as British Satellite Broadcasting, which merged with Rupert Murdoch's Sky operations in 1990 after an embarrassingly short period of 'competition'. The declining fortunes of ITV Digital will in turn have another effect on government policy, namely its desire to switch off (and then auction to telecommunications companies) the analogue broadcast signal by 2010 after everyone has converted to digital television. It now looks like the 95 per cent digital conversion required to switch off the analogue signal will not be in place until 2018–2020.

THE DISSOLUTION OF POLITICS IN THE MARKET

The state as a mechanism for class compromise and negotiating consent grew considerably during the twentieth century with the expansion of the political franchise which in turn provided the instrument for the state's mediation of class conflicts by the growth of social spending, the establishment of the welfare state and organisation of cultural entitlements (libraries, museums, arts funding, public service broadcasting). The expansion of the state's activities – in its mature form the 'strategic congruence between Fordism and the Keynesian welfare state' (Jessop 1997:261) – and its intervention into economic life were highly paradoxical. While it attempted to provide economic stability and ideological cohesion to the system, as the system entered a deep crisis in the 1970s, the extensive intervention of the state meant that it drew '*the economic class struggle increasingly on to its own* terrain' (Hall et al. 1978:214) which in turn exposed the limitations of the state's *post festum* sociality as it failed to resolve those conflicts and divisions to the satisfaction of either capital or labour.

The echoes of the crisis and its impact on broadcasting can be heard in Lord Annan's 1977 Report of the Committee on the Future of Broadcasting. The report notes a breakdown in social consensus and uniformity of public opinion and an array of 'divisions within society, divisions between classes, the generations and the sexes, between north and south, between the provinces and London, between pragmatists and ideologues' (Annan 1977:14). Insofar as a new generation of programme makers entered broadcasting and articulated this new mood of dissensus, tensions developed between the broadcasters and the state. At the same time, because public opinion was also fractured and divided, there was an increasing debate concerning the relationship between the broadcasters and their publics:

> [P]eople of all political persuasions began to object that many programmes were biased or obnoxious. But some with equal fervour, maintained that broadcasters were not challenging enough and were cowed by Government and vested interests to produce programmes which bolstered up the *status quo* and concealed how a better society could evolve. (Annan 1977:15)

Writing in the same decade as the Annan report was published, Jürgen Habermas argued that the extension of the state into social and cultural life *denaturalises* activities that were previously taken for granted and seen as outside social control (1976:68–75). The state's extensive involvements *politicise* social, cultural and economic life; in other words the separation of the political and economic realms is breached somewhat by the Fordist/Keynesian state. The post-Fordist strategic withdrawal of the state – not from regulation in general, which, as we have seen, even free market capitalism requires – but from social and cultural obligations on capital made by society, in turn can be read as an attempt to *re-naturalise* market relations, or at least expunge from market relations political questions of power, inequality and so forth.

Recalling the arguments from Chapter 1, we know that workers sell their labour power to capital in exchange for a wage. The first condition for the emergence and reproduction of capital is that labour owns no productive property of its own and so in order to survive must enter the labour market and for a period of the day sell his or her mind and body to capital which has the power to dispose of the worker's labour as it likes. We know also that the wage falls short of the actual value that labour produces; the difference between the wage and the full value of their labour power is the surplus controlled and absorbed by capital. There are, however, enough features of this transaction to give it the appearance-form of equality, fairness, freedom and individuality and at least minimise the sense of force and coercion that might make life intolerable. This transaction between buyers and sellers, whether workers selling their labour power to capital or consumers buying products, is the sphere of exchange. It is this 'noisy sphere, where everything takes place on the surface and in view of all men' that Marx famously conducts us from in *Capital* in order to penetrate to 'the hidden abode of production, on whose threshold there stares us in the face "No admittance except on business"' (1983:172). In the hidden abode of production Marx finds the invisible extraction of surplus value that speaks of social domination, class power, inequality, coercion and the crushing of individuality championed in the sphere of exchange.

The expansion of state activity as a means of fashioning consent during the period of mature Fordism does, however, begin to complicate and undo the separation of the political and economic arenas. Manifestly, the sphere of exchange requires the corrective action of the state to address the inequalities bubbling away beneath the surface of freedom, individuality and equality. What we have witnessed then over the last 30 years, as media and other corporate capitals have restructured themselves, is a new regime of accumulation and legitimation, a new mode of development that sees the state withdrawing from many social and cultural arenas where it had previously established universal modes of provision and the replacement of social and cultural obligations with regulation of a more politically 'neutral' administrative and technical character. The political crisis of the state has been resolved in the short term by its declaration that it had wandered into terrain that it ought properly not to be involved in, except as a guarantor of the free market. Politicisation and a visible central body responsible for collective rights is replaced by a new naturalisation woven by the atomisation of market relations which reproduces the labour market's appearance-form of equality in the sphere of consumption, dissolving the *inequalities between consumers and the unequal relations of power between consumers and corporate cultural providers.* Now universal provision becomes a series of economically differentiated lifestyle choices (this is true even in healthcare). What we are witnessing in public service broadcasting is the recasting of universal provision in terms of individual choice – determined by ability to pay and the corporations' willingness to provide – and the attempt to extract vastly greater sums of labour's disposable income for the profit margins of private capital. (The top end of BSkyB's satellite service runs to around £400 per annum for example, four times the cost of the universal licence fee.) In the vision of policy makers, analysts and economists, the citizen, a politicised term now seen as overburdened by the state's injunctions to improve itself, is replaced by the emancipated consumer. So deeply has this narrative of change penetrated, cast in the terms of a shift from politics and culture to economics, the marketplace and consumer desire, that even writers sympathetic to cultural goals concede it. Thus McQuail sketches the shift away from public service broadcasting in the following way:

> Non-commercialism was also expressed in a positive discrimination for educational and cultural content well beyond what could be justified on grounds of audience demand ... This feature of non-commercialism involved a widespread refusal to satisfy popular demand for television entertainment, as measured by normal audience market criteria. (1998b:110)

Here we see the binary opposition very clearly: non-commercialism is politically regulated and culturally goal-oriented, whereas commercialism is market-led and meets audience demands. The problem though is once again taking for granted the appearance-form of the separation of the political and the economic. In reality, the two cannot be easily separated. We have looked at and critiqued the supposed autonomy of the state *from* economics, but we now need to critique the neo-liberal market fantasy that the market operates autonomously *from* the state and its political frameworks. There is in fact no such thing as 'normal audience market criteria' neutrally measuring audience wants. We cannot abstract the market from the particular institutional and social conditions in which it operates. Popular culture is a construct shaped by those conditions. As the

Keynesian economist Will Hutton argued in his critique of the neo-liberal experiment, '[m]arkets are embedded in a network of social and political institutions which give them values and priorities' (1996:20). For example, within a given television ecology (say the public service one which was dominant up until the late 1980s) a 6–7 million audience rating for a documentary might well be enough to qualify as 'popular', that is it is considered sustainable as a share of the audience. However, a policy alteration in the competitive ecology, by, for example, increasing the competition for advertising revenue, and suddenly hey presto! documentaries need to hit 9–10 million to qualify as 'popular', that is sustainable within the new operating context. It is not the audience that has changed in such a shift, but other, political and economic, factors.

The shape and direction of broadcasting is far too important to be left to consumer desire. Audiences have hardly been invited into a public debate concerning what kind of broadcasting system they might want. Indeed the last time there was any substantive debate concerning the future of broadcasting was in 1977 with the Annan report. Since then, developments in broadcasting have been driven by corporate not audience needs. When public service broadcasting in the UK was established, media ownership was generally concentrated in single sectors. Thus the prospect of commercial radio opening up was not altogether welcome for newspaper capital since here was a new medium that would compete with the press for advertising revenue. The powerful press baron Lord Beaverbrook was primarily concerned that the new medium should not be dominated by radio manufacturers and if the public service model prevented that and competition for advertising revenue, then he was prepared to give John Reith, the BBC's first director general and public service architect, some support (Briggs 1961:160). But as media empires matured and diversified, changing from mono- to multi-media concerns, commercialisation of broadcasting was no longer a threat but an opportunity to generate more advertising revenue as long as the grip which the public service institutions had achieved on the industry could be broken (Hesmondhalgh 2002:112–13). Meanwhile, spending on advertising has become increasingly important for advanced capitalism, helping to accelerate the circulation of goods, differentiate essentially similar products and create brands, and raise barriers of entry to the market or marginalise competitors with smaller advertising budgets (Sinclair 1989:33). The media have also been important instruments in stimulating the debt-based hyper-consumption that writers have linked to the post-Fordist era (Heffernan 2000:21). Mattelart argues that there is a strong link between the growth of advertising expenditure, media corporate convergence, the consolidation and convergence of advertising companies and pressure on governments to liberalise the broadcast media (1991:49–50). The privatisation of the main French public television channel, TF1, in 1987 increased advertising space from 18 minutes a day to 12 minutes per hour (Mattelart 1991:106). In 1989 the Netherlands repealed laws that restricted advertising to 5 per cent of airtime, while between 1980 and 1987 television advertising in Europe grew by 181 per cent (Mattelart 1991:107). In 2001 the UK's Independent Television Commission, which regulates commercial television, changed its rules on the maximum amount of advertising allowed during peak time. This was increased from 7.5 minutes per hour averaged between 6 p.m. and 11 p.m., to 8 minutes per hour. The value of the 30-second increase accumulates further by using more adverts than average around a popular programme in peak peak-time and fewer adverts than average the closer one gets to 6 p.m. and 11 p.m. Thus Channel 4's *ER* (which starts at 9 p.m.) now has three commercial breaks (instead of two), at around 9.15 p.m., 9.30 p.m., and 9.42 p.m., totalling 10.5 minutes (the maximum allowed in any one hour). The extra 3.5 minutes of advertising is worth millions to the broadcaster. This small alteration in the regulatory regime of terrestrial commercial television is then just another micro-moment in the commodification of the public sphere with the effect that audiences have their viewing experience constantly interrupted and, more significantly, the threshold of the television broadcaster's expectations as to what constitutes 'popular programming' (quantity of advertising revenue to pour into share-holders' pockets) has been ratcheted up a few more notches.

The absence of any public debate on the direction of broadcasting means that the option of expanding television service within a public service framework was never even considered. While it may be reasonable to assume that people wanted more choice in provision, a modest expansion of choice could have been provided far more cheaply and universally within a public service framework instead of seeing universal provision (sport and good quality films) siphoned off into subscription services. It is clear, however, that public service principles and practices have become utterly incompatible with capital. The hostility of commercial broadcasters to BBC 3, which is aimed at young audiences (a crucial advertising constituency), illustrates well enough that any expansion of public service choice will be fiercely resisted by, and has financial implications for, the commercial sector. This is particularly so given the downturn in advertising spending which has hit the media since the late 1990s. This downturn suggests yet another case of overproduction, with supply (the commercial, advertising-funded media whose expansion has been driving media policy) and demand (the advertising spend) diverging just as they did with the dot.com crash. The government meanwhile has set strict limits on BBC 3's entertainment output in order to protect the commercial broadcasters, but, at the same time, the expansion of commercial broadcasting and multiple channels exerts a strong pressure on the BBC to compete for audience share so as to make the licence fee viable. Yet in shoring up the rationale for its financial base the BBC undercuts the rationale for its cultural distinctiveness by imitating the commercial broadcasters. This lose-lose situation is a contradiction for the BBC and stems ultimately from the contradiction in the broadcasting policy of successive governments. Where liberals would see the state as *balancing* between commercial and public service broadcast providers, the Marxian notion of *contradiction* suggests that policy proceeds not by even-handed weighting between different interests, but in an incoherent management of structurally irresolvable conflicts.

THE PROBLEMATIC HYPHEN IN THE NATION-STATE

The arguments of the preceding pages concerning the state's relationship with capital and labour have been summarised in Figure 4.1. But I want to now return again to what has been in many ways the blind spot in the Marxist theory of the state, and that is the question of culture and its role in securing consent or in opening up tensions between the state and some of its citizens. And the blind spot in much writing about the state in general has been, until recently, the assumption that nations and states are indissolubly tied together. However, contemporary writings on the nation-state have stressed how the two terms have become uncoupled to a large extent, both from 'below' by the migration of people which diversifies the nation in counterpoint to the elite dominated state, and from 'above' by the flow of culture and finance in the global market. One way of illuminating the issue of culture in relation to the state is to recast the nation-state as a linkage between culture and politics. The nation is then that realm of cultural resources and practices that the state wraps around itself to generate an affective bond between its machinery and its citizens. The latter are unlikely to be particularly committed to or willing to die for the Ministry of Agriculture, Foods and Fisheries (MAFF), but rolling green hills, babbling streams, dawn mists, grazing sheep and chirping birds mobilise the kind of resources which can forge a subjectivity highly, even ferociously, loyal to the state (Eagleton 2000:61). In return the resources of the nation are no longer merely an assemblage of local practices, representations and self-conceptions; by hitching themselves to the state they are attached to its globally prevalent, universal ideal as the centralised embodiment of the people's will. As Terry Eagleton puts it: 'Membership of the tribe thus yields to citizenship of the world' (2000:58). The poet and the film-maker are thus seen as representing the unique characteristics of a particular people organised around the highest form of social and political association. Within the international market, a narrow and dominant repertoire of images of and associations with national identity are mobilised to facilitate the exchange of commodities, whether media products such as film and television, manufacturing goods or tourism (Wayne 2002a). All of this then reflects back on the state, which hopes to improve its prestige and status by association, and if the representations are not suitably affirmative, the state can step into the field of cultural production and 'encourage' boosterism of one sort or another. Filtered through the market the nation projects back to itself and exports to others a highly selective and homogenised representation of itself, a narrowness which is reinforced by the state which is invariably dominated by an ethnic and class constituency which does not reflect the diversity of peoples actually living within the nation and under the dominion of the state. As a result of 'the uneven representation of social interests, cultures, and territories in the nation-state' (Castells 1997:270), the marginalised 'subdued identities' have historically sought to periodically renegotiate the national contract. Regional decentralisation, sometimes to the smaller nations that have been bundled into the larger nation-state, and campaigns against racism and ethnic discrimination are two indications of such renegotiations. In both instances, media representations become a crucial site in the battle of perceptions, ideas and identities.

If devolutions of power and migration are uncoupling the links between nation and state from 'below', the state's role in managing the nation's integration into the internationalised global economy is uncoupling the relations between nation and state from 'above'.

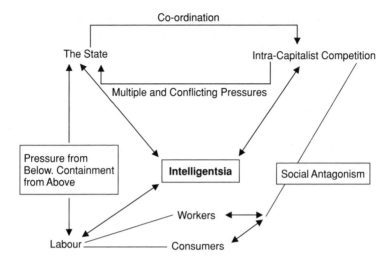

Figure 4.1   Class Relations of the State

One of the tensions within the world capitalist system that the separation of the political and economic realms opens up is that the political realm is still organised around nation-states while the economic realm is increasingly transnational and global in its reach and operations. This has led to the paradoxical development that while states cede control over the national economy to transnational business corporations, they become involved in providing the institutional framework for integrating the national economy into the international one (Jessop 1997:262). Thus the Chinese state has entered the World Trade Organization, balancing specific commitments to a very modest opening up of its film market to Hollywood majors with its own economic and political interests. For example, Hollywood has to share the majority of a film's revenues with the Chinese state, but the number of films that can be distributed annually has been increased and will climb to at least 50 by 2003. The Chinese have also opened up the market for direct investment in the retail infrastructure, permitting US companies to own up to 49 per cent of Chinese video and distribution companies and 49 per cent of companies building and owning cinema theatres.[8] It is a matter of speculation what the political effects on the Chinese state will be in the long term as it integrates its nation into the world film hegemony of Hollywood and Western popular culture generally. The combination of contradictory modes of production and development, which includes feudalism, Stalinist 'Fordism' and rampant deregulated capitalism, makes for a potentially explosive social cocktail, one interestingly explored in Zhou Xiaowen's film *Ermo* (1994 Ch). China may be a peculiarly sharp illustration of a conflict between a state's need to ensure the expansion of accumulation, which requires 'privileged appropriation of socially produced wealth', and the need to sustain its own legitimation on which that privileged appropriation depends (Habermas 1976:96).

However, it would be quite wrong to see the tension between national culture and states and the international market as simply a problem for developing countries. At a European level, the contradiction between regional film production and Hollywood famously flared up between American and European negotiators at the end of the General Agreement on Tariffs and Trade (GATT) talks in 1993, where the question of cultural protection, pushed vigorously by the French state but supported by producers across Europe, threatened to derail the free trade agenda (Grantham 2000). The cultural industries remain one of the most contentious areas of negotiation between the national and the international domains. At the Seattle World Trade Organization talks in 1999, which saw the spectacular birth of the anti-capitalist movement, the unresolved question of the European film and television industries' exemptions from the liberalisation of markets continued to exercise the US movie industry and US trade negotiators.[9] This tension between national culture/politics and the international media market was again illustrated when the German media empire controlled by Leo Kirch collapsed. The Kirch group had interests in television, film and print media and its collapse opened up the opportunity for its minority shareholders to seize control of key German media assets. The problem was that these minority shareholders happened to be Silvio Berlusconi, the Italian Prime Minister, and Rupert Murdoch. The German authorities regarded Berlusconi as compromised by his status as the Prime Minister of another country, while Murdoch was viewed as culturally and politically incompatible with German national conditions. Murdoch's championing of American-style free market capitalism (which his media interests have trumpeted in the UK) was viewed with considerable apprehension by Germany's political, financial and media elites brought up in the post-Second World War social democratic or 'Rhineland' market economy (capitalism with a human face).[10] The German Chancellor Gerhard Schröder was reported to have been involved in secret meetings with the German banks to cut a deal that kept Murdoch out of a controlling position in the Kirch holdings.[11] Meanwhile Julian Nida-Rümelin, a media affairs minister, suggested that the Kirch crisis raised questions about 'how much globalisation we can allow in the media sector and what dangers are posed by the growing domination of the media sector by just a few big concerns, interested exclusively in profit'.[12] One of the many contradictions of the state's relationship to capitalism is that such concerns about media concentration and profit orientation are less acute when it is 'their' capitalists doing the growing and profiteering.

A FINAL WORD ON CULTURAL POLICY

We have seen that the domination of the state by a narrow social and ethnic constituency tends logically to result in the projection of that narrow constituency onto the nation. And this is one source for what Stephen Crofts calls the 'homogenizing fictions of nationalism' (1998:386). For some writers, all forms of cultural protection fostered by state intervention, whether at a national or European level, are prone to delusions concerning the uniqueness and homogeneity of the 'national culture' (Collins 1999:165). If the traditional idea of the 'national' 'as a self-contained and carefully demarcated experience' (Higson 2000:64) is increasingly untenable, should the state cede all powers to the apparently more cosmopolitan global market? As we have seen, the state is a problematic entity for Marxists, but this does not mean that fruitful engagement with it should be ruled out. Indeed teachers and students are necessarily involved in one of the state's most important activities: education. It is possible for the state to put in place the material conditions that widen access to cultural production and diversify the repertoire of representations, and to provide those conditions with a certain stability that the rapidly shifting conditions of the marketplace cannot guarantee. For example, despite the commercial success of *East is East* (Damien O'Donnell 1999 GB) Gurinder Chadha was unable to secure private capital for her film *Bend it Like Beckham* (2002 GB) until the Film Council made an initial investment in it.[13] It is unsurprising but scandalous that, as an Asian woman, Chadha had to wait almost ten years before getting the chance to follow up on her first British feature film *Bhaji on the Beach* (1993 GB). It is to a certain extent in the interests of the state, through its role in forging consent, to respond to pressure and agitation for such state initiated concessions and support.

In order to develop a more radical cultural policy, one which does not fall foul of nationalist myths, we need to think of cultural materials being *sourced* and *circulated* at different geographical scales: the local, the national, the regional (e.g. Europe) and the international. In thinking of cultural exchange between these different scales, it is clear that the key doorway through which this takes place is between the international (dominated by the Hollywood media–industrial complex) and the national. We need cultural policies that can open many more doorways between the local, the national and the regional, and between all three and the international, rather than being simply subordinated to the international. And it needs to be made clear that, while porosity is to be encouraged, there should be the resources for a diversity of cultural expressiveness at the local, national and regional level, and that each of these geographical scales should connect with people's lives and be culturally specific and proximate to the way they think and behave in ways that Los Angeles or America generally, for all their pleasures and possibilities, inevitably cannot exhaust or, in many instances, explore.

This chapter has attempted to develop a dialectical account of the relationship between the political and the economic realms. That is to say it has described a conflictual and changing relationship between distinct social practices. Where media policy analysis takes the politics out of economics and the economics out of politics, it fails to live up to the complexity of this relationship. My account is dialectical too in the sense that a process or social phenomenon takes certain characteristics at one level of reality or stage in an ongoing process, only to turn those characteristics inside out and reverse them at another level or moment in the circuit of capital. Thus both the political realm and the economic realm have the appearance-form, generated up out of real relations, of autonomy from one another. This autonomy is real and has important effects. Without it one could not talk of the state having any scope for initiatives that might not please certain sections of capital. At the same time, the very separation of the political and the economic introduces real limitations into how far the state can control the productive life of society. In this regard at least, both neo-liberals and Marxists would agree. But, while the economic sphere really does have built-in resistance to being subordinated to the political sphere of the state, the neo-liberal fantasy of the autonomy of the economic is as implausible as the social democratic liberal fantasy of the state's role as balancing competing interests from some position outside them. Capital needs the state;

its interests are necessarily pursued through this distinct and separate social organ. In terms of media policy we have seen a shift from the role of the state as providing social and cultural obligations on capital, to its extensive involvement (not a withdrawal *per se*) in creating the conditions for intensifying international competition and multi-national corporate commodification of social and cultural life. This takes the appearance-form of the state conducting itself in a more politically neutral, technical and administrative manner than in the old Keynesian/Fordist era. But, of course, there is nothing politically neutral about extending the writ of capital. Yet, while the state's apparent withdrawal from taking any substantive responsibility for correcting market inequalities and chaos has enabled it to extricate itself from the corporatism of the preceding era, it has served to lay the long-term foundations for its own delegitimisation as the liberal democratic state. The political crisis of liberal democracy stems logically enough from the growing evidence that the agenda is set before and after and outside the electoral process. Whether the state can afford to continue to leak this kind of legitimacy and what impact that might have on media policy and on the conduct of current institutional regulators remain open questions.

5 Base–Superstructure: Reconstructing the Political Unconscious

> Any explanation must preserve *all the qualitative differences* between interacting domains and must trace all the various stages through which a change travels ... a process which emerges from the bas[e] ... comes to completion in the superstructures.
>
> Volŏshinov, *Marxism and the Philosophy of Language*

> Concrete analysis means then: the relation to society *as a whole*.
>
> Lukács, *History and Class Consciousness*

Many Marxists today are unwilling to defend the base–superstructure metaphor, so indelibly has it become associated with a crude model of determination. The separation of society into two domains has left the architectural metaphor in a bad state of disrepair, abandoned by a complex modern society in which culture cannot be safely contained in a particular quarter of the superstructure, but is in fact everywhere, not least in the base. Dispensing with the model (usually depicted as in Figure 5.1) may be tempting but in fact this only defers rather than resolves the crucial issue of determination: namely how the different parts of the social whole (the totality) relate to each other and are structured by the general social form or mode by which a society conducts its production. But if it is to be defended, the model will need more than a lick of paint: it will have to be reconstructed from the base up.

To put it at its most simple, the proposition of the metaphor is that the 'base' – usually but wrongly abbreviated to 'the economy' – determines the 'superstructure' – the political, cultural and civic domains of social life. In trying to develop a sophisticated account of the relationship between base and superstructure we will need to spend some time working the base up to an appropriately complex conceptual ensemble, the first condition of which is to dispense with the notion that it equals 'the economy' and insist instead on that more dynamic, process-orientated and above all contradictory foundational concept: the mode of production. We have already been

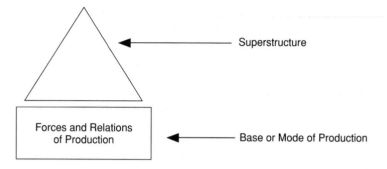

Figure 5.1   The 'Vulgar' Base–Superstructure Model

working with a complex model of the mode of production in relation to media technology, media corporations and the state. Part of the way in which I have tried to make the mode of production category adequately complex is by having the category mode of development 'sit' inside it, thus giving it a greater sensitivity to historical change than one necessarily gets from the brute abstraction of mode of production. The task of this chapter is now to apply mode of production/mode of development to the cultural products that the media produces. This chapter will conclude with an application of a renovated base–superstructure model to television and the international reality TV phenomenon known as *Big Brother*.

Raymond Williams has noted how in many uses of the base–superstructure model the base 'has come to be considered virtually as an object, or in less crude cases, it has been considered in essentially uniform and usually static ways' (1980:33). He argued that our understanding of the base had to be shifted away from 'a fixed economic or technological abstraction' and replaced with a sense of 'real social and economic relationships, containing fundamental contradictions and variations and therefore always in a state of dynamic process' (1980:34). Evacuating the base of *social relationships* which are in conflict with each other over the uses to which technology and other forces of production are put has, indeed, left it as an economic or technological 'thing'; fixed, inert, imposing itself on human beings as if it existed outside their activities and practices.

In the chapter on the state, I argued that the Marxist theory of the state had to navigate between 'reducing' the state to a mere puppet of capital ('crude' Marxism), on the one hand, and seeing the state, on the other, as autonomous from capital and therefore able to fairly accommodate the interests of diverse social forces. This latter position of course is the one favoured by liberals. The same dilemma and methodological choices face us with society as a whole and any other particular aspect of it. Is society as a whole to be understood as composed of a plurality of social forces with no systemic, structured and repeated hierarchies of power as liberalism would have us believe? Tony Bennett, for example, calls for cultural analysis to study the

> forms of social life and conduct that result from the interaction of multiple historical conditions and forces, without the form of their interaction being subject to any general form of determination ... arising from the effects of an underlying causal mechanism. (1997:53)

Now much depends on how one conceives the 'general form of determination' and how one in practice works through any 'underlying causal mechanism' (although the term 'mechanism' returns us precisely to that 'thing'-like automatic structure which we need to revalue the base away from). But one of the paradoxical effects of the liberal rejection of socio-economic determinations is that it usually involves introducing another form of determination through the back door. Often, this turns out to be culture itself, which collapses, as we shall see, back into the very idealism which the base–superstructure metaphor was trying to escape from. Bennett meanwhile, having insisted that there are no 'underlying causal' determinations, invokes what sounds suspiciously like an underlying causal determination when he argues that culture has become thoroughly 'governmentalized' (1997:54) (note not commodified) hence the need for intellectuals to start engaging with the state.

For some, like Dominic Strinati, Marxism is trapped in an impossible dilemma. If it tries to genuinely explore the interrelationships between what he calls 'the economic' (again abstracted from social relations) and culture, then it loses its distinctiveness, namely its claim that the former has priority in understanding the latter (Strinati 1995: 143). But if it stresses the priority of 'the base', it is then condemned to 'reductionism'. This is a major sin for contemporary cultural theory, although there is very little investigation into the difference between saying x influences y (without which we would pretty much have to give up *explaining* anything) and saying y has been 'reduced' to x and this is unacceptable if we are to fully understand x and y (McLennan 1996:53–61). It was after all mainstream journalists who were wondering how financial contributions from energy corporations to George Bush junior's presidential campaign in 2000, had affected his environmental policies, not raving 'reductionist' Marxists. The trap Strinati and others have set for Marxism – embrace plurality and you lose your Marxism, embrace your distinctive stress on the economic and you lose your sophistication – need not be sprung however. It will in fact be possible to formulate a way of thinking of the relationship between cultural life and the mode of production in such a way as to explore their *interpenetration* whilst retaining the priority of the mode of production. Without the mode of production, explanation tends to alight on and then inflate other factors that become symbolically overloaded, displacements for social causes that have been repressed. The mode of production is, as a number of Marxists have argued, a kind of political unconscious.

MATERIALISM AND IDEALISM

The methodology of Marxism is sometimes described as a historical materialism. The word materialism in particular has been subject to some misunderstandings and so it will be worth thinking through what it means, how it is related to the category mode of production and superstructure and what the role of ideas and consciousness can be within a materialist philosophy, since the latter was formulated in opposition to the philosophical tradition of idealism.

Why, we may ask, is the category mode of production foundational for Marxism? The basic argument is that production is foundational for human life; the activity of labour is required to produce the means to satisfy needs (eating, drinking, keeping warm, habitation, art, play, human reproduction, etc.) that expand and develop as our capacity to produce develops. This proposition is materialist in two senses. First, it is materialist in a simple physical sense; it stresses the physical requirements of the human body, its relationship to nature (its own natural requirements and nature as raw material for the satisfaction of needs) and the tools and means by which needs are satisfied. However, on its own, this definition of materialism, which is widespread within the bourgeois social sciences, is a merely crude or mechanical materialism. Along with sheer physicality, the concept of materialism also has a second meaning, which is often forgotten or not deeply appreciated. Marx argued that capital is not merely a brute material substance, a quantity of money, raw materials, machinery, technology or equipment (fixed capital). 'These material elements ... do not make capital into capital' (Marx 1973:98). What makes capital capital are the *social relationships* that it is embedded into. Thus materialism has a double meaning in the Marxist sense: it means sheer physicality *plus* social relationships. For production, labour is *social*. It requires, under class societies, antagonistic co-operation between individuals. This co-operation, however, is not haphazard and accidental; it is not open to voluntary change on a day-to-day basis. This co-operation has a definite pattern, a definite *mode* within a given society and in a given era. The identification of this mode, for us, the capitalist mode of production, maps out an entire historical period, with distinct characteristics and possibilities. This two-fold definition of materialism will need to be borne in mind because it becomes explicitly central to the argument in this and subsequent chapters.

It is important to sketch the philosophical context in which Marx and his long-standing friend and collaborator Friedrich Engels first elaborated their materialist method systematically in *The German Ideology* in the mid-1840s. The ideology referred to was a tradition of thinking that conceived ideas, consciousness, as developing *independently* from the kind of material conditions (physical and social) discussed above. This way of thinking, Marx and Engels regarded as ideological, which in this context refers to ideas and values that, for social reasons, repress their true social conditions of existence. The base–superstructure model attempts to combat this repression by returning to our cognitions the real *conditions of meanings and practices*. It compels us to ask what are the social conditions of the media text? What are the social conditions of the producers and production companies which produce the texts?

The repression of social conditions that Marx and Engels targeted in *The German Ideology* was practised by the philosophical tradition founded by the great German thinker G.W.F. Hegel. As German students, both Marx and Engels had been profoundly influenced by the Hegelian traditions that dominated the universities, but, in this text, they broke decisively with the *idealist* aspects of Hegelian philosophy. It is a point of debate within Marxism to what extent Marx remained, in subsequent work, influenced by Hegel. Certainly, *The German Ideology* is pretty tough on philosophy's ability to imagine that it could develop autonomously from material conditions. 'Philosophy', they suggest at one point, 'and the study of the actual world have the same relation to one another as masturbation and sexual love' (Marx and Engels 1989:103). Nevertheless, there is plenty of evidence to suggest that Marx did not abandon philosophy as the preserve of onanists, but that he remained indebted to philosophical methods, not least in his magnum opus, *Capital*. Philosophical categories such as mediation, dialectics, and contradiction remain crucial to historical materialism if it is to be sufficiently supple and complex in its responses to the world. What Marx did was not so much reject philosophy, but reject its idealism. He thus sought to synthesise a number of its categories with materialist ones in order to understand the actual world that was the condition of thought. Where Hegelian idealism took ideas and the categories of thought as its *starting point* and understood historical and social change as deriving from the development of ideas, materialism starts with the physical and social production of life.

> Morality, religion, metaphysics, all the rest of ideology and their corresponding forms of consciousness, thus no longer retain the semblance of independence. They have no history, no development; but men, developing their material production, and their material intercourse, alter, along with this their real existence, their thinking and the products of their thinking. (Marx and Engels 1989:47)

MEDIATING POLITICAL ECONOMY AND PHILOSOPHY

Now clearly this programme has implications for the study of the media, which after all are products of, and produce, values, ideas and ideals, identities and ideologies; in a word: consciousness. However, idealism flourishes today on the media studies curriculum for two reasons. First, idealism is not merely a scholastic error open to easy correction. As I have argued, one way of conceiving what the base–superstructure model is trying to do is to see it as a methodology for linking (social) parts to the (social) whole. Idealism (which splits consciousness off from the social whole) is socially generated and capitalism's material practices tend to encourage us to think more in parts than wholes. The private and competitive nature of production, for example, generates a fragmentary experience of the world where it becomes hard to discern the hidden connections between apparently remote, even global, forces and more local, even private, practices (Murdock 1997: 90). The autonomy of ideas may also be seen as a class fantasy on the part of the intelligentsia, a sort of quasi-real compensation for their real marginality as Adorno saw it (Best and Kellner 1991:231), but one which provides the intelligentsia with a cultural capital with which they offset their lack of that real economic capital owned by the bourgeoisie proper. Second, it must be admitted that establishing materialist premises for the study of culture and consciousness is the start of a problem, not a solution to a problem: for how exactly are the worlds of consciousness, or symbolic goods insofar as the media are concerned, to be related to the material world; to put the question more dialectically, how do we grasp the material constitution of culture and the cultural constitution of the material world while retaining the priority of the latter?

One way in which the attempt to re-materialise cultural studies has been formulated recently is to argue that the study of culture needs to draw on the traditions of political economy (essentially economic and institutional analysis) to provide cultural studies with its 'base'. Garnham, for example, notes how cultural studies has largely excluded material factors in favour of an exclusive focus on the symbolic world of texts (1997). Behind the rejection of the base–superstructure model by cultural studies lie a methodological objection to its supposed reductionism and a political interest in gender, race and sexuality as opposed to class, which is of course the central category of the mode of production. It has to be said that both political economy and cultural studies have yet to really explore the ways in which such social identities interlock with class. Kellner (1997) suggests that a combination of political economy and cultural studies approaches could be the way forward, particularly in reconciling class perspectives with the analytical tools that have been honed to critique gender, race and sexual domination. There is, however, a danger here in simply bolting together methods rather than working through the conceptual incompatibilities and contradictions between them to produce a new synthesis.

Murdock shows how the dominance of culture as the ultimate horizon in the study of culture has impacted even on the work of a Marxist cultural critic like Raymond Williams. Despite his own materialist methodology, Williams failed to 'mount a sustained investigation of the shifting interplay between the economic and symbolic dynamics of contemporary culture' (Murdock 1997:86). At issue here are the missing mediations, the social levels between the text and its wider social and cultural context. As Murdock notes, Marxist literary theory and cultural analysis can read texts as

Exemplars of new ways of thinking and feeling, produced by changes in social and economic conditions. But there is a link missing in this chain of argument. There is no sustained account of the institutions which mediate between 'remote transformations' and situated practices. Relations are established between texts and contexts, not between practices and conditions. (1997:89)

By practices Murdock means the immediate business of making meanings and by conditions he is referring to the institutional and economic underpinnings which make the making of meanings possible. One of the problems with contemporary political economy, however, is that it has developed as a specialised part of the social sciences and is thus often deeply reluctant to engage with such philosophical concepts as dialectics, contradiction, appearance-forms and mediation. For example, political economy is often rather functionalist, failing to accord a proper weight to the concept of contradiction. It also often fails to see how its domain of study is itself a mediation or production of a larger social totality. This totality accounts for social and cultural trends rather more persuasively than the *immediate* institutions and economics (Murdock's conditions) of the media (important though they are) which political economy takes as decisive.

The category of mediation is the counterpoint to the category of appearance-forms which we have discussed in relation to the apparent plurality and diversity of media capital (Chapter 3), and the apparent independence of the state from capital (Chapter 4). As a critical tool, the concept of mediation is deeply subversive since it cuts against the apparent isolation and independence of social phenomena.

Such momentary reunification would remain purely symbolic, a mere methodological fiction, were it not understood that social life is in its fundamental reality one and indivisible, a seamless web ... in which there is no need to invent ways of linking language events and social upheavals or economic contradictions because on that level they were never separate from one another. The realm of separation ... is merely the reality of the appearance. (Jameson 1989:40)

Within Hegelian philosophy the concept of mediation is used to deepen our sense and cognition of the immediate. When we study or observe a particular thing – say a text or institution – it is its immediacy that impresses itself on us most powerfully. In its immediacy we observe and study the text or institution as a discrete thing, cut off and separate from other texts and institutions in time and space. Thus, in terms of generating knowledge about the object, to stay at the level of its immediate appearance is to generate a fairly impoverished understanding of that object. Mediation then involves linkage; it reconstitutes the less immediate and visible relations that lie behind the appearance of the object. Its appearance, which strikes our senses so forcibly in the first (immediate) instance, comes to be seen, once it is mediated, as 'a moment in the movement of consciousness and the *totality*' (Aronowitz 1981:13). Like a brass rubbing, mediation makes visible the (social) patterns and connections that make up the complete picture. As Best and Kellner argue,

> The real issue – if one is to avoid an idealism which divorces social levels from one another and from economic processes – concerns the use of adequate mediations, of constructing a sufficiently sophisticated framework which can map the full complexity of cultural texts and social practices in a non-reductive way. (1991:187)

We will come back to this concept of mediation later because we have yet to formulate *how* the concept of mediation constructs these links. For the moment it is useful to simply identify what I consider to be the seven levels in the social process which can be analytically distinguished and which require mediation in the analysis of the media. The levels are:

> *The text.* This must itself be conceived as a production of existent cultural materials, a point we will come back to later.

> *Production Process.* A text is the product of a specific productive activity by particular people over a given duration.

> *Production Context.* This refers to the company/companies or organisation(s) in which the production process takes place, its/their history, strategies and philosophy which predate the production process.

Industrial Context. This refers to the industry (film, television, advertising, etc.) in which the company or organisation is operating in. Obviously, as we have seen in Chapter 3, there is increasing cross-industrial linkage in the age of monopoly, subsidiary and subcontractor capitalism. The later analysis of *Big Brother* will show how television can no longer be considered an isolated or stand-alone industry.

The State. As we saw in Chapter 4, the state has a major impact on the media through its policies and the regulatory regimes it establishes. Although there is no room here to discuss the role of the state in shaping the regulatory context of the media, I will suggest some allegorical connections between *Big Brother* and the crisis of the bourgeois state.

Mode(s) of Development. This is the category I have borrowed from Castells and used in previous chapters. Unlike Castells, however, I am keen to make the category work as a useful mediating link between the mode of production and superstructure. Mode of development refers to a particular configuration of technology and social and cultural relations. Castells uses the term informationalism, for example, to capture the rising importance of communication and information technology to capitalism and its resultant social, cultural and political effects (1996:17).

Mode(s) of Production. This is of course the master category, mapping out the fundamental social and technological antagonisms and priorities of an epoch. Like mode(s) of development, which this category encompasses, we can also talk in terms of plural modes of production in coexistence with each other. Indeed, one influential tradition of Marxism, deriving from the work of Louis Althusser and Etienne Balibar, virtually insisted that a dominant mode of production always coexists with other subordinate modes of production in any concrete social formation (Anderson 1980:67–8). This argument was seen as a means of making Marxism adequate to the complexity of any actual society and as a means of accounting for change between one mode of production and another (Jameson 1989:91–5). I will argue that, while it is true that different modes of production have coexisted with one another (for example, peasant and slave modes of production in ancient Greece and Rome), the expansionary imperative of capitalism more or less gradually dismembers and absorbs all rival modes of production. The *cultural resources* of alternative modes of production may well survive in very modified forms, because they are now articulated to the capitalist mode of production, but we should be absolutely clear in making the distinction between a cultural resource and a mode of production. Within Western capitalism in particular there really is only one mode of production and from a global perspective the trend is clear: the residues of feudal and peasant-based modes of production in the so-called Third World are in decline.

As should be evident, the seven levels are defined according to a series of increasingly wider contextualisations. The first five levels are recognisably those that would usually be located in the superstructure, while the final two levels belong to the mode of production and its internal transformations (modes of development). Figure 5.2 uses these seven levels to reconfigure and unpack the base–superstructure model. The mode(s) of production and mode(s) of

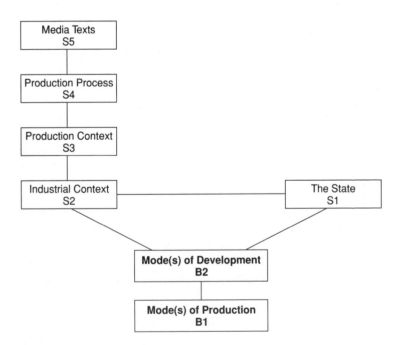

Figure 5.2   Base–Superstructure Unpacked

development constitute base one and two respectively. The other levels denote various levels of the superstructure, although, as we shall see below, this is only a schematic diagram and cannot represent such complexities as *straddling categories*, such as the state and the media, which, at some level, are both base and superstructure. Nevertheless the value of the base–superstructure model lies in the imposing presence of the problematic which it summarises, namely how we think through the determinations of class relations and division. Without that problematic, analysis of the different levels, such as production process and production context, can be easily evacuated of such central Marxian categories as class conflict and commodification.

RETURN TO MODE OF PRODUCTION

The problem and error with many attempts within Marxist cultural theory to make the base–superstructure model work have been to skip over the base and formulate the superstructure in various degrees of autonomy and independence from the base. We have to instead I think start from the base and work our way up. The category mode of production, as we have seen in previous chapters, is made up of that master couplet: social relations and forces of production. Under capitalism, the social relations are characterised by a fundamental antagonism and contradiction between labour and capital. This antagonism does not of course exhaust all the other antagonisms or classes still less groups in society. The proposition though is that all those other classes (intelligentsia, petit bourgeoisie) and groups and antagonisms (of geography, of gender, of race and so on) cannot exist in isolation from, and without taking up a relationship of some kind (to be discerned by concrete analysis and not assumed *a priori*) with, this fundamental antagonism. We have also seen that the social relations come into contradiction with the development of the productive forces (see Chapter 2 especially). From this it follows that the category of mode of production refers to a reality that is both riven with contradictions and highly dynamic.

The contradictions of the mode of production also derive from the fact that it is not uniform and homogeneous; internally it develops unevenly, as we shall see, but a mode of production also develops in temporal and spatial relations with other modes of production. It is historically the case (and it still continues to be the case) that the capitalist mode of production has on a global scale, as well as within nations, coexisted with *other* modes of production, particularly feudal patterns of ownership. Nevertheless, the expansionary dynamics of capitalism mean that over the course of time capitalism breaks down, absorbs and reconstructs what it can use from other modes of production and eliminates those practices and values and representations which it cannot. Thus many *traces* of those prior modes of production are retained as cultural resources within the capitalist mode of production.

At the cultural level, images and values associated with an earlier mode of production (feudal or quasi-feudal) are often grafted onto or integrated into the actually existing capitalist mode of production. Thus Britain, which has been a fully developed capitalist society since the eighteenth century (Thompson 1978:253), has nevertheless sustained the imagery and to a much lesser degree the values of an older feudal society, sometimes encapsulated in the notion of the organic community (Wayne 2002b). While a set of meanings and images requires a mode of production to be generated in the first instance, those meanings and images can be integrated into a quite different mode of production just as a quasi-feudal fantasy scenario such as *Harry Potter and the Philosopher's Stone* (Chris Columbus 2001 US) is deeply etched with the structures and values of a middle class dominated capitalist society. Thus the world of wizards turns out to be remarkably like our own drearily prosaic world, complete with banks, monetary exchange, class divisions, competition, hierarchy, divisions of labour and even specialised disciplines within wizard knowledge. Above all, evil is incarnated in individuals and has no systemic, structural roots. It is vitally important politically to make the distinction between *actually existing modes of production* which *might* be coexisting (with decreasing frequency today) with capitalism and the *cultural residues* of prior modes of production. For many political strategies have been launched on the basis of confusing the two, with the result that, in the case of Britain, political critiques have identified 'feudal' antecedents (the monarchy, the House of Lords, the dominance of the City) as responsible for economic or political decline rather than the contradictions of capitalism itself. Bearing this distinction in mind, we can endorse Fredric Jameson's argument that

> every social formation or historically existing society has in fact consisted in the overlay and structural coexistence of *several* modes of production all at once, including vestiges and survivals of older

modes of production, now relegated to structurally dependent positions within the new, as well as anticipatory tendencies which are potentially inconsistent with the existing system but have not yet generated an autonomous space of their own. (1989:95)

Jameson here also makes the important point that culture may anticipate future modes of production, and, indeed, archaic and future visions may often converge or be mapped on top of one another as visions of alternative ways of living. The cultural outlines of a different mode of production embryonic within capitalism can be glimpsed in the utopian images and representations of a transcendence of unnecessary limitations, of a reconciliation of social divisions, of a successful expression of desire, of a liberation from bonds of domination, of a reconnection to creativity and so forth. Such prefigurations of another mode of life are not only 'textual' in their manifestation, but, as we saw in Chapter 2, articulated by new technologies even as they remain snared in the current mode of production. Yet such 'anticipatory tendencies' are not the same as a fully-fledged mode of production, a distinction hinted at but not fully acknowledged in the above quote from Jameson. Without such fantasies and prefigurations the socialist mode of production cannot be created, while the socialist mode of production is itself a condition for these subjective forces and sporadic counter practices to be authentically realised *as a mode of production*, rather than just tapped into and exploited by consumer capitalism which sells back to us solutions (from private healthcare to bottled water) to the problems which it has created (Wayne 2002c).

As the idea of coexisting modes of *development* suggests, a mode of production is also internally contradictory because it (and this is especially true of capitalism) does not develop in a linear and consistent fashion. The antagonism between capital and labour becomes inextricably entwined with the uneven historical development of capital's own dominant structures. This manifests itself in the contradictions that arise between bourgeois economics on the one hand and bourgeois culture and politics on the other. In other words, base and superstructure need not fit snugly together but developments within a differentiated base can come into contradiction with different aspects of the superstructure.

For example, when Christopher Dunkley, the television critic for the *Financial Times*, complains about the sorry state of programming on British television, then we have a good example of the base (the capitalist economic priorities the *Financial Times* exists to serve and champion) and the superstructure (the cultural values of the upper middle class) confronting each other as sworn foes:

> *Big Brother* exemplifies many of the most significant characteristics of British television in this new millennium. The participants are seen as having a celebrity status which would once have been acquired by a world-class violinist or a scientist who had won the Nobel Prize. Today's TV producers, with their terrified adherence to relativism, attribute celebrity and consequently respectability as readily to Mad Frankie Fraser, one-time gangster; or the discredited former MP Neil Hamilton and his wife, as a previous generation would have reserved for Albert Schweitzer. Indeed the very idea of holding fast to certain values, whether moral or artistic, is giving way in television (as in other areas of life) to the dictates of focus groups and the ratings figures. If popular, then good.[1]

Here we see the conflict between two different models of value; in one celebrity value derives entirely from media *performance*, and in the other an older model of the classical bourgeois subject derives value not from the media, which merely brings people and events to a wider audience, but from the contribution to social and cultural life which the people and events have made outside the media. We can correlate these different models of value to two conflicting modes of development: informationalism and industrialism respectively. If the postmodern emphasis on media performance and spectacle has a 'base' it is to be found in the post-Fordist mode of development which has seen capital flow into the culture industries, into the communication and information industries and promote extensive debt-based 'hyper consumption'. This has developed a particular model of the subject (the socialised individual) constructed at the point of consumption around a 'dispersed, decentred network of libidinal attachments, emptied of ethical substance and psychical interiority, the ephemeral function of this or that act of consumption, media experience, sexual relationship, trend or fashion' (Eagleton 1986a:145). Terry Eagleton is one of the few Marxist critics who have been unembarrassed by the base–superstructure model, using it to explore the tensions between bourgeois economics and bourgeois culture (Eagleton 1997). There is, he notes, something of a contradiction between this model of the subject and older models of the bourgeois subject which require some sense of rational decision-making, some sense of rights and responsibilities (as a parent or political citizen for example), some sense of continuity (that who you are today is not radically different to who you were yesterday) in order to be effective in the workplace, aspire to have a career, pay your bills on time or be a good legal subject if called upon to do jury service or be a witness at the scene of a crime or accident.

One can find this contradiction between the classical rational bourgeois subject and the irrational and fragmented bourgeois consumer at work in the dialectic between the declining fortunes of the sphere of political representation (voter turnout is dropping precipitously in the West) and the increasing participation in the corporate-driven representations of an expanding media. The crisis of bourgeois democracy, operating within increasingly narrow margins, increasingly defined by failure (rather than the self-realisation of the world of consumption), by remoteness, by elites, is both offset and highlighted by media representation where a more authentic participation and representation without representation (that is elite mediation) *appear* to be on offer. In such promises the populist media makes its own apparatus of production, control and manipulation disappear (although this repression is not entirely successful, as we shall see in relation to *Big Brother*). Similarly our *Financial Times* critic, Mr Dunkley, makes the production apparatus disappear not by celebrating the presence of the masses but by blaming the television audience for the cultural debasement of the medium. The audience is a convenient displacement because it confirms Dunkley's values (those proles really have no taste!) rather than challenging them (why am writing for a paper which champions the destruction of every cultural value I hold dear?). This is an example, in critical discourse, of what Fredric Jameson, in relation to cultural products themselves, calls a strategy of containment, meaning a strategy of managing, containing and ultimately *repressing* a contradiction (the mode of production).

THE SUPERSTRUCTURE

If the mode of production is a category denoting activities primarily concerned with the production of economic value, then the superstructure refers to those activities whose 'product' or outcomes are primarily non-economic but which are nonetheless, to varying degrees, crucial to the reproduction of the mode of production. The superstructure is conceived as operating within the parameters of the socio-economic relations mapped out by the mode of production. Thus superstructural activities are often described as 'regulating' or 'reproducing' the conditions that further the continuance of the mode of production, although, as we have seen, this does not mean that different parts of the mode of production and superstructure cannot come into conflict with one another. Such superstructural activities are usually differentiated into two types: first, regulation and reproduction can be and are achieved by *coercive* means (the police, the judiciary, the army); second, reproduction is also achieved (even in dictatorships) through the more *consensual* modes of culture, that is through the production of values, ideas, knowledge, habits, identities, and so forth. Here the key superstructural agencies are politics, education, the media, the family and religion. What imme-diately becomes clear though in making the distinction between the production of economic value and superstructural practices is that some agencies are *straddling* categories. The media are both a business, an increasingly important site for capital investment, accumulation and employment, *and* a producer of ideas, values and so on. It is precisely this split between their economic and cultural operations, and attempts to understand the relations between them, which are the sources of tension and debate between political economy and cultural studies approaches to the media.

Once we start thinking about the superstructure and the economic and cultural dimensions of the media, it becomes apparent that we need to distinguish between two levels in the foundational category, mode of production. We can think, for example, of the mode of production (B1) as a *general* category with no particular content, which is to say that it does not refer to particular kinds of production, industry, services or whatever. At this very abstract level, to talk of the capitalist mode of production refers to the *social form* which all or at any rate almost all production must take within a given society. At this level of abstraction the distinction between a mode of production and the superstructure holds firm. But then we can also talk of mode of production in a more *concrete* sense, referring to actual industries (S2), actual companies (S3), actual production (S4), and so forth. Clearly there can be a considerable variety of concrete productive arrangements or practices that can be housed within the general social form. How the mode of production as a general social form sets limits and exerts pressures (Williams 1980:32) on media producers and products cannot be read off from the general abstract mode of production category, but requires analysis of the mediations between the general social form and specific media, their institutional and economic relations or 'base' and their cultural forms.

Nevertheless Marxism does expect that the institutional and socioeconomic forms of specific media will manifest in particular ways the socio-economic relations of a *general* mode of production (capitalism in our case). And, further, that the dominant social and economic relations will be manifested in the politics of the cultural values that the media produce so that the media will in general further the reproduction of the relations of production (although this almost always involves arguments concerning the best way to ensure that reproduction). In *The German Ideology*, Marx and Engels write that: 'The ideas of the ruling class are in every epoch the ruling ideas, i.e. the class which is the ruling *material* force of society, is at the same time its ruling *intellectual* force' (1989:64). Now, things are no doubt more complicated and variable than this bald statement suggests. For example, are the ruling ideas always directly the ideas of the ruling class? Such a statement would seem to dissolve the specific and contradictory class position of the intelligentsia who staff the means of 'intellectual production'. One might want to rephrase it as this: the ruling ideas are by and large *compatible* with or at least do not openly confront the ideas or (an important distinction) *interests* of the ruling class.

This opens up the question of hegemony, the struggle for moral and intellectual leadership. Williams introduces an important temporal dimension to the base–superstructure model with the concepts of emergent and residual practices, vying with the dominant culture. He then crosses this temporal dimension with categories which evaluate their political character with the terms oppositional and alternative cultural values (1980:39). Oppositional cultures, such as the emergent anti-capitalist movement, confront the *values* of the dominant social relations, but, because they actively seek to change those social relations, or, at the very least, some significant aspect of them, they also confront the *interests* of the dominant social forces. Alternative practices by contrast offer, to varying degrees, value systems which conflict with the dominant values, but, because the limit of their ambitions tends to be to carve out an autonomous space of their own, they do not constitute a threat to the socio-economic interests of the dominant classes (youth cultures tend to be a good example of alternative practices). Obviously, the relations between dominant, residual, emergent, alternative and oppositional have to be considered dialectically. These are not in the real world mutually exclusive forces, but dynamically interacting and overlapping to some extent. Thus rephrased, is the proposition concerning ruling material forces having a strong correlation to ruling intellectual forces a reasonable starting point for media analysis? If it were *not* a reasonable proposition and starting point then one would expect to see the mainstream news media calling capitalism into question on a regular basis; one would expect to find them attacking the profit motive routinely, pointing out the irrationality of capitalism's priorities, highlighting its wastefulness, attacking *wealthy* minorities that control vast resources rather than the poor and the vulnerable (such as asylum seekers), and linking the various tragedies, discontents and crises which they find in the world *back* to the capitalist relations of production. No one could seriously suggest that this is in fact what the mainstream media do (even its liberal wing), and so Marx and Engels' proposition of a link between ruling ideas and the ruling class does indeed seem to me to be a reasonable proposition from which to start.

It is vitally important that we do not map the earlier discussion of the distinction between materialism and idealism onto the mode of production and the superstructure. If we do, we separate the world of production from the world of ideas and consciousness, assigning them respectively to the mode of production and the superstructure. This turns the mode of production into brute matter (this is indeed one of the reasons why the base gets conceived as a technological or economic objective 'thing' external to human consciousness). A moment's reflection though makes it clear that consciousness, knowledge, thought and values are indispensable to any real productive activity, including of course media production. In his bluff common-sense critique of Hegel and Marx, Leonard Jackson argues: 'Tools are useless without concepts but if you take that point too seriously you might as well go back to Hegel and make ideas the driving force of history' (1994:86). Not quite. Ideas, consciousness, and so forth are crucial to the labour process, but only those ideas that are articulated to that process can become 'productive forces' and only those ideas that are seen as compatible with the dominant social relations of production at any one time will have a chance of being developed in systematic and dominant ways in the labour process. This does not rule out contradictions, such as the growth of digital file swapping discussed in Chapter 2, but such contradictions are very evidently a threat to capital accumulation which will have to be tamed if they are ever to become an institutionalised and legal part of the mode of production. In this formulation then, the materialist doctrine is retained without separating social and economic forces and ideas. In a formulation that bears repeating, *it is the social and economic forces that determine which ideas will in turn determine the social and economic forces.*

However, as I have suggested, material forces should not be equated with the mode of production and ideas with the superstructure. Not only does this impoverish the base (turning it into brute matter) it also impoverishes the superstructure by 'de-materialising' it into a realm of pure consciousness (Eagleton 1989:168). If you view the superstructure as merely the realm of ideology, values, consciousness (as some of Marx's formulations suggested), then it becomes easier to see the superstructure as a secondary domain whose movements and character can be read off from an analysis of 'the base'. It is not only the media institutions and organisations which have a material existence, but even culture, language and consciousness itself. The Russian Marxist linguist Vološhinov had no problem in arguing that signs are a 'material segment' of the real world and require 'some kind of material embodiment' (1996:11). Marx and Engels in *The German Ideology* made the link between the materiality of consciousness as expressed in language and its interpersonal, *social* character:

> From the start the 'spirit' is afflicted with the curse of being 'burdened' with matter, which here makes its appearance in the form of agitated layers of air, sounds, in short, of language. Language is as old as consciousness, language *is* practical consciousness that exists also, for other men, and for that reason alone it really exists for me personally as well; language, like consciousness, only arises from the need, the necessity, of intercourse with other men. (1989:50–51)

Here we see quite clearly the *link* between those two definitions of materialism discussed above: *sheer physicality and social relations are linked because it is only through social relations that the capacity to manipulate the physical material world can grow.*

The superstructure then is material as are culture and consciousness. There is though a danger in such a formulation that all such materialities are then treated as equally determining. Raymond Williams once famously complained that 'it is wholly beside the point to isolate "production" and "industry" from the comparably material production of "defence", "law and order", "welfare", "entertainment", and "public opinion"' (1988:93). His argument, against 'vulgar Marxist' currents that reduced the superstructure to mere reflexes of the mode of production or base, was that we needed to extend the concept of production and materiality to all social activities. The result, if we did, would be that these activities would acquire a weight and efficacy that demanded study in their own right: 'From castles and palaces and churches to prisons and workhouses and schools; from weapons of war to a controlled press: any ruling class, in variable ways though always materially, produces a social and political order' (Williams 1988:93). This is a shallow rather than deep materialism. The sheer materiality of castles, churches, schools and so forth is not, as Terry Eagleton pointed out, at issue (1989:168). Without the deep materialism of mode of production, there is nothing substantively weaving these apparently discrete organisations together, except the 'intentions' of the ruling class (Eagleton 1989:170, Williams 1980:36). But we then have to ask why they have such intentions and what activities take place (such as economic crises) irrespective of their intentions. The extension of materialism in both its senses to all social activities does not negate the base–superstructure model, it merely demonstrates that for Marxism a hierarchy of determinants governs the capitalist world. Thus in Chapter 4 we saw that the state is a powerful determinant on social and economic relations, but that it was the social and economic relations of capital which, to repeat the earlier formulation, determined the manner in which it *could* be determined by the state.

LOUIS ALTHUSSER: OVERDETERMINATION OR MEDIATION?

Any analysis of the social order has to navigate between two pitfalls: on the one hand, can the concept of mode of production avoid collapsing into a *monocausal* account of the social order in which the hierarchy of determinants is asserted but at the cost of reducing the complexity of the world to a single essence; and can it avoid this pitfall while avoiding the liberal model of sheer *multicausality* in which a variety of factors can be admitted to have powerful effects but any sense of a systematically structured social hierarchy of forces disappears in favour of more or less equal plurality? One such attempt to resolve this dilemma was made by the French Communist Party theoretician Louis Althusser. In the late 1960s and up until the mid-1970s, Althussarian Marxism was extremely popular in cultural, film and media studies (Clarke 1980). Its swift decline is testimony to its failure to address the dilemmas posed by the base–superstructure model. But the failure is worth briefly charting because it can help us clarify what kind of conceptualisation of mediation we need to be able to link the mode of production to the superstructure without reducing the latter to a mere expression of the former. While Williams' notion of determination as setting limits and exerting pressures is useful, it does not tell us what is going on *inside* the process which is being determined. Hence the need to return to the concept of mediation.

Yet it is precisely this Hegelian concept that Althusser sought to eradicate from Marxism in his famous essay 'Contradiction and overdetermination' as part of his broader project to separate out all Hegelian influences from a 'scientific' Marxism. Let us begin with Althusser's destination before reconstructing his route. Towards the end of the essay he famously formulated the base–superstructure model like this:

> Marx has at least given us the 'two ends of the chain', and has told us to find out what goes on between them: on the one hand, *determination in the last instance by the (economic) mode of production*, on the other, the relative autonomy of the superstructures and their specific effectivity. (Althusser 1996:111)

Here we have an attempt to reconcile the mode of production category with multicausality (the superstructures and their 'specific effectivity'). Except the formulation and therefore reconciliation dissolves almost immediately. The mode of production is either a determining force or it is not; to relegate its determination to 'the last instance' is highly undialectical, stressing not interdependence but a rigid temporal externality between it and the superstructures. Even then, the formula 'in the last instance' merely returns Althusser to the reductive (Stalinist) Marxism he seeks to escape from, and so he is forced to conclude that, from 'the first moment to the last, the lonely hour of the "last instance" never comes' (1996:113). Thus it was that Althussarian Marxism laid the foundations for post-Marxism and discourse theory. This then was Althusser's destination which was little different from the standard liberal relegation of the economic sphere to a narrowly conceived, specialised and non-determinant role. But how did Althusser get there?

Conceptually, his starting point is promising enough. He argues that Marx's relationship to Hegel is rather more complicated than is often supposed. He notes that 'as Marx said twenty times, Hegel explains the material life, the concrete history of all peoples by a dialectic of consciousness' (1996:107). Marx's relationship to this explanation is often characterised as a simple *inversion*, so that the productive life of society (and as we have seen this often becomes abstracted into 'the economy') becomes the 'essence' of history and all other social forces become its simple *expression*. Althusser sees this impoverished and reductive version of Marx as deriving from the Hegelian category of mediation against which he counterpoises his own concept of overdetermination. Althusser argues that in the Hegelian model of how the different parts relate in a whole we have not multiple determinants (overdetermination) but the 'cumulative *internalization*' of a general contradiction (1996:101). This is the crucial concept: internalisation. It is clear that if all parts of the social whole are simply internalising a general contradiction (the economic base in 'vulgar Marxism') then all we need ever do is devote our critical and practical energies to that general contradiction and relegate everything else as secondary. And yet without *some* conception of internalisation the superstructure disengages from the mode of production entirely and we are left with Althusser's concept of overdetermination in which all the other non-economic factors converge from disparate sources and are apparently unrelated to the socio-economic relations which remain rigorously external (not internalised) to those other determinations. We appear to be in an impossible bind, caught between crude reductionism and liberal pluralism.

Althusser is in fact only half right on the question of mediation. If internalisation is one side of the mediation process, linking the particular to the general, the other side involves a necessary process of *reconfiguration* (necessary because of the material – in the double sense of the word – character of the entire social formation). The mode of production does not pass through into all the other levels of the social formation unhindered and in a uniform and homogeneous manner. Mediation involves a double process of internalisation *and* reconfiguration, so that the logic of the mode of production – which itself must be differentiated by distinct categories such as social class, productive forces, commodification, use-value and so forth – enters into the social formation but gets reworked according to the practices, agency, institutions and technologies of a differentiated social whole. To take one small example, live Web streaming for television increases in cost the *more* people log on to use it, in stark contrast to the way costs fall per copy for every consumer of a film. Here the technology of the Internet and Web-broadcasting reconfigures the general logic of the mode of production which it internalises, thus calling forth in turn particular responses from the social agents involved. All that the mode of production category insists is that all social phenomena take up *some* relationship to the socio-economic antagonisms of production; but it does not insist that all phenomena take up the *same* relations to it. Indeed, any authentic materialist philosophy will *expect* the concrete materiality of practices to produce nuanced reworkings of, say, the accumulation imperative. It is only capital which harbours the *fantasy* that it can do away with the concrete materiality of social practices and use-values. With the emphasis on reconfiguration as much as on internalisation, Marxists can learn to be surprised again at what they find.

JAMESON'S DECODING GEIGER COUNTER: FROM TEXTUAL TO MODE OF PRODUCTION

In the next section I am going to sketch out how the base–superstructure model might be deployed in relation to a popular television text: *Big Brother*. Here, however, I briefly want to sketch out how we can move from analysis of a single text up to the general category of mode of production. Unquestionably it is Marxist literary theory and in particular its engagement in the late 1960s and 1970s with formalist and structuralist theories of language which have led the way in developing a sophisticated understanding of textual production and its relations to the mode of production (Macherey 1978, Eagleton 1986b, Jameson 1974b, 1989). This engagement brought a new sophistication to Marxist literary criticism through a new attentiveness to the formal properties, the formal strategies and hence the *specificities* of literary language, while, at the same time, transcending the ahistorical and idealist tendencies of formalism and structuralism. However, this transcendence was only partial. Such Marxist literary theory is a prime example of Murdock's complaint concerning the missing mediations which political economy focuses on. In part the lacuna in literary theory derives from the fact that literary production, while obviously requiring publishing companies and involving marketing strategies, still involves a direct artisanal relationship between individual author and text which is displaced within the culture industries proper where collective production under capital's social relations and technology interposes rather more directly. Thus the case study of *Big Brother* will still sketch out the immediate institutional and economic mediations at work on the text, particularly as they relate to new technology and the corporate alliances of the media–industrial complex. Fredric Jameson has often been criticised for missing these and other mediations and this needs to be borne in mind because I am going to sketch out his model of historicising textual production first elaborated in his book *The Political Unconscious*. I have chosen Jameson because he offers a comprehensive model (within its textualist limits) and because his is also well known for diagnosing the cultural trend which *Big Brother* can be located in: namely, postmodernism.

Jameson identifies three dimensions of analysis of the text, what he calls interpretive horizons, with each one moving out to a wider frame of reference. In the first instance, analysis takes the text as a 'symbolic act' (Jameson 1989:76), which is to stress that the text is a *production* of pre-existing cultural and ideological materials (see also Eagleton 1986b:64–101). Seeing the text as a 'production' is vital if we are to move away from the more passive notion of a text simply 'reflecting' the wider society. If it is a production then the task is to investigate it as a reconfiguration of existing materials, a combination of those materials which has some element of 'uniqueness' about it no matter how generic or formulaic its materials and operations. And one of the things that the text produces is its own imaginary resolution to real social contradictions. As Jameson puts it,

> the relationship between art and its social context can be freed from inert conceptions of reflection by the proposition that the social context (including the history of forms themselves and the condition of the vernacular language) is to be grasped as the *situation* – the problem, the dilemma, the contradiction, the 'question' – to which the work of art comes as an imaginary solution, resolution or 'answer'. (1992:164)

This, from Jameson's *Signatures of the Visible*, is fully consonant with the model mapped out in *The Political Unconscious*. The resolution is imaginary because the social problems that the text diagnoses can only in fact be resolved through social practice. When that practical resolution is blocked (by the dominant social relations), culture performs a mythical reconciliation. Cultural texts use *formal* strategies, such as narrative oppositions, imagery, particular points of 'entry' or focalisation on the action, in order to manage and contain

problematic social content. This implies that strategies of containment are a complex process in which that problematic social content
simultaneously surfaces, only then to be repressed by the formal
strategies deployed (Jameson 1989:213–14). Jameson's interpretive
model then is like a Geiger counter passed over the text; the distinctive clicking of the Geiger counter here picks up not just what is
emitted but what is omitted by the text, what has been repressed
(Jameson 1989:215). Jameson is seeking to decode the political
unconscious (essentially the repressed mode of production) that
haunts the text, leaving its mark on the text's form and content. As
we shall see, the *Big Brother* phenomenon ('text' is really too narrow
a word) is haunted by the unequal exchanges of value, power and
ethics which are indispensable to capitalism.

In the second dimension of analysis, the discrete text's imaginary
resolution of real social contradictions is seen as part of a larger social
'conversation', specifically the 'antagonistic dialogue' between classes.
If the first dimension stresses the formal completeness of the text,
its success in arranging its materials in such a manner that it can
perform its resolutions and containment strategies, this second level
of analysis unpicks that apparent closure and situates the text in a
more open-ended process where signs become, following Volŏshinov,
'multiaccentual', pulled in different directions in the 'arena of the
class struggle' (Volŏshinov 1996:23). To identify this class struggle
in particular signs means specifying minimal units of signs around
which the class struggle is conducted. Jameson calls these units *ideol-
ogemes*. An ideologeme, such as say 'nature' or 'new technology', is
an 'amphibious formation' insofar as it can be developed either as a
concept, philosophical system or doctrine, or it can be developed as
a narrative, a story, with characters or other representations
embodying its essential theme (Jameson 1989:87). The ideologeme
that we will need to consider in relation to *Big Brother* is that of 'surveillance'; this is the minimal unit, the sign around which we can
locate *Big Brother* as a 'move' or stratagem in the 'ideological confrontation between the classes' (Jameson 1989:85).

The final interpretive horizon is larger still and is nothing less than
the mode of production itself. Here the dialogue between classes as
it is organised in relation to a particular text is reframed as a moment
within the struggle to achieve a complete cultural revolution, which
is to say the struggle for cultural hegemony (leadership) appropriate
for an epoch. However, there are problems with this final interpretive horizon. Jameson argues that each mode of production has a

'cultural dominant', a cultural paradigm best suited to 'program-ming' (to use Jameson's somewhat functionalist term) the subject so that they are fit to live (with few questions asked) within capitalism. Jameson has famously diagnosed the cultural dominant for advanced capitalism as postmodernism (1991:4). The problem with this is that it rather prejudges the extent to which postmodern cultural production can be seen as 'dominant' and encourages a certain inflation in the use of the term postmodern whereby it ends up covering and including everything. Certainly in the case of *Big Brother* one could plausibly situate it in a postmodern 'cultural revolution'. The programme was much commented upon and can be seen as indicative of wider cultural and economic trends as well as sympto-matic of certain directions contemporary television is taking. However, television is a heterogeneous medium and the impact of commercialisation is uneven and takes a variety of directions not all of which could be classified as postmodern. So I think we would want to be cautious about claiming that there is a single cultural resource which best reflects the dominant culture and that postmodernism is it. There are in fact a variety of cultural forms which can be mobilised to manage and contain social contradictions.

The other problem is with Jameson's formulation of the mode of production category. I earlier suggested that there is a distinction to be made between a mode of production coexisting with another *actually* existing mode of production and one which has appropriated the cultural residues of an earlier but now dismantled mode of production or the cultural use of anticipations of a future (socialist) but not yet realised mode of production. However, for Jameson, the 'form contradiction takes' at this level of analysis is *between* modes of production (1989:94). It is here, in the conflict and contradictions between different actually existing modes of production that Jameson finds the dynamics of social change and political hope. This formu-lation is unfortunate because it is quite clear within the heartlands of advanced capitalism that there is in fact no coexistence between different modes of production. There is only one mode of production in what is called 'the West', and that is capitalism. If we want to talk about the coexistence of different modes, it makes more sense to situate *Big Brother* along the fault-line of modes of *development* as I indicated in my discussion of Mr Dunkley's defence of the old, arguably now *residual* (to use Williams' category) high bourgeois subject against the consumerist and mediatised subject of advanced capitalism. The upshot of Jameson's insistence that contradiction is generated between modes of production is that contradiction then logically disappears given the 'prodigious expansion of capital into hitherto uncommodified areas' (1991:36) which characterises postmodernism. This leaves Jameson looking to the non-capitalist or less capitalised developing world for resistance or hope. Those of us living within the advanced capitalist mode of production need instead to recover our sense of contradictions *within* the capitalist mode of production, between capital and labour, exchange value and use-value, unnecessary alienation and necessary universal emancipation.

BASE–SUPERSTRUCTURE MEETS *BIG BROTHER*

Or rather the model of base–superstructure that I have unpacked into seven levels of mediation meets *Big Brother* (see Figure 5.2). I will begin with levels S2 and S3, the industrial context of television and the production context of the companies involved. *Big Brother* is a format devised by a Dutch company called Endemol Entertainment, one of the largest independent European producers, which by the late 1990s had interests in more than two dozen production houses in over 15 countries. The show involves contestants who are locked inside a house, cut off from all contact with the outside world and monitored twenty-four-seven. In the UK version of the show contestants are nominated for eviction by their 'house-mates' every week. The two contestants with the most nominations are then subjected to a public vote where their fate is decided. A cash prize goes to the last person left in the house. The Dutch *Big Brother* first ran in 1999 and the format was subsequently sold or subcontracted out to local producers in Germany, Spain and the US. The UK version of the show (which first ran in 2000) is produced by Bazal, the production company run by Peter Bazalgette, and part-owned by GMG Endemol, the British offshoot of the Dutch parent company. The 'GMG' refers to the Guardian Media Group who also part-own the UK offshoot. *Big Brother* did not come out of a cultural and televisual vacuum but was preceded by *Survivor* (whose makers indeed sued Endemol after claiming that *Big Brother* was a virtual copy of their idea) and other reality TV shows which followed the daily activities of law enforcement officers and public service agencies (Dovey 2000:80–81).

The success of such shows in both Europe and crucially the United States generated large broadcaster demand for producer ideas around what are known as 'scriptless' shows involving ordinary people. It is important to note how congruent reality TV is with the political economy of television. In terms of the number of editions of such shows which a given outlay can produce, and therefore the airtime they can fill, reality TV is considerably cheaper than those other staple fares of the schedules: situation comedies and drama.[2] Moreover reality TV lends itself to 'continuous originals' (with all the attendant publicity that generates) rather than having to show repeats.

Within the UK television industry the general logic of the capitalist mode of production does not unroll uniformly but is instead reconfigured differentially by the various broadcasting organisations (BBC, ITV, Channel 4, Five, BSkyB). Thus the material conditions of existence for any particular text depend on the broadcaster's identity, public service remit (if any), main audience constituency or target and the particular problem or gap in the schedule which the programme aims to fill. Consequently, within UK terrestrial television, there was probably only one broadcaster who could have commissioned *Big Brother* and that was Channel 4. It had the right demographics (a younger audience base than ITV which tends to be skewed towards an older audience profile) and it was looking for a response to ITV's phenomenally successful *Who Wants to be a Millionaire?*, which was being stripped across the schedules (Wayne 2000). The success of the programme in Europe probably already made it too upmarket and expensive a franchise for Five. Meanwhile the programme's competitive elements made it vulnerable to charges of it being exploitative and the controversies that it had already generated in other European countries made it emphatically not a BBC programme (which instead developed the more public service oriented, co-operative and idealistic *Castaway*).

One of the important features of *Big Brother* is that it has become a showcase for developing an evolving multimedia, cross-platform and interactive 'experience'. Live feeds to a *Big Brother* web site twenty-four-seven gave a crucial reinforcement to the theme of surveillance beyond the restrictions of the edited highlights broadcast on Channel 4. (The Channel's digital channel, E4, also ran hours of live footage.) Thus *Big Brother* saw the first real convergence between television and the Internet, between an old technology's content and a new distribution technology. The integration of the Internet and the web site into the television programme was profoundly attractive to the corporations involved, since it facilitated worldwide marketing opportunities. The *Big Brother* web site markets not only the usual books, magazines, caps and T-shirts, but also has links to bookmakers and *Big Brother* branded gambling games. The Dutch site for the first series generated 53 million online impressions.[3] The UK *Big Brother 1* web site registered 7.4 million page impressions on the night the pantomime villain Nasty Nick was confronted by his housemates.[4] The UK's *Big Brother 3* (2002) meanwhile generated an average of 4 million hits per day.[5] *Big Brother 3* was also important in shifting from free 24-hour web streaming to a subscription service costing £10 a month. Important here was the need to break with the cultural expectations of the Internet distributing free services. 'We always knew there would be a bit of a backlash from the internet community', noted Chris Short, head of interactive services at Endemol. 'The problem is that they have been used to the internet being free ... By next year people will have got used to paying and it won't be such a big deal.'[6]

The continuous nature of *Big Brother* generates daily newspaper copy while live feeds to cinema-size screens in public places spread the *Big Brother* text inescapably into every pore of the public sphere. The other 'interactive' dimension of the programme is the phone votes that generate yet more cash for Channel 4, Endemol and British Telecom (around another £4 million for the second series). The programme's spin-off series, *Big Brother's Little Brother*, uses the discussion format to encourage endless mini-votes and phone-ins. With the third series (sponsored by the mobile phone company O_2) viewers were able to vote using their mobile phones' text message facilities. On top of this viewers could receive news updates as text alerts on their mobile phones, costing another £5 (for 36 'alerts'). Interactive television then essentially means various companies inter-acting with your pockets. The levels of surveillance and manipulation of the *Big Brother* audience are carefully fostered. As Chris Short admits: 'We're trying to be increasingly clever about how we move our audience around from one platform to another.'[7] The accumu-lation logic of all this interactivity is closely woven into the feedback mechanisms which increase the levels of surveillance and manipu-lation of the *Big Brother* audience. For example, phone votes on *Big Brother's Little Brother* not only bring in the cash but also provide data on audience attitudes to both the contestants and the *Big Brother* apparatus itself. The programme producers can then respond flexibly to audience attitudes and concerns as each series unfolds. The multimedia and interactive components of the programme fit exactly into contemporary corporate strategies that have seen Internet companies and content providers, such as AOL and Time Warner, merging. Thus it is no surprise to find that Endemol was subsequently bought up by the Spanish telecommunications giant Telefonica for £3.5 billion, up from a pre-*Big Brother* valuation of £700 million.[8] This corporate base in turn underpins the technological construction of a multi-platform national experience, and crucially national *community*. The society of the spectacle 'is not a collection of images', wrote Guy Debord, 'but a social relation among people, mediated by images' (1983:4).

An analysis then of the political economy of the media can tell us why the reality TV genre is congruent with commercial pressure and strategies and it can even explain the development of certain features such as the multimedia and interactive components of the show. It begins to shade in some of the crucial mediations at work on the cultural product. In his textual/ideological analysis of reality TV, Bill Nichols notes that it 'has a vested interest in subsuming everything beyond itself into its own support system of circulating exchange values' (1996:396). We have seen that there is a real economic infrastructure, a web of interlocking financial interests, underpinning this hermetic quality of the genre. At the same time, it is but one scale of determination we must attend to. Political economy of the media is a blunt instrument when it comes to understanding why *this* particular format has developed now and not some other format equally congruent with the industry's economic priorities; it cannot in other words account for the cultural origins of reality TV nor can it explore the particular programme as a *production* of that cultural milieu (Dovey 2000:85). For that we have to move (if we are using the seven levels of mediation) both 'down' into the broader social, political and cultural environments that the institutions of the media are mediating, S1 (although I am going to say little about the state as a policy organ here), B2 (modes of development) and B1 (mode of production), and 'up' into the strategies of the production process and text itself (S4 and S5).

I suggested earlier in my summary of Jameson's methodology that we needed to select an ideologeme, a sign that is to be analysed as the site and stake of class struggle. The title of *Big Brother* itself suggests the relevant ideologeme: surveillance. This will be the key category by which we link B1 and B2 to S5 (the media text). The development of technologies of representation, communication and information, such as video, the Internet, mobile phones, computer software programs, global positioning systems and so forth, has massively expanded the capacity to generate, store, access and analyse data. There is an inextricable link between surveillance and the cutting-edge mode of development, Castells calls informational-ism (B2). Once again the technological forces of communicative production become the site and stake of the class struggle (B1). New technology allows you unprecedented access to a plethora of information, data and communication channels, but it also allows corporate and state agents unprecedented access to you. Thus the meaning of surveillance – think, for example, of the debates around closed-circuit video monitoring of public space – whether it is essentially benevolent and protective or whether it is malevolent and directed by interests inimical to those who are observed and classified, acquires the multi-accentuality of a sign being pulled in different directions by the conflicts and contradictions of class division and struggle.

A full analysis of *Big Brother* would want to show how it mines this cultural seam/seme in both directions. In relation to the house-mates it generates some of the negative signifiers associated with a remote institution (the set design of the house, the motif of the mechanical camera eye, the capricious tests and surprises which *Big Brother* sets for the contestants) in order to generate a certain dramatic frisson; but, in relation to the audience, the programme works very hard to develop strategies to contain and manage any anxieties which might cause them to distrust the *Big Brother* apparatus. There are, for example, the strategies of inclusion (the public's vox pop commentaries on the contestants, the 'fans' gathered around the house on eviction nights) and presentation (the performance of Davina McCall, or even the Northern accent of the narrator, Marcus Bentley; market research for call centres has found that the Northern accent connotes a trustworthiness and honesty which helps contain anxieties around the remoteness and anonymity of such consumer services). The tension within the ideologeme of surveillance between representation for public good or observation for some private (or state) self-interest runs back to the aesthetic origins of reality TV itself. Where once the extension of representation to the ordinary in documentaries or social realist films was a subversion and critique of professional codes of representation, now the ordinary is co-opted as a badge of professional authenticity, a sign of the proximity of the professionals, including stars and celebrities, to the vernacular and the plebeian. This is one master strategy of containment in which class is simultaneously acknowledged and conjured away at a stroke: the ordinary is valued precisely because of its difference from the elites, but then we discover that, since the media elites and their codes of representation can adopt the style of the ordinary at will, there is no class difference of any note. Reality TV's production of this cultural tension has its roots in the camcorder revolution which made it economically possible and aesthetically legitimate for the ordinary to break into the fortified bastion of broadcasting (Wayne 1997). Video technology is obviously central to the feasibility of *Big Brother*'s twenty-four-seven surveillance but it is also central to the rationale of the form, the aesthetic of reality TV. For reality TV at its purest (and *Big Brother* is reality TV at its purest) is premised on the myth of real time, where both the gap between action and representation is closed by the eternal presence of the cameras and the gap between the recording and audience consumption (and feedback) is narrowed by technologies of rapid assemblage (digital editing) and dissemination (Internet, satellite, broadcasting).

Big Brother produces a surprising twist on earlier 1970s debates concerning the illusionism and pseudo-transparency of dominant audio-visual discourse. In *Big Brother* the authenticity and spontaneity of the events is paradoxically confirmed by the very visibility of the representational apparatus. All those banks of monitors recording the events unfolding in the house which we see when the programme cuts to the inside of the control room, or when Davina quietly watches the inmates behind the two-way mirror, are signifiers of catching reality on the run. This was the explicit and conscious intention of the executive producer, Ruth Wrigley, who tells us: 'I wanted viewers ... to see the control room, to get an idea of all the behind the scenes work ... We were filming it for real, and it was a virtue of the programme that viewers understood that' (Ritchie 2000:10–11). But the contradictions of the surveillance ideologeme – and the class divisions that underlie it – nevertheless resurface via this selfsame strategy of containment. The show is caught between flaunting its elaborate apparatus and trying to persuade us that they are *not really in control*. In the *Big Brother* book accompanying the first series, the writer is at pains to convey the producers' sense of not being able to control the events going on in the house. But, rather like the base in relation to the superstructure, the producers have already determined the parameters within which their lack of control will run. The contradiction between displaying the apparatus as a sign of authentic connection with the ordinary and its display as a sign of the apparatus' ability to control and manipulate is the mediation, the *internalisation–reconfiguration* of the more general contradiction already discussed around the ideologeme of surveillance.

It is a contradiction that surfaces when ex-contestants complain about how they were represented by *Big Brother*'s editing decisions. And it is a contradiction that surfaces in this passage from the *Big Brother* book on the computer software used to log and retrieve actions by the contestants (S4):

> For example, if a producer was trying to put together a film package on two contestants, he or she put their names into the computer and it would deliver every instance when they were filmed together. By adding the keyword 'touching' this would be refined to any sequence of them making bodily contact with each other. (Ritchie 2000:12)

These contradictions at the level of form between the authenticity of the ordinary and manipulation are also played out in relation to the content of the show. Despite the postmodern qualities of *Big Brother*, it mobilises powerful Utopian desires which would be left untapped in a more thoroughly postmodern artifact (given that Utopianism implies some desire for those very concepts that postmodernism tends to eschew, namely progress and transcendence beyond what is). Within the Utopian promise of the ordinary there lies a desire for transparency in our relations with individuals and institutions, which the capitalist mode of production and its cultural spectacles are structurally quite unable to deliver (Dyer 1985). So the hope that twenty-four-seven observation will reveal, through emotional revelation, confession and action, such transparency, and thus provide the viewer with the authentic basis on which to judge and vote for the contestants, is cancelled by the very structure and premise of the show. The competitive relations between the contestants coupled with the monitoring of their every move mean that they must instrumentally calculate their performance both to each other and to us, the watching audience. Under such circumstances, every action and gesture and confession becomes tainted with some hint of what the public relations industry calls perception management. The electoral element of the show thus now stands revealed as something of an allegory of the crisis of legitimacy bourgeois democracy now finds itself in.

The world of *Big Brother* is also very similar in many ways to the world of work: along with the instrumental calculation of performing to colleagues and superiors, there is the tension between co-operation and competition, the rules and conditions already imposed, the futile tasks and the boredom. *Big Brother* is etched with the world we recognise as much as *Harry Potter and the Philosopher's Stone*. Once again, the real surfaces only for its potentially troubling antagonisms to be recontained, not least by the fantasy compensation of mastery and control offered to the spectator by their alignment with the all-seeing *Big Brother* eye. Furthermore, while there is class, ethnic, gender and sexual diversity in the selection of the contestants, this only becomes converted into elements of their media performance (working-class contestant wins because he does not seem bright enough to be dissembling; gay man wins because he embodies emotional honesty). For the audience, this social diversity works in a contradictory fashion. On the one hand, it offers multiple points of identification, on the other, the text encourages the social or political basis for that identification to be converted into an individual's media performance. Indeed, were the *Big Brother* contestants actually drawn from a more homogeneous group, say white men, the show would be much more political, more evidently about a social constituency. The social diversity of the contestants is depoliticised in the editing out of any reference points to the social reality the contestants are drawn from, partly through fear of libel action (even the web feeds have a ten-second delay to provide enough time for controllers to stop broadcasting should libellous material be produced) but largely because of the nature of the programme (premised on isolating the group from any contact or stimuli from the outside world) and the narcissistic contestants selected. This strange abstract social unit masquerading as a social microcosm is projected by the techno-spectacle as the raw material of relatively risk free 'national conversation' in the interstices of work (so-called water-cooler television). An ethnographic study of the reception of the programme would very likely find the ghostly traces of the *social* and *political* basis for judgement and evaluation beneath the surface reduction of opinion to the merely personal, but it can hardly be said that the programme itself encourages this. Similarly, an ethnographic study would in all likelihood find an intermittent awareness within such conversations of how the production apparatus of *Big Brother* manipulates and controls the events and warrants ethical judgement on its role. But, again, it can hardly be said that the programme itself encourages this.

Instead *Big Brother* is a symptom of certain regressive trends within the public sphere whereby the foundations for making rational and informed decisions about socially constituted persons and events are eroded by a welter of mediatised interests (both corporate and individual). The first series of *Big Brother* ran alongside mobs being whipped up by the *News of the World* around fears concerning listed paedophiles. At least one newspaper commentator made the link between *Big Brother* and 'a season of media witchhunts and the opportunistic exploitation of "ordinary" people, of fake intimacy and knee-jerk emotional outpourings'.[9] When everything becomes reduced to perception management, the postmodern subject dissolves, as Jameson argued, into a fragmented series of intense experiences (Jameson 1991:6) with little rational continuity and prone to powerful feelings of either exhilaration or fear, love or hate. Thus the public narrative of *Big Brother* is characterised by a series of displacements in which most of the contestants eventually – particularly once on the cusp of eviction – become the focal point of dislike and public condemnation orchestrated by the media. The case of Jade Goody in *Big Brother 3* was merely the most extreme example of a general tendency to vilification. Within Jameson's methodology then, *Big Brother*, far from being harmless entertainment, is a transient moment of a cultural revolution 'reprogramming' the subject for integration into advanced capitalism's mode of production (Jameson's third, widest horizon of interpretation). Yet Jameson's notion of a thoroughgoing cultural revolution at this level of interpretation tends to cancel out the stress on cultural struggle and contradiction found at the second level of interpretation, the ideologeme (the dialogic tensions inscribed into 'surveillance'); the notion of a *cultural* dominant tends to smooth over the contradictory and multiple resources of cultural domination and resistance and compound the problematic implication that the rapid decline of older modes of production in the face of capital's 'prodigious expansion' in turn makes the capitalist mode of production less contradictory and less prone to challenge from alternative cultural resources.

In *Big Brother* we see one possible future direction of television, namely the thorough penetration of commodified information and communication technology into our rapidly shrinking public spaces and public services. Such public spaces are perhaps best understood as the residual traces of an older, still present, but embattled mode of development that was characterised by nation-states regulating national markets and capital (Fordism). New information and communications technology has been one important element in the globalisation of capital that has undermined that old order. The new political economy of the media evidently has parallels with the globalised economy generally. This is the reality of reality TV. In *Big Brother* we see the cultural contradictions of this political economy manifest themselves around the closely connected question of surveillance. The tensions between accessing the ordinary and being 'spun' by the media performance, between the authenticity of representation and its manipulation by the technological controllers, between participation in an event and being a mere object to be controlled and exploited, are all swimming around the programme as a reconfiguration of the class struggle between capital and labour. In offering a materialist analysis of all this, I have sought to unpack the somewhat monolithic and immobile base–superstructure model, and argue that its problematic is of continuing importance for media analysis.

6   Signs, Ideology and Hegemony

> That the definitions which make the object concrete are merely
> imposed upon it – this rule applies only where the faith in the
> primacy of subjectivity remains unshaken.
>
> Adorno, Negative Dialectics

This chapter will focus on the question of the internal structure of
representation, the question that is of signs. How do signs signify?
How is meaning generated by certain kinds of inscriptions? In the
previous chapter we were concerned with the conceptual problems
of thinking through how to situate representations in their social
contexts. Here we are more concerned with the process of representation, or signifying practice itself. This does not mean that we
abandon the crucial question of the relationship between signs and
society, just that we are starting from the other end of the process as
it were, from the 'texts' themselves. Indeed the question of how to
think through the relationship between signs and society remains
an important point of disagreement between Marxist theories of the
sign and those developed out of Saussurean and post-Saussurean linguistics. There are points of contact between Marxism and these other
contesting theories of signifying practices, but there are, as we shall
see, important and fundamental differences. However, the conceptual
foundations for exploring the world of signs, developed initially by
the Swiss linguist Ferdinand de Saussure (1857–1913), have come to
dominate, although in modified forms, the study of media representations. This domination needs to be challenged if we are to
understand the relations between the world of signs and the world
around signs. Such an understanding also requires us to think
through the relationship between signs and ideology, which will here
be defined as those values and beliefs which contribute to the reproduction of the social order on terms most beneficial to those already
occupying powerful positions within capitalism. The struggle to
sustain a pattern of such belief systems across a wide range of issues
and phenomena, from Nigella Lawson's television cookery series
(with its upper-middle-class *mise en scène*) to whether or not the West
should drop bombs on this or that part of the developing world, is
a crucial part of the struggle to sustain hegemony. My examples will

focus on the written language, drawn from the UK daily national press, but the principles concerning signs, ideology and hegemony, are relevant to other media.

THE WORLD OF/AS SIGNS

Towards the latter half of the nineteenth century, the fragmentation and specialisation of tasks which the bourgeois economy was developing in the factories also penetrated into the world of philosophy and the social sciences. The production line became the emblematic image of a social totality minutely divided and broken down into specialised tasks. This principle was generalised throughout the capitalist social and cultural structure. As a result there is a peculiar dialectic between fragmentation – as the world is broken up into separate fields and domains (economics, law, politics, science, culture, etc.) – and formal unity – as each field and domain develops highly elaborate *closed* systems in which all the parts slot seamlessly into place *within* a particular domain even as that domain's relations with other domains becomes increasingly opaque and difficult to fathom. As with the development of capitalism as a whole, this fragmented world is an ambivalent one in which progress and regression walk hand in hand. In the factories (and today in the service sector) productivity is enormously expanded, but at a crippling cost to the mental and physical life of the individual. In the world of theory, specialisation vastly develops the formal rigour and 'productivity' of intellectual enquiry with specifically honed conceptual tools while simultaneously the humanities and social sciences break up with each field losing its connectedness to the other and the social world (Lukács 1971:229–30). The study of literature, for example, is routinely separated from the study of history, politics and economics. This process affected not only the bourgeois social sciences, but also Marxism in the late nineteenth and early twentieth centuries. Karl Korsch criticised the Marxism of this period, arguing that

> A unified general theory of social revolution was changed into criticisms of the bourgeois economic order, of the bourgeois State, of the bourgeois system of education, of bourgeois religion, art, science and culture. These criticisms no longer necessarily develop by their very nature into revolutionary practice; they can equally well develop into all kinds of attempts at *reform*, which fundamen-

tally remain within the limits of bourgeois society and the bourgeois State, and in actual practice usually did so. (1972:57)

If this is true of Marxism, how much more true is it of a bourgeois science of linguistics such as that developed by Saussure and his followers, with its dissection of the 'internal' laws of language? For the moment, though, we need to appreciate the productive power of Saussure's theoretical system. For Saussure, the laws of language constitute an objective unconscious grammar or *langue* which individual utterances or *parole* must utilise. The signs of parole are made up of two parts. The first part is a *signifier*, the physical mani-festation which the senses (the eye, the ear) must register, whether a sound or word. A sign also requires a *signified* which is the concept attached to the signifier. Once combined, the signifer and the signified make a sign. Now, the Saussurian argument is that the world around us is divided up into signifiers that can be read because of their *differences* from one another (cat, mat, hat, sat) while the relations or bond between the signifer and the signified (four legged furry pet, floor decoration or utility for wiping your feet, cloth which you wear on your head, at rest on your posterior) are purely *conven-tional*. The importance of this will be drawn out in later developments of Saussurean derived cultural theory, where the meaning of the sign comes to be seen as a socially derived convention rather than natural fact. For the moment though we need to note that not only is the bond between signifier and signified conventional and not only does the signifier require differentiation from other signifiers, but the signified too generates meaning because of its differences from other signifieds. For example, a hat is conceptually different from a coat, from gloves, jumpers, and so on. Such items may be said to belong to a *paradigm*, a pool of similar signs, in this instance, articles of clothes (cats may be said to belong to another paradigm, that of pets). Words are selected from different paradigms and combined into *syntagms* (that is ordered into a pictorial or linear relationship according to the rules of langue).

Blair In Crisis Talks To Heal Rift With Unions

This newspaper headline from *The Times*[1] might have selected other signs from the paradigm which 'Blair' belongs to, such as 'Prime Minister' – but the formality of the title would have conflicted with the urgency which the headline is trying to convey. Similarly, if 'talks' had been replaced by another word from the same paradigm, such as 'discussions', the resonance of the sentence would again have been altered, softened, with a greater sense of 'exchange' between the two sides than the monosyllabic 'talks' can muster. The selection of signs, a process of inclusion and exclusion, is important to the overall meaning which the configuration of signs is generating. Consider dropping the adjectival paradigm 'crisis' for example:

Blair In Talks To Heal Rift With Unions

This alternative dramatically lowers the temperature of the headline. Yet not only is the selection of signs important for the generation of meanings, so too is the particular combination of signs, their syntagmatic arrangement. Consider this:

Blair In Crisis Talks With Unions To Heal Rift

The same sign selection is here reordered in a different combination, again producing a rather different feel to the sentence. Now Blair (the subject) and the unions (the object) no longer occupy opposing ends of the sentence as in the original headline, but are brought closer together in the word order to give a sense that they are working together to heal the rift which already seems on the mend, already less central and divisive a gulf between them.

The great pedagogic value of structuralism (the method which derived from Saussure's analysis of the structure of signs) is that it teaches us that language is a construct, a system. After Saussure it is difficult to subscribe to the view that meaning derives from some innocent one-to-one relationship between signs and the real world. Language, as we have seen, does not passively reflect the world but actively shapes our understanding and take on it. Language requires choices and decisions concerning sign selection and combination, and different choices and decisions produce different effects, although the language user may by no means be conscious of or anticipate the different patterns of meaning their choices produce. However, the real world – now termed the referent – was of little interest to Saussurian linguistics. The Hungarian Marxist Georg Lukács noted in *History and Class Consciousness* how under monopoly capitalism the sciences turned 'away from the material substratum of their conceptual apparatus' (1971:109) and no more apt description of Structuralism can be found. Structuralism stressed the 'physical' materiality of the sign but at the expense of the social relations which, as we saw in the previous chapter, also constitute an authentic materialist philosophy. Saussurian linguistics isolated language from the social material world, making it impervious to its demands, contingencies and conflicts, and instead projected language as a self-sufficient system of formal laws (lange/parole, signifier/signified, sign/referent, paradigm/syntagm). Cut off from its material roots or substratum, language floats free into its own specialised autonomous realm. And despite the modifications which cultural theory subsequently made on Saussurean linguistics, this fundamental problem concerning the relationship between the sign and the referent (a term which reduces the real to a passive object) was never sufficiently addressed.

Saussure died in 1913 but by the time the Soviet theorist Volŏshinov came to write his book *Marxism and the Philosophy of Language* in the 1920s, Saussurean linguistics was already dominant within the field. Like Lukács, who traced a series of splits and fissures in bourgeois philosophy (subject and object, nature and culture), Volŏshinov saw that bourgeois linguistics had split into two camps. On the one side there were philosophies of language that Volŏshinov characterised as individualistic subjectivism (1996:48) where the individual psyche is seen to be the source of the meanings of language. While such philosophies could stress the creativity and agency of the language users, they could not situate that use within a larger system of language rules and conventions which had accumulated over time. By contrast, structuralism was the supreme example of the other trend in language philosophies which Volŏshinov called abstract objectivism. It stressed precisely a supra-individual linguistic structure in which the rule governed system (langue) determines the utterance (parole) absolutely without any reciprocal effect of parole on langue (Volŏshinov 1996:53). If individualistic subjectivism was unable to account for the shared nature of language – that it is inevitably an inter-individual structure – Saussurean linguistics grasped language as a structure but emptied it of not only individual creativity but also of social conflict. It is a language structure uncoupled from the social structure, 'pervaded by laws of a specifically linguistic nature' and nothing else (Volŏshinov 1996:54). Saussure championed the cause of what he called the synchronic study of language. Prior to Saussure, the diachronic study of language, the study of its historical development, had been dominant. But to really get at the internal structure of language, its constructed quality, Saussure advocated the study of language outside its historical evolution, a move which followed logically from the wrenching of language away from social relations and politics. Volŏshinov traces the roots of abstract objectivism back to seventeenth- and eighteenth-century rationalism. What concerns this tradition of linguistic theory is 'the relationship of sign to sign within a closed system ... they are interested only in the inner logic of the system of signs itself' (Volŏshinov 1996:58). It is hardly co-incidental that it is this tradition, in its Saussurean manifestation, which triumphs in the twentieth century, where rationalism is integrated into such dominant forces as industry, science and technology. Nor is it surprising that such a theory of language eclipses individual agency so thoroughly at the very moment that monopoly capitalism, in its Fordist mode of development, sweeps aside the individual entrepreneurs of an earlier, *laissez-faire* phase of capitalism. Contemporary cultural theory's analysis of the production of meaning is still very much in thrall to a closed system of signs, although not quite in the way it manifests itself in Saussurean linguistics. Again, the shift and difference can be related to the wider context of capitalism, now in its post-Fordist mode of development.

If Saussurean theories were dominant in linguistics by the 1920s, the second half of the twentieth century saw the principles and concepts which underpinned the theory of the sign expand into the fields of mass culture, literature, anthropology and psychoanalysis. Structuralism (the search for the deep structures or 'langue' of different kinds of utterances) and semiotics, the science of signs, transformed the study of culture and meaning. The anthropologist Claude Lévi-Strauss drew on structuralist principles to analyse the myths of tribal communities while Vladimir Propp used similar methods to study Russian folk tales. Both were to be influential sources for new methods of reading cinema in film studies (Caughie 1990, Wollen 1970). Roland Barthes' application of a loose form of structuralism and semiotics to analyse mass culture in his book *Mythologies* was perhaps the most widely influential demonstration of these new critical tools. The left semiotics of Barthes' *Mythologies* underline the formal affinity between structuralism, with its mapping of the 'deep structures' (or langue) of underlying principles that codify and organise cultural representations, and Marxism, which, as we have seen in relation to base and superstructure, also operates with a 'deep structure' model. But, despite this formal affinity, in substantive terms, the structuralist resistance to history and nonlinguistic materialism makes it ultimately incompatible with Marxism. Nevertheless, as with Saussurean linguistics itself, these developments had much pedagogic value, bringing a newly rigorous vocabulary and approach to signifying practices (although claims that they represented a 'scientific' approach to cultural analysis were wide of the mark) and a refreshing suspension of (elitist) judgement as to what was considered worthy of study (although, within literary studies, semiotic analysis often simply concentrated on the same old canon). Just as importantly, because the basic principles of structuralist analysis could be taught and learned in an educational system, this was also a movement which undermined the elitism of critical practice itself. Criticism was no longer the preserve of a privileged few who could demonstrate an 'innate' sensitivity to the text (in reality a class determined acquisition of cultural capital learned in the course of growing up) but a method which could be acquired pretty quickly and deployed at a basic but nonetheless illuminating level, by anyone. This levelling dimension to the new critical tools remains within a pedagogic context a valuable component in any *first stage* honing of critical powers.

Structuralism and semiotics were then to be modified by post-structuralist philosophies of language. Post-structuralism broke with the scientific pretensions of structuralism and semiotics and pressed the logic implicit in Saussurean linguistics to its limits. If the link between signifier and signified was conventional rather than natural as Saussure had argued, then it could no longer be seen as so secure and fixed. If language and indeed all signifying practices were seen as generating meaning by difference, then any particular sign, any particular ensemble of signs creating meaning, could be seen as shadowed by an interplay of other signifiers and signifieds that constantly threatened to unsettle any fixity, unity or firmness of meaning. The rise of post-structuralism in the late 1960s was certainly mediated by the political defeats that began to accumulate after the high-water mark of 1968. As Eagleton notes, 'Unable to break the structures of state power, post-structuralism found it possible instead to subvert the structures of language' (1993:142). But the rise of post-structuralist methods also had deeper ontological roots. Again, it is surely no coincidence that just around the same time that capitalism begins to develop a new mode of development for monopoly power, one which overcomes the rigidities of Fordist corporate and market structures, one which develops new modes of flexible accumulation and apparent decentralisation through profit centres and subsidiary and subcontractor modes of inter-corporate relations, along comes a new paradigm of language and meaning-making, which also stresses change and mutability, decentralising the language system while still retaining a strong sense of language as a system.

The work of the philosopher Jacques Derrida formulated a vision of language that was far more unstable, shifting and slippery than that envisaged by Saussurean linguistics. There was also a political critique, of sorts. Derrida's target was a Western metaphysics of authenticity which, Derrida contended, constantly sought to fix meaning, curtail the play of the signifier, bond it to the signified and propose a 'truthful' connection between sign and referent. Such a *fixing* of meaning (Derrida calls it logocentrism) became indeed something like one definition of ideology in much cultural theory, while, implicitly or explicitly, difference and the potentially endless proliferation or deferral of meanings became an ethical ideal to be promoted. Take our earlier headline:

Blair In Crisis Talks To Heal Rift With Unions

A Derridean reading of this mini-text begins by treating it, as it would any text, as a literary one. Derridean decodings explode genre distinctions such as between factual/informational discourse and fiction. Deconstruction works to 'bring to light the suppressed surpluses of rhetorical meaning in ... texts – against their manifest sense' (Habermas 1987:191). There is even in this short, apparently uncomplicated, sentence an excess of signifiers and signifieds which undermines the attempt to pit Blair and the unions at odds with each other. There is a shifting play of imagery around the body and nature. One signified of 'crisis' refers to the decisive turning point in the course of a disease. However, this turning point can be for the *better* as well as for the worse. A crisis can be resolved in different ways. The signifier 'heal' with its etymology in bodily repair seems to confirm this imagery, but this suggests that Blair/Labour and the unions are one indivisible body while the sentence structure puts them at opposite ends of the spectrum. With 'rift' the natural imagery is maintained but, with its geological meanings, shifted outside the body to the very foundations Blair and the unions are standing on, which again suggests shared ground as much as division while also locating the crisis outside the body and external to them, perhaps hinting at a right-wing wish-fulfilment on the part of *The Times* and its readers that both Blair and the unions would have the ground from under them collapse. There is then, even within this short sentence, a certain 'undecidability' concerning the presentation of the relations between Blair and the unions. The conflict between Blair and the unions is at odds with the slippery imagery deployed.

If Derridean deconstruction seems a bit like a scholastic game, a more explicit worldly politics was developed via Foucault and discourse studies. Discourse is language understood as woven into particular ensembles of concepts in circulation through the institutions of the social order. The excavation of a discourse's 'langue' Foucault called archaeology, while its historical development he called genealogy. For Foucault discourses are the means by which power circulates through the social order, the means by which subjects frame, classify, define, and generate knowledge (which is power) about themselves and others. The historical development (genealogy) of discourses of the body, in terms of madness, criminality and sexuality, were key studies in Foucault's work. Edward Said famously analysed the discourses of *orientalism*, the way in which writings and other representations by the West (French and British colonialism in particular) of the rest are integral to generating knowledge about and authority over the Orient. Orientalism is 'a Western style for dominating'; the systematic means by which 'European culture was able to manage – and even produce – the Orient politically, sociologically, militarily, ideologically, scientifically and imaginatively during the post-Enlightenment period' (Said 1978:3).

With discourse analysis in particular we seem to have broken with the insularity of Saussurean linguistics, structuralism and semiotics. Discourse analysis can stress the way language mobilises material forces. However, as Habermas notes, Foucault was unclear as to how the relationship between discourses and material practices was to be conceptualised (1987:243). This only reinforced discourse theory's reluctance to mediate institutional practices within larger social totalities. For example, the discursive figure of 'balance' within news and informational media is inscribed into media practices and procedures when reporting on social conflicts. Yet 'balance' is also a mediation of the practices of bourgeois politics. The democratic state, with all its weaknesses and strengths, has been *made* more democratic (more 'balanced') by the struggle of the disenfranchised. Discourse theory, however, resists such mediations between institutions, politics, labour and capital, since they ineluctably draw analysis back towards an understanding of the social totality that discourse theory sees as a prime case of Marxian 'reductionism'.

With discourse theory, history, institutions and power enter into language, but at a cost that has made the failure to really confront the autonomy of the sign in Saussurean linguistics critical. Jacques Lacan, in a famous example of the new trend towards what became known as the linguistic turn, declared that the Freudian unconscious could be best understood as being structured like language. As in the Derridean system where meaning is always deferred, unconscious desire is always moving on down the chain of signifiers, never complete and present to itself because it is always defined by what it is not at any one time (just as the signifier and signified of 'crisis' in our earlier headline were defined and shadowed by a chain of other signs). It was only a matter of time until cultural theorists came to regard the real as, in effect, structured like language. The relationship of sign to sign within a closed system had imperiously expanded to absorb politics, society, history, culture, even economics. The caveat which proponents of discourse theory make to the implications of this argument goes something like this. Yes of course there is a real world existing *outside* language, but we cannot know it except through language. Yet the conceptual structure of Saussurean and post-Saussurean linguistics is such that in practice, since we cannot know the real except through language, the impact of the real *on* language and on signs generally, whether written or visual, largely disappears in favour of a more or less *one way* investigation into the power of language to name, classify, order, define, map and signify the real. The conceptual underpinnings to Saussurean and post-Saussurean theories of meaning production are rarely challenged but are on the contrary routinely recycled.

Take, for example, the Open University course book *Representation, Cultural Representations and Signifying Practices*, edited by Stuart Hall. Here we find a classic statement of the current position dominant within cultural and media analysis of the sign: 'Meaning does not inhere *in* things, in the world. It is constructed, produced. It is the result of a signifying practice – a practice that *produces* meaning, that *makes things mean*' (1997:24). There is another way of understanding 'the world', but first of all we would have to get away from thinking of the world in terms of *things*; that is, inert, passive, isolated objects (or referents) awaiting the power of language to imbue them with meaning. Discourse theory is unable to grasp the world, the real, as the *accumulated, collective, interdependent outcome of our own social activity.* In Hall's passage the world is presented as an assortment of passive things while language is credited with being a *practice*, that is, a creative, active process of meaning production. But it is not only language which is a *system*. The world in fact is not made up of discrete things – natural or social – but of relationships or practices which like language are material, but which have a deeper materiality about them because they constitute our very mode of production, our very mode of physical interchange and reproduction with nature and each other. Language is part of that interchange, but the interchange itself cannot be understood by privileging language within it.

A popular example, which Saussurean inspired arguments concerning the primacy of language like to use, concerns snow. The Inuit (Eskimo) language has, on one estimate, 22 words for snow and twelve for ice. This appears to be rather more than most groups have for the same phenomena. Here we seem to have a supreme example of the blank whiteness which we 'see' with the aid of our *one* sign, 'snow', being turned into a nuanced, highly differentiated, graded and ordered phenomenon by the very power of language to name (Hall 1997:23). In fact, as an example of linguistic relativism – the idea that different language systems 'produce' different conceptualisations of the world – the Inuit example has been somewhat discredited in recent years as something of an urban legend (Pinker 1994:44–82). We can see the problem clearly enough when we turn to Hall's table of Inuit terms helpfully translated into English (1997:23). The fact that different Inuit words *can* be translated into different adjectival descriptions of snow (watery, wet, light, soft, blowing, etc.) actually suggests that they do not have a linguistic universe that 'sees' snow differently and which causes them to experience snow differently. What they do have is a greater *material need* to differentiate snow on a daily basis than someone living in Manchester or even Moscow. This in turn undermines the linguistic determinism of much contemporary cultural theory. According to linguistic determinism, language *produces* meaning. In fact the example – even if it was based on solid evidence – demonstrates precisely what Saussurean and post-Saussurean theories repress. The mode of production of the Eskimo requires an interchange with nature and each other which makes the finer elaboration as to the different qualities of snow and ice and the uses to which they can be put necessary and essential. It is not language as some free-floating autonomous power to classify which is demonstrated by the example but the determination of a given set of social relationships at a given level of productivity in a given set of natural conditions which are shaping language and which are mediated by language. It is not snow, conceived as the isolated 'referent', that determines its meaning(s) in Inuit (the old and now discredited reflectionist account of language), but equally it is not the Inuit language system, an autonomous set of conventions, which determines the meanings of snow. Instead it is social being, understood as a practice, as a system of social relations, through which language must pass, which presses meaning and language into particular patterns of differentiation.

We need to be able to make a simple but effective distinction that language can be conventional (a social construct) without it thereby being arbitrary, in the sense that it freely determines its own meanings. Marx, by the way, made a similar distinction concerning money, which is at once both merely a conventional symbol and a sign of real-world material relations determining that symbol from the outside (1983:94). The conventionality of all symbols is an indication that signifying practices constitute a realm of creative and flexible practice, in which choices are made between alternative forms of expression influenced by wider cultural patterns. But this creative practice is intertwined with social necessity. Meanings must have a practical function for structurally conflictual and overlapping modes of social being (overlapping because a class position is always gendered and ethnicised for example). Meanings are interwoven into the means by which society as a whole and classes and groups within it sustain and reproduce themselves.

THE HISTORICAL MATERIALIST CHALLENGE

None of this of course is to say that Saussurean and post-Saussurean theories have not produced good work in the field of cultural analysis. But there is always this undertow pulling such work away from a historical and materialist understanding of the conditions of symbolic production and meaning. This has in more recent times accelerated into a veritable descent into discourse (Palmer 1990). Yet there are other theoretical resources which are not premised on the insularity of language from the real or its expansion and absorption of the real. The trick is to grasp the intersection of rhetoric (the figurative strategies of language to persuade, to make sense, to classify) and the real, understood as not external to us but as the product of our own activities as social beings. Vološhinov formulates the situation like this: 'Consciousness takes shape and being in the material of signs created by an organised group in the process of its social intercourse' (1996:13). Signs and social intercourse have a dialectical relation, one of reciprocal influence, although social being (emphatically *not* to be reduced to 'the economic') has primacy.

Within this conception we can certainly give the constructed quality of language its due. It was the Italian Marxist Antonio Gramsci, before Foucault or Derrida, who insisted that language 'is always metaphorical' (1967:111), composed that is of a series of endless comparisons.

> It is evident that East and West are arbitrary, conventional, i.e. historical, constructions, because outside real history any point on the earth is East and West at the same time. We can see this more clearly from the fact that these terms have been crystallised not from the point of view of man in general but from the point of view of the cultured European classes who, through their world hegemony, have made the terms evolved by themselves accepted everywhere. (Gramsci 1967:108)

Like other writers, Gramsci describes language as both conventional and arbitrary, using these terms interchangeably, when in fact they pull in opposite directions. As I have already suggested, the conventionality of language refers us to the social parameters, context and historical relativity of its use and meaning, while the notion of arbitrariness suggests that language escapes its social determinations by implying that *any* other sign conventions could also have been developed and deployed in the same context and with equal validity to sign users. The notion of arbitrariness represses the historical reasons why the signs we have before us (either as historians or observers of the contemporary scene) are there and others are not, or are, but only in a marginal way. Gramsci's main point, however, is one we can readily agree with. 'East' and 'West', imaginary constructs, are a projection of power. But if left at that Gramsci's argument is indistinguishable from the Foucauldian one. Gramsci, though, goes on to say (and this also cuts against the notion that language is merely 'arbitrary') that while they are conventions, East and West

> correspond to real facts, they will allow one to travel over land and sea and reach a known destination, to 'forsee' the future, to objectivise reality, to understand the objectivity of the external world. The rational and the real are identified. (Gramsci 1967:109).

Language then is an indispensable tool in our navigation (literally in this case, but also metaphorically) of the world. It allows us to operate within it, shape the world and also negotiate with its objectivity, its independence from our means of apprehension. This objectivity means that the world cannot be reduced to how we conceive it. If it could, then the dominant class could always linguistically resolve any crisis or revolt which threatened it. When, invoking Hegel, Gramsci notes that the 'rational and the real are identified', he is saying that for language to be effective it has to have *some* correspondence with the real. This is so because in order to develop and change the productivity and quality of our social activity and its outcomes (to develop the relations and forces of production) some correspondence between our language practices and social practices is necessary. The seeds of rationality in discourse are planted in our necessary co-operation with each other and growing interdependence. However, the real is the outcome of conflictual and antagonistic social relationships and not just co-operative ones, and so consciousness of the real is a site of contestation and dispute. Insofar as social relations develop the forces of production and win from that development generalised improvements, the real is rational and consciousness corresponds to it. Insofar as the social relations are built on relations of domination and exploitation which thwart co-operation, deny our interdependence and skew generalised improvement into generalised destruction or private gain, the real and consciousness of it are shot through with irrationality. When the necessities of production which plant the seeds of rationality are combined with the ethics of human freedom and needs, which derive not from outside or above the class struggle, but from the struggles of the subordinated classes and groups, the conditions for and the pressure of rationality and the critique of irrationality (or ideology) in reality and in our signifying practices grow.

Consider the dialectic between rationality and irrationality in this front-page headline from the *Daily Mail* on the same day as *The Times* headline already analysed:

<u>Union militants are back and the next target is your holiday</u>
SUMMER OF
AIR CHAOS

There is some correspondence between the rational and the real here insofar as baggage handlers and airport staff were indeed preparing to go on strike (it was not just a fantasy on the part of the paper, one which could be easily refuted) and this would indeed disrupt holidays. But after that, the rational and the real begin to fray at the seams. The particular claims and grievances of the workers are framed as part of a systematic campaign, indeed a war with targets ('militants' is a word closely associated with the military and here inflected with the connotation of aggressive violence). It is the readers of the paper directly and personally who are being threatened ('your holiday') while the 'are back' has the double function of hinting at an almost personal revenge against such decent citizens while also tying in with the 'Summer of Air Chaos'. For this reinforces the 'are back' by its intertextual associations with that other famous seasonal definition of 'illegitimate' strike activity and general national malaise, the 'Winter of Discontent', all the way back in 1979, just before the *Daily Mail*'s heroine, Margaret Thatcher, won the general election that year. If conflation is one of the typical rhetorical devices of ideology, then we have conflation here in spades, with the particular claims of airport workers being merged with a generalised sense of contemporary threat from 'militants' and that in turn being merged with events dating from as far back as 1979.

The mismatch between the breakdown of all order and reason ('chaos') which conflation here produces, and the utterly reasonable claims of the workers is revealed on the inside page towards the end of the article. Here the reader finds out that the threat of strike action is over a meagre 1.5 per cent wage offer by the employers, while the workers live in the most expensive part of the country. That the article feels compelled to engage in a dialogue here with the claims of the workers is a weak gesture towards 'balance'. That such information as the size of the employers' offer comes after the article has attempted to define the workers' response as negatively as possible is an indication of the deep reluctance with which the article yields to such a *moment* of rational engagement. We have here an example of what Habermas calls a performative contradiction (1987) where the communicative rationality of language as a shared resource for the exchange of meanings is thwarted by conceptual contradictions (the tension between 'balance' and the heavily anti-union position of the newspaper). Furthermore, the fact that the reader may also be a worker whose interests might be aligned with other workers struggling to raise the bar on what is seen as acceptable as an annual wage rise is repressed. If conflation is one trope of ideology, the repression of connections (here between the reader and the potentially striking workers) is another.

The front page of the *Daily Mail* is surely an example of what Roland Barthes called myth, a virtual synonym for ideology, at least in one of its many guises or definitions. Myth, Barthes argued, takes a sign, the sum of a signifier and signified, and converts it into another semiological system. Thus the possible strike by airport workers is hijacked by a second order semiological system (myth) which entwines it in a chain of *connotations* dredged up from the bottomless pit of bourgeois fears and fantasies.

> In passing from history to nature, myth acts economically: it abolishes the complexity of human acts, it gives them the simplicity of essences, it does away with all dialectics, with any going back beyond what is immediately visible, it organises a world without contradictions because it is without depth, a world wide open and wallowing in the evident, it establishes a blissful clarity: things appear to mean something by themselves. (Barthes 1986:143)

Of course in another discourse the ensemble of signs mobilised to signify this or any other strike may have very different meanings. Even individual signs or signifiers can be inflected in different directions. Militancy, for example, could be a sign not of some embittered worker who enjoys strikes because they like disrupting the public but of people who are intelligently politicised, well organised and prepared to defend their interests against those of capital. Volóshinov referred to this ability of signs to be inflected in different directions as their 'multi-accentuality' (1996:23). The theorist most associated with developing our understanding of this quality of the sign was Volóshinov's colleague Mikhail Bakhtin. His concept for the multi-accentuality of the sign was dialogism. In some ways the concept of the dialogic is rather similar to Habermas' idea that language is intrinsically communicative, presumably because it is, as Volóshinov argued, an inter-individual chain of signs connecting 'individual consciousness to individual consciousness' (1996:11). However, Bakhtin stressed that the individual consciousness and the words or signs which constitute it are not a unified whole but exist, as Michael Gardiner argues, 'in a tensile, conflict-ridden relationship with other consciousnesses, in a constant alterity between self and other' (1992:28). For Bakhtin, no utterance, no discourse, no word is self identical; it is always shaped and defined by its relations with other words (or different uses and meanings of the same word) in other discourses or utterances. It is in this sense that signs are dialogic, which of course includes a 'dialogue' between intensely conflicting utterances. We have seen how for structuralist and post-structuralist theory the word is always incomplete in itself, always depending on other words around it to define its meaning which remains partially dependent on what it is not. Bakhtin has a more 'humanist' and materialist take on this, grounding the relations between words in the utterances of concrete people in concrete circumstances rather than a language 'system'.

> The word, directed toward its object, enters a dialogically agitated and tension-filled environment of alien words, value judgements and accents, weaves in and out of complex interrelationships, merges with some, recoils from others, intersects with yet a third group. (1992:276)

For Bakhtin, the sign, within any historical context, 'cannot fail to brush up against thousands of living dialogic threads, woven by socio-ideological consciousness around the given object of an utterance' (1992:276). Let us, for example, take the black American golfer Tiger Woods as a sign. In July 2002 Woods arrived at the Scottish golfing Open Championship at Muirfield as the world's number one player. Fabulously wealthy, incredibly talented and black, Woods was asked in a press conference about the Muirfield golf club's rules banning women members. He replied that while it would be 'nice' if there was a chance for everyone to participate, he thought that clubs had the right to set their own rules and that 'there is nothing you can do about it. It's just the way it is.' Suddenly, as a sign, Tiger Woods found himself brushing up against a number of 'living dialogic threads', entering a 'dialogically agitated' environment in which the meaning of wealth, the meaning of blackness, the meaning of sport, the meaning of gender, were suddenly unlocked from their mythic simplicities and naturalisation (Barthes) and came bubbling to the surface. Woods was roundly criticised for his apathy, especially in the American press, with the *New York Post* labelling him a gutless hypocrite. (Presumably, if Woods had ironically mused whether Muirfield should be bombed by the US airforce in the name of female emancipation, which was one of the arguments put forward for the bombing of Afghanistan, he would have stirred up a different kind of flak in the US press.) Woods' wealth suddenly became a sign not of glamour, but of insularity (his gated or 'fortress' home was mentioned frequently); his blackness suddenly became a sign not of a role model for the black community, but of someone who had cut themselves off from black American civil rights struggles of the past; his celebrity became a sign not of popular ubiquity, but of a bland, safe, well-managed depoliticised commodity (he has commercial sponsorship deals with Nike for example) unfavourably compared to Muhammad Ali who put his political convictions first.

How though are we to judge and assess this signifying agitation around Woods' star image? Bakhtin is less useful here. He does coun-terpoise another concept against that of dialogism, which he calls monologism. This is quite similar to Barthes' notion of myth or Derrida's logocentrism, where the fixing of meaning, the containing of meaning and the simplification of meaning by repressing contra-dictions or difference or dialogue are seen as something to criticise and as the special provenance of the powerful. Yet, in the case of the Tiger Woods example, the media response to Woods' unconcerned do-nothing attitude to institutionalised sexism constitutes precisely a dialogising of the golfer's star image, opening up its safe 'monologism'. Indeed one could say that this is what the media does routinely, dialogising around various signs, from celebrities to war. But, if this is the case, how are we to get a critical purchase on the media? For there are assumptions underpinning the media response to Tiger Woods (or war) which need more sensitive instruments of analysis than the concepts of dialogism and monologism. 'Since Muhammad Ali, sport has not had a single champion brave enough to shout loudly against global injustice' writes one journalist in relation to the Tiger Woods affair.[2] There is something of a displace-ment going on here. It is surely the job of the media also to shout about injustice, but the fact that it feels compelled to go through surrogates (media personalities) to do this is part of the problem and only confirms that the media is interlocked into a sporting industry where the likelihood of such champions of injustice emerging, are in fact pretty slim. The appeal to a *black* figure who would see parallels between the civil rights struggle and other forms of discrimination assumes that race exists in isolation from class (Ferguson 1998) while also forgetting to ask why such expectations are not equally applied to white sportspeople. Of course one could argue that what is at work here is the interplay between dialogism (the opening up of Woods' star image as a site of contestation) and monologism (the containing of such questions around a single individual where the role of the media's own complicity with the system goes unacknowledged). Yet even this still lacks a precise, radical analysis of the relations between signs and social relations. We must turn instead to the concepts of ideology and hegemony for that.

IDEOLOGY AND HEGEMONY

Ideology is itself a multi-accentual sign, which has been pulled in many different directions in the course of its history and requires far more space than I have available to do it justice. There is a general consensus that the term refers to ideas values, beliefs, imagery and assumptions, but the status of ideology is far more contested. As I have indicated, there is one strand of thinking which associates ideology negatively with a certain fixing or containing of meaning and the transformation of social and cultural convention into nature (myth, logocentrism, monologism). There is another definition which is more neutral and which expands the term, making it equivalent to the production of meaning in general or consciousness itself (both Vološhinov and Bakhtin sometimes use ideology in this sense). Yet another version of ideology keeps the expanded sense of it as co-terminous with the sign/signifying practices but casts it now as in some way inherently disabling as far as knowing and understanding the world are concerned (see, for example, Althusser 1971), in which case it is difficult to know how anyone can escape ideology.

There are many definitions of ideology (Eagleton 1991:1–2) and there is no need to restrict ourselves to a single one, but I am going to concentrate on one version which it seems to me needs to be fairly central to any Marxist deployment of the term. This version has the critical and negative sense of ideology which we have already seen in the 'fixing of meaning/naturalisation' critique, but is rather more precisely focused in tying ideology to social relations of domination. For Thompson, ideology is at work whenever signifying practices 'establish and sustain relations of power which are systematically asymmetrical ... Ideology, broadly speaking, is meaning in the service of power' (1990:7). Terry Lovell offers a similar definition but one which emphasises the effect on the *validity* of ideas when they are pressed into sustaining asymmetrical power relations: 'Ideology ... may be defined as the production and dissemination of erroneous beliefs whose inadequacies are socially motivated' (1983:51).

Ideology then is not the same as error, or mistakes due to a lack of information or the quality of the tools (methodological or techno-logical) used to generate knowledge. Ideology is not the same as assumptions *per se* although it often uses unquestioned assumptions as part of its repertoire of strategies. It is not ideological to assume that the sun will set tomorrow, but if I say that the poor will always be with us just as long as the sun is in the sky, then that would be ideo-logical, harnessing as it does the imagery of nature to erroneously naturalise social and historical relations. Ideology is what happens to signs when they are pressed into the service of sustaining exploit-ative social relations, and, because of those social motivations, such ideological signs are impoverished in terms of generating knowledge about the world. Ideology works in the popular media by mobilising imagery and mini-narratives, stirring us at a 'gut' level of fear, feeling and desire. It is by definition irrational. Yet it still requires a certain systematic quality insofar as it provides a grid or framework or set of organising principles and values (remember Saussure's concept of langue) by which to respond to and interpret new data and phenomena in such a way as to be conducive to the reproduction of the exploitative social relations. The example of the *Daily Mail's* 'utterance' on the possibility of an airport strike is very much in line with its response whenever it sees workers asserting their collective rights and strengths. It is not that the next day or week we will read a *Daily Mail* article championing the cause of a particular group of downtrodden workers any more than one would expect to find the paper sympathetically investigating the plight of asylum seekers.

However, interestingly, the *Daily Mail* did take up the case of Stephen Lawrence, the black teenager killed in South London by a gang of white racists. The subsequent police investigation was so botched that a public enquiry was held. In a memorable front page the *Daily Mail* named the suspected killers and challenged them to sue if they were wrong. Championing the cause of black people is not what one expects from a paper that in the 1930s welcomed the rise of Mosley's black-shirted fascists. If there is a stronger connection between the rational and the real in the paper's reportage of the Lawrence debacle than in its coverage of strikes, it is still operating within definite ideological *limits* and trying to define and shape the meaning of the Lawrence case (and the public debate about it) within certain parameters that are less threatening to the paper's core values and belief in institutions like the police than other (very) possible interpretations. As a contested dialogical sign, one interpretation of the Lawrence case is that it is an appalling instance of police incompetence, where British justice let down an aspirational young man with 'respectable' parents. This is the *Mail*'s preferred interpretation and their central targets in their representations of the case were the accused white youths. However, the public enquiry (led by Lord Macpherson) into the botched investigation identified not police incompetence but institutionalised racism as the cause of their failure to bring the case to court. Here, the Lawrence case as a multi-accentual sign is inflected in a direction in which the police as an entire public body come under scrutiny. This was broadly the position of the more liberal establishment and its media. There is a third position in the dialogic struggle around the Lawrence case, even further away from the *Daily Mail*'s interpretation. This one would situate what happened in the course of the botched investigation in the wider context of black people dying, not at the hands of white racist 'thugs', but at the hands of white racists wearing uniforms that look remarkably like those of the police. The film *Injustice* (Ken Fero and Tariq Mehmood 2001 GB), for example, reminds us that more than a thousand black people have died in police custody in the UK since the 1950s without any charges being successfully brought against the police officers involved. The relationship between ideology and signifying practices in the *Daily Mail*'s discourse can be revealed not just by what it says, but by what it omits, by exploring the gaps and limits of what it can acknowledge or explore. As Eagleton notes, '[a]n ideology exists because there are certain things which must not be spoken of' (1986b:90).

I have so far stressed that the utterance, the sign or the discourse is very far from being fixed, rigid and homogeneous but that it is instead a fluid site of contestation and dialogic struggle. Yet at the same time this fluidity takes place within certain parameters and patterns; it is still possible to identify *dominant* ideologies corresponding to the interests and values (not remember the same thing necessarily) of the dominant class. To say that there are such things as dominant ideologies, does not mean that those ideologies fit seamlessly together and that they do not articulate real differences. An authentic Marxism will always be alive to contradictions in the realm of signs as much as in the realm of the real. Gramsci, for example, argued that even within the Catholic Church, beneath its superficial unity, there is in reality a multiplicity of distinct and often contradictory religions: there is the Catholicism of the peasants, the Catholicism of the petty bourgeoisie and of the town workers, the Catholicism of the women and the Catholicism of the intellectuals, and this also is varied and disconnected. (1967:91)

Yet despite (and perhaps also because of) this internal differentiation and contradiction, the Church can still function with a sufficient degree of institutional co-ordination to enable its daily reproduction. The same is true of society generally. Not only are dominant ideologies contradictory but so too are the values, beliefs and perspectives of the subordinate classes. It has often been assumed that in order for society to reproduce itself there has to be a consensus of values which integrate people into the norms and belief systems that sustain the dominant social relations. However, it is increasingly recognised that advanced capitalist societies are characterised less by value consensus than dissensus (Gardiner 1992:149); that the further one travels down the class system, for example, the less integrated into the norms and values of the dominant ideology people appear to be (Abercrombie et al. 1980:147–8) and that indeed it may be the very 'diversity of values and beliefs, a proliferation of division between individuals and groups, a lack of consensus at the very point where oppositional attitudes might be translated into political action' (Thompson 1990:8) that are conducive to the reproduction of the social order.

This would seem to be close to Gramsci's conception of the popular classes as having a 'contradictory consciousness' made up of a patchwork quilt of belief systems, outlooks and values drawn from often incompatible sources and which it is the task of revolutionary theory to develop into the sort of systematic and coherent world view which bourgeois philosophy has attained (1967:58–66). Gramsci made a distinction within popular consciousness between common sense or 'folklore', which is most likely to be interwoven with dominant ideologies past and present, and good sense, which represents those elements of popular consciousness that are the more robustly sceptical, questioning or dismissive of the claims and values of the dominant order. A paper like the *Daily Mirror* is a good example of a contradictory amalgam of common sense and good sense, rational critique and ideology. After the 11 September terrorist attacks on the Twin Towers, the paper relaunched itself as a serious left-of-centre newspaper, inviting such campaigning journalists as John

Pilger and Paul Foot, who had been sacked from the paper during an earlier drift to the right, to return. The paper has made front-page attacks on the Prime Minister, Tony Blair, with the popular vernacular of good sense that the broadsheets, with their more formal and deferential language, would steer clear of. Blair's subordinate position to US President George Bush in the 'war on terror' has been regularly criticised as has Blair's backing for the arms trade, including British arms sales to the Israeli state (despite its war on the Palestinians) and Pakistan and India (despite the potential for these two nuclear powers to go to war over the disputed territory of Kashmir). Yet, jostling alongside these positions, the paper continues to devote many of its pages to the usual fare of celebrity-driven entertainment. This material is heavily suffused with the backward and ideological threads of common sense. For example, the *Daily Mirror* led a campaign against *Big Brother 3* (2002) largely on the basis that the people in the house were 'halfwits'. This hardly amounts to a critique of the production apparatus which is responsible for the creation of this and other exploitative reality television shows.

The moral and intellectual lead of the dominant classes, what Gramsci called hegemony, is clearly uneven and contradictory. Gramsci, who spent the last years of his life languishing in Mussolini's jails, was concerned to explore why the militancy of the industrial working class in the years after the First World War did not translate into the revolutionary transformation of society. Despite political and economic crisis, and despite industrial militancy of the workers, particularly in Turin, the working class were unable to develop themselves into a force that could convince enough people, inside and outside that class, that it had a viable political alternative to capitalism. Gramsci argued that protecting the capitalist social order from short-term economic and political crises was a network of social organs that had developed the *cultural* dominance of the dominant class to such an extent that economic and political crises alone did not automatically lead people to break with the capitalist order of things. But Gramsci did not conceive hegemony as simply a top-down process of imposition of values and ideas. A deeply dialogical thinker, Gramsci was well aware that defending and sustaining a hegemonic position involved a continual process of the dominant class adapting to changing circumstances, incorporating, if necessary, ideas and values generated from outside itself and channelling them in directions that were compatible with its own interests and the structural requirements of the capitalist system.

It is unclear whether Gramsci thought the terms ideology and hegemony were interchangeable. My own feeling is that it makes more sense to distinguish between them. I have already suggested that the terms sign and ideology are not to be conflated and that ideology critique consists precisely in thinking through their convergence and divergence. The reason why hegemony and ideology are analytically distinct (although potentially often closely interwoven) is that the struggle for hegemony also requires the dominant class to make real concessions to the claims of subordinate classes. Insofar as those concessions are made, for example, the extension of the popular vote, or the formation of the welfare state, the moral and intellectual lead of the dominant classes is enhanced by the demonstration that these claims can be accommodated within capitalist relations of production. Yet to reduce such concessions to ideology *per se* would seem to say that the subordinate classes and groups struggling for such progressive changes are generating up their own ideological domination. The struggle for universal franchise by the labour movement by women and black people (in America) was not itself ideological even though its accommodation does help sustain the hegemony of the dominant classes. It becomes ideological though when the limits of political democracy (today becoming ever more evident) are conceived as the limits of reason itself, a position which of course sustains the tyranny of unelected power in the production process.

Hegemony involves the winning of consent to the social order and particular directions which that social order may take. Insofar as the winning of consent is a *cultural* battle (which is to say it is not just a cultural battle) it is fought out across a range of social organs including electoral politics, the media, charities, consumer bodies, schools and universities and religious groups. However, one needs to be careful not to forget that the structural weighting of ideas and values towards relations of domination is not the only reason why the social order reproduces itself. Consent could involve a very wide spectrum and should not be conflated with a uniform non-contradictory consensus. Pragmatic acceptance of the social order rather than enthusiastic belief in it may be just as powerful a check on social change as anything else. There may be a lack of viable ideas for alternative systems and there may be a shrewd assessment of the risks involved in trying to effect major social transformations, while, on individual policies, politicians, voted in every four to five years, can often resolutely ignore the popular will and major threats to the social order in the form of social movements for change, can be beaten back not by rhetorical strategies but good old-fashioned coercion and force. Above all perhaps, people working 40–50 hours a week, with families to look after, are constrained by what Marx called the 'dull compulsion of economics', which saps the time and energy required to engage in oppositional politics. Such considerations provide a useful corrective to the tendency to overestimate the 'moral and intellectual lead' of the dominant classes. This argument was well made by Abercrombie et al. (1980:153–4), who pointed out that rather too much was being asked of ideology by radical theorists hoping to explain the reproduction of the social order, and it is a theme that has been picked up and developed by Lodziak (1995). Yet it is difficult to endorse the view that: 'We have to take into account the limiting case of an economy which does not need ideology at all, and it is our contention that late capitalism is very nearly such a case' (Abercrombie et al. 1980:173). For it is hard to explain with such a view why across a range of issues and sites of conflict, one can find systematic patterns, one can find systematic limits and one can find positions being fiercely defended and extended which just so happen to have the handy quality of supporting dominant social relations although within a range of conflicting positions. Lodziak, for his part, argues that ideologies do not generally *motivate* people (1995:40), that in other words they are motivated by more quotidian, everyday realities rather than abstract explicitly articulated doctrines, such as Thatcherism, socialism, Christianity, and so forth. While a good many people *do* model their behaviour (at least in part) according to such philosophies, ideologies weave their way into thoughts and actions outside such explicit frameworks, attaching themselves to a range of popular (rather than just scholastic) expression and motivating at the level of emotional 'gut instincts', while their philosophical or doctrinal roots (such as racism or sexism) remain tacit and unstated.

Take, for example, the question of the family. Representations of the family are like everything else, a site of dialogic agitation. The sexuality of the family, the composition of the family, the size of the family, the legal status of adults (married or unmarried), the relations between the family and the state, the internal power relations between members of the family (is it right to smack children?) – all of these and other questions are potentially and actually sites of dialogical agitation. But there are also strong hierarchical patterns to the meanings in circulation and these just so happen to be the patterns of meaning *least* requiring an examination of the family structure as a microcosm of the inequalities of the social structure. It is a very popular representation within Hollywood cinema, for example, to see the family as embattled by forces threatening it from the *outside* (Red Indians, aliens, psycho nannies and so forth). This is something which is also reproduced in news media coverage concerning the deaths of children. Both print and television news give extensive coverage when a child is killed by a stranger, by someone outside the family. If the child has disappeared, then an enigma is set up which the media can run with on a daily basis for days, even weeks. Another enigma is then generated concerning the identity of the killer, while the progress of the police investigation, with all the appeals for witnesses which that generates, becomes a key media theme. It is not only that the stranger as killer is narratively attractive to the media, it is also simultaneously ideologically attractive. One starts to see the ideological implications of such media representations when one looks at the actual statistics concerning the homicide of children. Murders of this nature are in fact carried out very rarely (around five cases each year in the UK) by the dark, evil, unknown stranger or monster invading the life of the family from the outside. Usually in fact it is either daddy and/or mummy who are the killers:

> Between 70 and 80 children are murdered each year by their mother and father, and 10% of all homicides are by the victim's parent. Most of these deaths are impossible to predict; only hindsight gives us clues to the agonies inside so many homes. But our response to them is not so unpredictable. It is apathy and silence.[3]

The media quietly report such stories and move on. There is no enigma or narrative for them to construct their stories around because the killer is known. When the parent takes their own life along with their children's, this further closes down the possibility for a news narrative within the personalising and individualising terms which dominate the media. Ideologically such stories are explosive. For they locate violence and threat within the family itself and this begs questions as to the structure of society and its values that can lead to such acts. Internalising economic competition and crisis, authoritarian relations and casual and routine violence (such as smacking children), the family can implode in all sorts of directions and homicide is clearly one variation of a multiple crisis in this institution. Far better then to give a huge media profile to the odd killer as stranger or lone monster, since then both society and the family escape any sustained investigation. The above quote, it is true, comes from a national newspaper and is one of a handful of articles which raise questions as to the values and assumptions built into media representations of child killers. Yet such critical articles, written often in the personal commentary pieces rather than as 'news', are both quantitatively and qualitatively marginal to the *dominant* mode of representation on this issue. The effects of this dominant mode are illustrated in the article which compares the case of Sarah Payne, the little girl murdered by a stranger, with that of Jade and Keiren Austen, killed (along with their mother) by their father and discovered around the same time as the Payne story broke. Whereas Sarah Payne's parents became national 'celebrities', receiving condolences from royalty and politicians and thousands of cards from as far away as Russia, meeting media celebrities, having an audience with the Home Secretary to discuss the registering of paedophiles, getting a memorial made for Sarah and so forth, the story on the other side, for the relatives of Jade and Keiren, was rather different. The grandmother, Carol Quinn,

> triply bereaved, received just one letter and no floral tributes. When she asked to use the money raised by the elderly people her daughter had looked after, to plant a memorial tree on the local village green, her request was refused.[4]

Thus ideology does indeed have effects on the conduct and behaviour of both elites and ordinary people, it does indeed work to organise emotional energies and intensities around particular foci and not others, according to their compatibility with the social order.

This chapter has argued that the main weakness of Saussurean linguistics is that its theory of the structure of language and its capacity to generate meaning is wholly internal to language which is cut off from social determinations and relations. Post-structuralist linguistics did not fundamentally challenge this but instead developed some of its implicit 'internalist' logic by absorbing the social world into language and discourse. I argued that the one-way determination of language over the real must be reformulated, with language passing through social being. I drew on Gramsci, Vološhinov and Bakhtin to show how the sign can be theorised as constructed and contested (which post-Saussurean theory can also show), but also that the sign world must have *some* correspondence – even if limited – with the real world because of the necessity for some (if desperately limited) co-operation which interdependence thrusts upon human beings in the production of social life. This rational correspondence post-Saussurean theory cannot accommodate. I worked with a definition of ideology as socially motivated, systematically limited or partial and irrational ideas and value systems which contribute to the reproduction of unequal social relations. The struggle against ideology then involves developing that rational correspondence more fully and adequately, sifting representations for their entanglements with ideology as well as for their 'rational kernal' as Marx put it when describing his relation to Hegel. Since the partiality and one-sidedness of the sign's ideological legitimisations are intrinsically connected to relations of social domination, the struggle against ideology is also a counter-hegemonic struggle against such relations.

7 Commodity Fetishism and Reification: The World Made Spectral

> A commodity appears, at first sight, a very trivial thing, and easily understood. Its analysis shows that it is, in reality, a very queer thing, abounding in metaphysical subtleties and theological niceties.
>
> Marx, *Capital*

If the previous chapter explored how the media, as part of the super-structures, produce ideological representations of the world, this chapter will conversely explore how the general organisation of social and economic relations exerts a determining pressure on and contradictions within consciousness and its modes of representation. I began the previous chapter, for example, by suggesting that the socio-economic relations that led to a division of labour and task fragmentation in the industrial sector, also penetrated right through into philosophy and the social sciences, hence the conceptual structure of Saussurean linguistics. In this chapter the media will be examined as symptomatic barometers of such dynamics coming 'from below' as it were – with a special emphasis on film, which, because of its narrative base, its emphasis on the visual (a potent medium for fetishism), the scale of its storytelling canvas, and its technological and economic underpinnings, seems to articulate the contours of fetishism and reification with particular clarity. These two closely connected terms, fetishism and reification, are perhaps more familiar to the reader in their philosophical conceptualisation: alienation. This term has acquired a general popular currency as signifying some sense in which the individual subject has lost touch with their own feelings and desires on the one hand, while the external world seems unremittingly hostile and unfathomable on the other; in short both self and society become alien to the individual. Yet the popular grasp of the notion of alienation has been won at the expense of an explanation as to why alienation occurs. It seems to have become a code word for a generalised human condition. Marx's theory of commodity fetishism grounded the concept of alienation in the specific historically determined characteristics of capitalism's social and economic relations. That analysis was then extended, via the work of Georg Lukács and the concept of reification, to cultural and philosophical practices. The theory of commodity fetishism, I shall argue, helps us develop a distinctively Marxist theory of the subject, necessary if we are to explore the psychology of lived experience under capitalism. Fetishism, Michael Taussig argues, 'denotes the attribution of life, autonomy, power, and even dominance to otherwise inanimate objects and presupposes the draining of these qualities from the human actors who bestow the attribution' (1980:31). Accordingly, to explore this draining away of essential qualities from the human actors or subjects, I develop the concept of the subjectless subject, which refers to the way subjects acquire agency and autonomy by internalising the very logics of the system which has emptied them of authentic autonomy, power and free will in the first place. However, the subjectless subject is only one dimension of the process of reification; it is the ideal subject which capital strives for but which it can never wholly achieve because of the resistances which the *materiality* of the biological and social world generate. We shall see that the figures of the ghost, of possession and of spectrality in general function as signs of capital's 'dematerialising' logic. This may sound odd given that Marx's critique of Hegel in effect turned the World Spirit (collective abstract reason) into the world market, an institution that could hardly be more brutally material. But, as we shall see, capital's dematerialising materialism is central to the spectral qualities of commodity fetishism.

COMMODITY FETISHISM AND THE SUBJECT

It is often said that Marxism lacks a theory of the subject or at least one sufficiently different – and not just a collective version of – the bourgeois subject/monad (Soper 1986:20–21). Althusser famously used the term 'subject' to play on its ambiguity. To be a subject on the one hand implies being at the centre of things, having some autonomous agency, a fairly strong sense of internal coherence and free will. This is the idealised subject of bourgeois philosophy, politics and economics. But, in the twinkling of an eye, such a subject can be turned into its opposite and become an object, which is to say it becomes subject*ed* to the will and power of someone or something else: the big Subject (Althusser 1971:178–80). This twinkling of an eye corresponds to the Marxist distinction between the surface forms, phenomenal forms or appearance-forms of society, where the subject operates in the first positive sense of the word, and the real relations, where the subject operates or is operated on according to the second subjected definition of the word subject. To lack a theory of the subject is to be unable to account for the psychology, experiential world, culture and consciousness of the individual and the collective as they navigate between appearance-forms and real relations. This apparent gap in the theory of the subject has been filled by some combination of Marxism with psychoanalytic theory, such as the Freudo-Marxism of the Frankfurt School or the combination of Marxism and Lacanianism during the Althusserian interlude (Coward and Ellis 1977) or more recently by the left Lacanian, Slavoj Žižek (Žižek 1989).

Yet the theory of commodity fetishism provides the basis precisely for a distinctively Marxist theory of the subject, or more precisely of the subject as commodity and the commodity as subject under advanced capitalism. Dominant economic models, whether neo-liberal (new right) or Keynesian (left/liberal), are also underpinned by a theory of the subject: this is the subject which makes 'rational' choices in order to maximise resources for itself (Amariglio and Callari 1996:187). Within Keynesian economic models this theory of the subject may be modified by pointing out that the individual subject does not have all the information to hand to always make rational choices in the marketplace or that its choices are circum-scribed by its own financial resources. But such modifications essentially leave the model of the subject intact, thus excluding the possibility of contradiction *within* the subject and between subjects, the choices they make and society as a whole. Figure 7.1 maps out the four co-ordinates that need to be explored in order to grasp the contradictory dynamics of the subject under conditions of commodity production. We have already seen in other chapters, but most extensively in Chapter 5, that repression of the mode of production constitutes a central feature of culture and theoretical apprehension within capitalism. Together with repression, the other co-ordinates, inversion, immanence and splitting, will help us map our crippled subjectivity under capitalism.

The theory of commodity fetishism, which Marx developed most systematically in *Capital*, is the social and economic counterpart to the philosophical concept of alienation, which refers precisely to that process through which the subject in the autonomous free will sense becomes subjected to the powers of someone or something else. The force of the term fetishism depended on Marx subverting

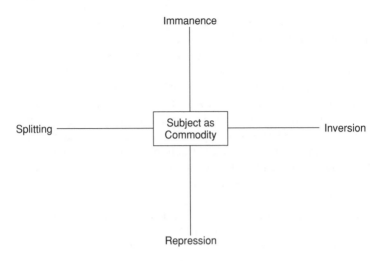

Figure 7.1   The Subjectless Subject

its prior history within Eurocentric and emerging colonial discourses. It was a derogatory term which Europeans applied to the pre-capitalist communities they were increasingly trading with as capitalism emerged out of medieval feudalism (Pietz 1996:131). For the Europeans, primitive forms of religion were marked by the fetishistic worship of material objects that were accorded magical powers of their own. For the rationalist European, the primitive was unable to *value* things properly. In terms of trade, this meant that the primitive was characterised by its overvaluation of relatively valueless 'trinkets' and their undervaluation of precious natural and mineralogical resources (Mulvey 1996:125). The moment of exchange between Europeans and pre-capitalist communities is a familiar one in countless examples of popular culture, where tribal chiefs are won over by ordinary commodities of the advanced society while the white traders nervously eye the riches they have come to extract. In *Mutiny on the Bounty* (Lewis Milestone 1962 US), a more critical text, the undervalued commodity extracted from the tribal community reveals its own fetishistic overvaluation within the capitalist economy. Captain Bligh (Trevor Howard), the professional middle-class captain, puts the breadfruit plants which he and his men have secured from the Tahitians before his own men on the return trip home, rationing scarce water supplies to the latter in order to keep the plants alive. The sailor-proletariat meanwhile have had their own historical moment radically relativised, simultaneously stepping backwards in time in their encounter with the primitive communism of the tribe (with its freedoms from the fetishistic drudgery and divisions of wage-labour) and, through their later mutiny/insurrection, forward in time as an embryonic anticipation of the socialist mode of production. To the capitalist, primitive communist and socialist modes of production (or its prefiguring) the film also adds a fourth in the figure of Bligh's second in command, Fletcher Christian (Marlon Brando), a dandy not averse to pleasure, whose aristocratic heritage and potentially anti-bourgeois value system are forced into a class alliance with the sailors against Bligh's puritanical single-minded subordination of every need and value to the commercial success of his mission.

So fetishism is a potentially double-edged concept for the European to deploy against pre-capitalist societies. Marx exploited this, choosing his slings and arrows carefully, knowing that to describe capitalism, with its worship of money and material objects transformed into commodities, as a new form of fetishism was a provocative insult to those who believed capitalism was the last word in rationality and human progress. In the early 1920s, the Hungarian Marxist Georg Lukács drew on Marx's theory of commodity fetishism to suggest how this process through which the subject is emptied of meaning and agency, turned into a 'thing', can be extended into the culture and philosophy of capitalist society in general. He called this reification. Thus the socio-economic dynamics of commodity production impact on 'the *total* outer and inner life of society' (Lukács 1971:84). Drawing on Max Weber's concept of rationalisation, Lukács links commodity fetishism and reification to the way reason, science and knowledge have been turned into things. In its formal structure or appearance, reason appears rational, but it becomes progressively indifferent to the diversity of human contents to which it is applied. Indeed, for formal rationality the *more* indifferent it can become to the diversity of contents the more rational and universal it proves itself to be while, conversely, anything or anyone who tries to insist on particular and local conditions, materials and needs (such as the sailors' demand for water in *Mutiny on the Bounty*) becomes associated with the irrational and is excoriated as 'anti-science' and anti-progress (Lukács 1971:126). This is why Captain Bligh is such an anticipatory figure for today's captains of industry and global institutions such as the World Bank and the IMF.

Thus, for example, if vaccination works in particular times and places then it 'stands to (formal rationalistic) reason' that it works in all times and places; and if it works as protection against one disease then it works equally well against others; and if it is necessary for polio, then it is equally necessary for measles or, very probably, soon, chicken pox; and if it works for one child then it works equally well for all children; and if it works in single doses then it works equally well, indeed more efficiently, in combined doses. And so by turns we come to the debate about the measles mumps and rubella vaccine (MMR) in which any evidence which indicates resistance to this expanding empire of reason, whether resistance from the body of the child or concerned parents, is dismissed by orthodox science and mainstream politicians as 'irrational'. For Lukács, there is an intimate link between such formal rationality with its indifference to 'concrete content' (1971:137) and the economic exchanges of capitalism, which, as we shall see, are equally indifferent to the concrete content of human needs and uses. The fact that vaccination policies are a central plank in the business strategies of the pharmaceutical industries is not then unconnected with such formal rationality.

For Lukács, the expansion of the capitalist system went hand in hand with 'the structure of reification [which] progressively sinks more deeply, more fatefully and more definitively into the conscious-ness of man' (1971:93). This sounds a little economistic on Lukács' part, but the main thrust of his great text *History and Class Consciousness* is to stress (and in passages overstress) how conscious human agency and politicised activity can break down reified thought and practice. Commodity fetishism and reification are generated up out of the very *structure* of capitalism but do not constitute a fixed state of affairs within capitalism, nor a unilinear and symmetrical process progressively and inevitably entrenching itself in all social, economic, political and cultural practices. Instead they are extended, affirmed and contested by social agents in specific institutional locations and cultural practices. We saw in Chapter 3 that cultural production is, like pharmaceuticals, powerfully penetrated by the economic practices of corporate capital. Specific product and brand name tie-ins have been routine practice for Hollywood cinema since the 1920s at least, and more generally, the glamour and high production values of Hollywood have swathed a cornucopia of consumer goods in a shimmering aura of optimism, scale, desirability and cool, effectively turning Hollywood into the promotional wing of America Inc. both at home and in foreign markets (Wasko 1994, Eckert 1996:98, Doane 1996:121). However, as I have already argued, we cannot reduce the text to its immediate mediation by the production process, for then we would be unable to explain how cultural texts are not only reified, at the level of both form and theme, but are often also commentaries (particularly in narrative-based media) on that selfsame process of reification. Cultural texts that are reified examinations of reification must clearly be drawing on the wider cultural dynamics of the class struggle than simply the immediate production context.

THE SOCIAL MODEL OF FETISHISM

I am going to present the model of fetishism and reification in two parts, the first stressing its social dimension, the second, its economic dimension. I do this partly for the purpose of a more easily under-standable exposition, but also because, as with previous chapters where I have dealt with the mode of production, I want to stress the *social* nature of the theory as something of a correction to the tendency to view the theory of commodity fetishism (and *Capital* in general) as largely about economics. In between the social and economic dimensions of fetishism I want to explore some of the cultural figurations of repression, inversion, splitting and immanence which social and economic fetishism generates.

The basic formal structure of fetishism/reification/alienation according to Marxist theory is mapped out in Figure 7.2. At a formal level, it is rather similar to the psychoanalytic theory of fetishism which 'epitomises the human ability to project value onto a material object, repress the fact that the projection has taken place, and then interpret the object as the autonomous source of that value' (Mulvey 1996:127). In the first part of the process (a), the subject's own powers are re-routed into the object. Within the Marxist model, the social relations that are responsible for this process by which the object gathers up the powers of the subject constitute the *real relations* of commodity production. The powers of the subject, which the object has accumulated or seized (and here there is a difference in even the formal similarities between Marxian and psychoanalytic models of fetishism, where, for the latter, that seizure is replaced in the first instance with projection), then confront the subject *not* as its own re-routed powers but as powers that emanate originally from the object itself. In the second part of the process (b), the subject's own powers return to it as the reified 'thing' powers of the object (what

I have called immanence). As I have stressed in previous chapters, the term appearance-forms does not refer to mere illusions or tricks of the mind. A 'form' here refers to real objects such as money and real institutions such as the market. Yet, whilst real in both physical and social senses, the term 'appearance' refers to the qualities and characteristics of these forms that in various ways repress the real relations on which they are founded. As a category then, fetishism refers to real practical activities as well as particular forms of consciousness implicit in those practices. It is *both* these components of fetishism which are at work in the appearance-forms. The final part of the model (c) represents the extent to which the subject identifies with those practices or generates representations of them which are congruent with the appearance-forms. Here, what is implicit in our practices gets elaborated, extended and affirmed by social agents in concrete cultural activities. It is not that the subject invests the object with a power it does not have (fetishism then would be mere illusion or psychoanalytic projection) but that it misrecognises that the basis for the power which really does confront it is its own collective self-alienation (repression once again). It is at the level of the appearance-forms and their corresponding cultural elaborations that we find the subject subjected to the realities and fantasies of immanence, splitting, inversion and repression.

Clearly the media will play an important role in constructing symbolic goods, which internalise and promote certain modes of consciousness, identification and fantasy that correspond at some level to the appearance-forms. The theory of commodity fetishism is useful because it offers an explanation as to why media representations may have powerful ideological effects. Media representations have a sticking power not because they peddle in mere illusions, for, if they did, those illusions would be so much easier to combat and dispel. Their power stems in fact from the way they correspond with

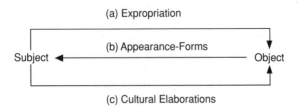

Figure 7.2   The Model of Commodity Fetishism

the social relations when they are fetishised into appearance-forms (Mepham 1979:141, Rees 1998:88). This would seem to suggest that commodity fetishism is less a theory of ideology than a theory which explains why ideological production (ideas and values which systematically legitimise the dominant social relations) is effective. There is some ambiguity within the Marxist literature on this score, a residue perhaps of that rigid distinction between material practices (in this case appearance-forms) and ideas/representation. Yet, as Žižek has argued, the practices which constitute the forms and appearances of the subject's life world do indeed secrete ideological fantasies into the tissue of their experience. Ideology resides in what people do as much as in what people think (Žižek 1989:31). The ideological fantasies of commodity fetishism, like the ideologies produced in specialised domains such as the media, religion, politics, education, philosophy, theory and so forth (the cultural elaborations of the superstructures), are inscribed into real material practices. Yet commodity fetishism is a very particular theory of ideology and can be distinguished from the ideological production of the superstructures. The theory of commodity fetishism locates ideology as being generated up from 'below' as it were, from the mode of production itself. As we saw in Chapter 5, the category of mode of production explains the *social form* which concrete production takes under capitalism. Similarly, commodity fetishism explains why ideological production, in quite different institutional domains and with quite different *content*, shares the substantive *structural* features of immanence, splitting, inversion and repression.

Let us now return to the first stage of the process which constitutes the real relations and fill the formal categories of subject and object with some real social content, labour and capital respectively. Labour, which owns no productive property, must sell its labour to that class which owns the means of production. It is labour which produces value (above and beyond the wage it gets in return) and this surplus is converted into money-capital by capitalists during the circulation of products on the market before a portion is reinvested into the production process for the further accumulation of capital. Labour then produces capital and in doing so produces itself as an object, a mere factor in production to be shunted around and dispensed with at will. Here is one example of the process of inversion but it is also simultaneously an example of splitting. Insofar as labour produces itself as an object, it is both a subject and an object and thus internally fissured as a subject producing its own objectification just as surely as there is a fissure between labour and capital. Not only this, but capital, this fetishised offspring of labour, becomes the subject (inversion again) insofar as its forms and appearances imply that its powers stem autonomously from itself in much the same way that share prices seem to go up and down without any correlation to the human labour which produces wealth (immanence). Yet capital cannot be a real subject, being the institutionalised and externalised expression of the subject's own alienation. Thus individuals who occupy key controlling positions within the structure of capital (personifications of capital) and whose role it is to facilitate the subjection of the true subject (labour) to the object (capital) are themselves hollowed out subjects and objects of the capital system. For capital is essentially *uncontrollable* and, even though a small minority benefit outrageously from the system and even though they occupy positions of power within it, the system's imperatives are not amenable to human control. Capital is a 'peculiar mode of *subjectless control* in which the controller is actually controlled by the fetishistic requirements of the capital system ... because of the radical separation of production *and control*' (Mészáros 1995: 66).

PI AND SUBJECTLESS SUBJECTS

In *Capital* Marx found an analogy between the secular world of commodity fetishism, with its separation of control from the direct producers, and the 'mist enveloped regions of the religious world. In that world the productions of the human brain appear as independent beings endowed with life, and entering into relation both with one another and the human race' (Marx 1983:77). Confronted by products and outcomes which it no longer recognises as derived from its own practice, consciousness splits into one or other characteristic response in order to regulate its relations with the alienated products. One response, which governs the world of business, is to develop formal rational models of behaviour and analysis (such as political economy); the other, apparently antithetical, response is to develop anti-rational models based on faith and magic. These two poles, as with all poles, are not only evidently oppositional to one another, they are also linked. The juxtaposition of capital and religion is the subject of Darren Aronofsky's film *PI* (1997 US), a narrative which turns on the fetishistic desires of its protagonists. The story focuses on Max Cohen, a mathematical genius who is trying to develop a formula that would predict the movements of the stock markets. Unlike Karl Marx, who developed a critique of the formal rationality of bourgeois political economy, Max Cohen's mathematics are the epitome of formal rationality, an attempt to make sense of social relations merely by formal, quantitative means that are entirely indifferent to social content. Max is pursued by ruthless stock market analysts who are after any discoveries he makes, but also, intriguingly, he is being courted by a group of Jewish Kabbala mystics who are trying to use number theory to decode the hidden meanings of the Torah (believed to be the word of God), thus combining formal rationality with mysticism. The film explicitly forges parallels between the god of accumulation and the word of God. These domains produce very different and in some respects conflicting ideologies at the level of content, but their ideological forms are strikingly similar. For both groups, the stock market analysts and the Jewish Kabbalists, their objects of desire, as alienated products of their own activities, are mysterious, their movements and meanings need to be divined, whether through rational or irrational frameworks, or some combination of both. Capitalists and spiritualists alike seek to draw back into their control that which has been collectively sundered from them. Thus formal rationality and mysticism attempt to return some power and agency to the subject by internalising the very logics of the system which has separated them from control in the first place. What we see here is the creation of subjectless subjects, subjects who have internalised the objectifying logic of the social relations in a doomed attempt to become subjects once more. The narration of the film is filtered through Max's consciousness, and is increasingly fractured and dissonant as Max slides towards some sort of psychological breakdown. But his 'madness' is merely the individual mirror of the objective madness of the profane and sacred worlds.

IMMANENCE

Immanence refers to the process whereby the networks of social relations are rubbed away, in practice and in consciousness, only returning (as the repressed) in the form of social and economic crises. It is precisely because these social networks (the real relations) which comprise the social totality do return in the form of crises (such as the environmental crisis) that we can postulate the appearance-forms as appearance-forms. For a postmodernist such as Jean Baudrillard, there is nothing but appearance-forms, or what he calls simulacra. These are signs which are the 'death sentence of every reference' (1994:6), signs which do not in any manner refer to the real and which the real itself cannot call into crises as a result. The problem of the simulacra in the aesthetics of alienation is something we shall return to later in an analysis of the film *Dark City* (Alex Proyas 1997 US), but, needless to say, historical materialism can grant this problem only a limited power, or at least insist that it is one part (and not the sum) of a contradictory reality. But let us return to the question of decontextualisation (a form of dematerialisation). Lukács, in a useful phrase, writes of how reification erodes the overlapping 'gradations of reality' (1971:127). Commodity fetishism represses, rubs away and dematerialises the social relations of an activity or commodity and just leaves us with its physical materiality, isolated or with its interdependence with everything else fading away. This sense of the social context of a practice or activity being only faintly detectable gives the social totality a somewhat spectral, ghostly quality. As we saw in Chapter 6, Marxism counterpoises the concept of mediation to capitalism's remorseless decontextualisation/dematerialisation:

> Thus the category of mediation is a lever with which to overcome the mere immediacy of the empirical world and as such it is not something (subjective) foistered on the objects from outside, it is no value-judgement or 'ought' opposed to their 'is'. *It is rather their manifestation of their authentic objective structure* ... Mediation would not be possible were it not for the fact that the empirical existence of objects is itself mediated and only appears to be unmediated insofar as the awareness of mediation is lacking so that the objects are torn from the complex of their true determinants and placed in artificial isolation. (Lukács 1971:162–3)

Michael Taussig captures something of this dematerialisation process when he speaks of 'self-encapsulated things' (1980:32) and autonomisation as the 'privatised cell of self-enclosed thinghood' (1980:136). Immanence follows logically on from the erosion of the overlapping gradations of reality which the subject/object has been prised from. Freed from its contextual interdependencies, the subject/object can act *as if*, and can be perceived *as if* its powers and agency emanated largely from *within* its own body and form (and when 'things' go wrong blame can be apportioned on an individual rather than systemic basis). Power, agency, error: under commodity fetishism, 'What is really a structured effect, an effect of the network of relations between elements appears as an immediate property of one of the elements, as if this property also belongs to it outside its relation with other elements' (Žižek 1989:24).

The waning of sociality has traditionally been central to male identity and masculinity which has invested heavily in the immanence of 'self-encapsulated things' while women have been traditionally portrayed as signifiers of dependency and interdependence which are often framed as threatening to masculinity. Yet with the threat there is also an appeal, as if conventional masculinity sensed the loneliness and impossibility of pure immanence. Impossible because value – whether the value of being a man or economic value – cannot be measured, cannot signify, unless it can be compared to something else. The notion of women as redemption and as threat is evident in such deeply flawed films as *Fight Club* (David Fincher 1999 US) and *American Beauty* (Sam Mendes 1999 US), both critiques of consumer culture. Paradoxically, immanent versions of masculinity do not see in consumer culture their own mirror image of a faded sociality, but instead associate consumerism's dependency on material objects with femininity and weakness. The male protagonists in *Fight Club* and *American Beauty* come to see the home, replete with consumer items, as a trap; in *Fight Club*, Jack (Edward Norton) fires his plush condominium and launches himself into bare-knuckle fighting to toughen himself up, while Lester Burnham (Kevin Spacey) in *American Beauty* relocates to the more masculine domain of the garage where he lifts weights. In *Fight Club*, the image of masculine immanence has a collective manifestation (in the fight clubs). Collective immanence may sound like an oxymoron, but 'self-encapsulated things' need not just be individualistic. The collectivity of men in *Fight Club* (quite apart from reproducing relations of inter-male subordination just as crippling to autonomy as the bonds of consumerism) does indeed see itself as transcending sociality, which is why the fight clubs morph into a terrorist network later on. The anti-commercial violence of *Fight Club* is now unthinkable within Hollywood post 11 September; but the imagery of vandalism and terrorist violence in that film, as with the spectacle of violence on 11 September, graphically demonstrates that terrorism is an act of political immanence. The blow is struck from a position which does not see itself as transforming the world from within it – and therefore transforming it collectively and democrat-ically – but from a transcendent position outside it, a necessarily elitist or authoritarian position. Ultimately, immanence is a religious conception of the world.

SPLITTING

The split between the subject and the object comes to dominate philosophy, but, for Marxism, it is a split which can be grounded in precise historical circumstances. In the quote from Lukács on mediation, he is concerned to point out that the concept is not a mere value judgement or 'ought' imposed onto the actual unmediated 'is' of reality. He makes the point to distinguish his own position from the bourgeois philosophy he critiques. He finds the split between ought and is, values and facts, to be quite typical of bourgeois culture. This is because the world of the bourgeois economy is essentially amoral and unable to sustain any value other than economic calculation and accumulation. Thus value judgements ('oughts') and morals tend to be located elsewhere, in politics, art, religion, the family and so forth, and left contemplat-ing and very often legitimising an economic system that lies outside its own sphere of reference and is taken as an immutable fact. One can only wonder at the psychical impact which the dawning real-isation of a gulf between is and ought has on the subject. Children's television, for example, is shot through with 'oughts' concerning the need to be kind to people, to share resources, to look after people, to not be selfish and greedy, to be co-operative, to be tolerant and under-standing and so forth. Yet all this stands in stark contrast to the fact that such values are largely evacuated from the world of production, with consequent effects on family and school. The sense that for the adult world children then become the repositories of this contradic-tion in which they are expected to conform to some idealistic 'ought' but continually fall short and so come to symbolise that society is going to the dogs is evident from the way media representations of children are split along the dichotomous line of angels and demons.

Guillermo del Toro's *The Devil's Backbone* (2001 Sp) is set in an orphanage during the Spanish Civil War and the republican/socialist fight against Franco's fascist/monarchist/Catholic/bourgeois coalition. The orphanage is haunted by a young boy called Santi, who has been secretly killed by Jacinto, a former student himself at the orphanage but now the janitor. Jacinto is trying to steal the gold hidden in the orphanage safe by the republicans to finance the cause. The film opens with an image that profoundly reveals the gap between is and ought. There is hardly an ideology on the planet (fascist, liberal, socialist) which does not, in theory, value children. Yet the film begins with an aerial bombardment and our point of view is from within the belly of the plane as its doors open and the bombs fall away through the clouds towards the ground (and the orphanage) below. As an image, this is a rebuke to the watching audience as much as the ghost is to the complacent adults in charge at the orphanage who think the boy has simply run away. For the Spanish Civil War was the first war in which civilian populations – including of course children – were subjected to aerial bombardment – a horror which inspired Picasso's *Guernica*. It is salutary when surveying the contemporary wreckage of the post-Cold War era to be reminded that the ghostly origins of aerial bombardment lie in the fascist deployment of the technology of death.

Yet socialists too can be prone to the is/ought antinomy when their rationalist doctrines concerning what people ought to be like and ought to do are confounded by the fact of their recurrent irrationality. Doctor Casares in the orphanage does not believe in ghosts or supernatural forces. The title of the film refers to the spine of babies who die in childbirth. Superstitious locals explain this in terms of the Devil's curse. Casares is right of course to point instead to poverty, but there is something complacent and high-handed about not engaging with the need for the irrational and the desires which fuel it. Carmen, the older woman who runs the orphanage, despises herself for succumbing to her sexual desire for Jacinto, while he in turn sleeps with her in the hope of getting access to the key which opens the safe. Carmen, with her wooden leg, and the embittered orphan Jacinto are, like all of us, deeply marked by the repressions and renunciations which the social order has inscribed into our psyches. As Sartre wrote in relation to Genet: 'we must bring to light the subject, the guilty one, that monstrous and wretched bug which we are likely to become at any moment' (Taussig 1996:217).

The paradox of commodity fetishism is that it is at one level a material practice which acts as it really is, as an autonomous practice; but it is also a practice which disavows a deeper materialism, that complex of determinants which Lukács writes of. Thus material practices and activities have that classic fetishistic split structure: *as if*. In popular vernacular discourse, the phrase 'as if' indicates a cool scepticism towards certain claims. It implies a model of the subject who can identify the gap between appearance/claim and reality, a gap which the subject locates outside of themselves. But in fact under capitalism such a gap is driven deep into the interior of the subject. In practice, in our everyday lives we act in an 'as if' manner all the time. Recall that revealing quote from Chapter 2 when a commentator on the dot.com implosion remarked that it was as if 20 players thought they would each grab 30 per cent of the market. The as if structure of fetishism involves a suppression – or at least its simultaneous cohabitation – of evidence or knowledge which contradicts what is implicit in the performance being engaged in or consumed.

In *Last Resort* (Pawel Pawlikowski 2000 GB) Dina Korzun plays Tanya, a Russian immigrant who ends up applying for political asylum when her British boyfriend fails to turn up at the airport. While her application is processed she is dumped by the authorities in a bleak seaside resort that has seen better times and is enlisted by a seedy Web porn merchant as his latest live performer. In the middle of her first act for the Web consumers, she breaks down and breaks off her performance. Later, however, the porn merchant visits her and begs her to come back. Apparently she was a hit with the punters who loved her 'crying schoolgirl act'. Confronted then with the evidence that the performance was painful, that it was conducted under conditions of economic coercion, the consumers disavow this knowledge and reinterpret the breakdown in the performance as part of the performance. And is this not true of consumption generally, epitomised in the increasingly Americanised service sector by the consumer's desire for the worker to act as if they really were happy and dedicated to their role ('have a nice day!') even though we know full well that they are not? And is the consumer when occupying their other social identities not continually playing a similar role like actors in a drama they have no control over? Think, for example, of all those middle-class bums in the UK sitting on church pews acting as if they were there for religious and spiritual reasons, but there largely in fact to ensure their children get access to reputable church schools. And of course Anglican and Catholic churches, who know exactly why these people have suddenly found their faith, are themselves, like the porno-punters in *Last Resort*, in a similar disavowal. The pervasiveness of the performance principle in a consumer culture and the disavowal of the conditions of performances, splits the subject of advanced capitalism into the most credulous suspender of disbelief on the one hand and the most jaundiced cynic who trusts no one on the other. As we saw in

Chapter 5, this split spectator/subject exactly captures the mode of address of *Big Brother* in which the authenticity of emotions and relations is continually being affirmed and unmasked all at once.

INVERSION

Capitalism is characterised by perverse dialectical inversions that attend its peculiar fading (dematerialisation) of sociality. Social relations, notes Marx, 'appear ... as what they really are, material relations between persons and social relations between things' (1983:78). Here Marx is writing of the fetishising process whereby the *physical* materiality is separated off from the *social* relations or materiality in which it is embedded. Historical materialism combats such commodity fetishism by rejoining the physical and social materiality that has been sundered apart. Within popular culture, one very evident example of this process of sundering can be found in the way advertising personifies things, bringing commodities to life and attributing to them the human qualities of agency, interaction and value (Marx's 'social relations between things') which capitalism is steadily draining away from human beings who relate to themselves and others via material (in the merely physical sense) objects (primarily money). In his archaeological excavations of the origins of consumerism in nineteenth-century Paris, Walter Benjamin unearthed this review of one Paul Siaudin. Active for many years in the theatre, he opened a confectionery shop where, 'from the large display window in the Rue de la Paix ... the sugar almonds, bonbons, honeycakes, and sweet crackers [are] offered to the public in the form of one-act dramatic sketches at the Palais-Royale' (Benjamin 1999a:178). This fossil of consumer capitalism finds its terminus today in such contemporary phenomena as company logos being protected by a battery of legal rights and enforcement mechanisms while workers and human rights are continually downgraded and ignored. Logos can even have (as with Siaudin's confections) a dramatic life or career independent even from the company that originally brought them into being, such as when the bankrupt ITV Digital company found that one of its most valuable assets was the well-liked stuffed monkey which they had used to advertise the service. As the company's workers received their redundancy notices, an ownership tussle between ITV Digital and the advertising company that created him broke out. Such is life when things acquire social agency and people are turned into mere material things.

Consider too how a commodified media and consumer culture have inverted the political challenge of feminism. As part of the broader feminist claims for female equality, feminist cultural analysis dissected the representational strategies which sexually objectified women, consequently emptying them of agency. Complex social changes have indeed brought about a new equality between men and women, but it is the equality of objectification rather than emancipation (MacKinnon 1998). In the television series *Sex and the City*, the four main female characters are the sexual hunters, the men are the interchangeable objects of the female gaze and desire (although the scenario of sexually active women with no interest in long-term commitment clearly can also function as a male fantasy). Thus the former sexual objects have become subjects by appropriating the objectifying mechanisms which they were once on the receiving end of. But such subjecthood is no more fulfilling than when subjects try to use formal rationality to acquire social agency. Like formal rationality, desire that objectifies is indifferent to human content. In both cases the subject becomes the vehicle or personification of the logic of the system rather than an authentic agent, they become, as in *PI*, subjectless subjects. A similar dynamic to the subjectless subject is described by Adorno when he writes that: 'The subject's real impotence has its echo in its mental omnipotence. The ego principle imitates its negation' (1973:179).

It is no accident that the women in *Sex and the City* belong to the professional middle class who socially are always better located to adopt and adapt the system's imperatives. The narration of each episode's events by the lead character Carrie cuts down on narrative exposition, allowing for the swift alternation between scenes and the love lives of the women and this underlines the incoming and rapid outgoing trajectory of the objectified males. And yet because equality of objectification essentially reduces human relations to the mechanical, interchangeable world of the commodity and formal rationality, the representation of the liberated sexually active female is split and continually prone to invert back into the more traditional gender roles of yesteryear. Thus, as one commentator noted, in *Sex and the City*, 'what the girls want, what they really, really want, apart from giant organs and monstrous orgasms, is exactly the same as their mothers: marriage to Mr Right'.[1] This is because some fantasy semblance of sustained human commitment and connection can be imagined via backward projection.

REPRESSION

Another way of thinking about the implications for the subject of a fading, dematerialising sociality is in terms of repression. In exploring the bourgeois repression of its own conditions of existence, Marx famously invoked the 'spectre of communism' on the opening page of *The Communist Manifesto*, which, he argued, was haunting the bourgeoisie. Marx wanted to stress how frightened the bourgeoisie were of something that had yet to materialise. With the spectre, Marx 'announces and calls for a presence to come' (Derrida 1994:101) anticipating a future yet to happen rather than, as ghosts usually are, the trace of something already past. The bourgeoisie represses an alternative historical trajectory as well as the collective agent that harbours that alternative future. Like all repressions, this stems from not wanting to acknowledge something that hurts, something that questions the very basis of your existence and your values. At the margins and yet at the centre of the bourgeois world were the working class, that 'body' which Marx's spectre of communism wanted to enter and possess in order to bring both the spirit (or theory) and the flesh (or practice) together in a real revolutionary life. The body of the working class, labouring away in the factories of the bourgeoisie, scarred, divided, a mere factor of production, impoverished mentally as much as materially, was marked by countless social crimes. And it was these crimes which the spectre of communism wanted to redress.

In *The Communist Manifesto* we have the basic template of many ghostly apparitions in contemporary cinema today. A dominant and often complacent social order repressing that which challenges its existence and values, marginalising opposition, kicking over the traces of violence which it has performed, and the appearance of some spirit crying out for past injustices to be recognised, for its memory to be redeemed, or for good old-fashioned bloody vengeance to be wreaked. This is the case at least in such films as *Candyman* (Bernard Rose 1992 US) or *Ring* (Hideo Nakata 1998 Japan) and *Ring 2* (Hideo Nakata 1998 Japan) and, as we have already seen, *The Devil's Backbone*. Alejandro Amenábar's *The Others* (2001 US) does not quite work in the same way but is once again an interesting meditation on repression. Here there is in fact a triple repression. First, Nicole Kidman's Grace does not know she is a ghost, having repressed her murder of her own two children and her subsequent suicide. Second, the film stirs up the tricky issue of wartime collaboration, being set very specifically in Jersey just after the Nazi occupation has come to an end. Like many others, Grace isolates herself from the historical conjuncture – the fight against fascism – and holes up in her house while raging against her husband who has committed himself to fight in the war. Although Grace has a legitimate excuse at one level for her isolationism – her children are light sensitive – the lesson surely is that any authentic protection of the private sphere in times of crisis – a permanent state of affairs today – requires public engagement. And, finally, there is a class repression. Grace does not recognise the trajectory of class relations that have transformed her own class and the working class in the course of the twentieth century and in the course of the war in particular.

The sense that she is an historical and class anachronism with her 'Lady of the Manor' attitudes is only underscored by the three servants who come knocking on her door looking for employment and who, as one immediately suspects, turn out to be vintage nineteenth-century ghosts. The presence of the masses in the Second World War accelerated their impact on political and social life in such a way as to make the Upstairs/Downstairs scenario, with its limited opportunities and deference, a thing of the Victorian and Edwardian past. As the film progresses, the ghostly servants clearly appear to be in some kind of spectral revolt, with their own designs and increasingly open disobedience. But this revolt is not all that it seems and is certainly not the kind envisaged by Marx; nor does it even have the class resentment of say Henry James' *The Turn of the Screw* (Jameson 1999:39). Rather than wanting to teach this representative of the dominant class that her time has come and gone, they merely in the end want her to learn a more moderate message. They want to alert her to her new status and her altered condition of existence, while at the same time preserving the fundamental relations between employer and employee. The limitation of their revolt is that they are merely seeking to continue their old role with a new mistress in the house they have haunted since they were carried off by TB. This is the film's secret and unconscious message in fact. For all the changes which the war has wrought in the land of the living, the ghostly continuities with what has been remain. The film's narrative structure makes the ultimate revelation of Grace's true ghostly status the most important and cathartic moment in the film, the point at which our knowledge of events and Grace's knowledge finally converge with the servants who have known all, all along. After this point, there is nowhere else to go, certainly not into the terrain of class struggle. Yet there is still something to say about that startling moment just before all is revealed, when the spectator is flipped over into the land of the living and we see for the first time the poltergeist-like effects that Grace is having on the new bourgeois owners of the property. For while secretly comforting the spectator with the conformist message that continuity is really all the working class desire, the very fact that we see here in this scene what is otherwise the faded, ghostly temporal continuity of the dominant class, as one generation replaces another, hints at a different assessment of such continuities, one which Marx described in *The Eighteenth Brumaire of Louis Bonaparte* as the 'tradition of all the dead generations weigh[ing] like a nightmare on the brain of the living' (1984:10).

THE ECONOMICS OF COMMODITY FETISHISM

We are now in a position to establish the economic dimensions of commodity fetishism, which Marx elaborated most systematically in *Capital* and particularly in the difficult opening chapter of that book. Marx begins his analysis of capitalism with a forensic deconstruction of the commodity, the 'economic cell-form' of bourgeois society (1983:19). The commodity – apparently so ordinary and banal – is a microcosm which crystallises the outlines of some of the fundamental contradictions within capitalism. Marx's critique of the commodity form is also a critique of the consciousness which attends the commodity form.

A commodity, Marx argues, is divided, split, between its use-value and its exchange value. The use-value of a product is realised in its uses (which are potentially multiple and changing) rather than being essential and fixed within the product itself. As Thomas Keenan notes: 'This formulation implies not an infinity of uses – one cannot do everything with anything – but simply an unpredictability, a structural openness to new contexts' (1996:160). Use-values are not only potentially open they are also diverse in their variety and concrete in the specificity of human needs they satisfy. Yet the heterogeneity of use-values is only one pole of the commodity, its other and dominant pole is what Marx calls value and exchange value. These categories represent the 'commerce first' logic of capital and they penetrate and structure use-value, blocking off its 'structural openness' (as we saw, for example, in the case of Napster and P2P technology in Chapter 2) and only sustaining those use-values that can coexist with value at any particular time.

Value is simply that which gives commodities their *economic* value or weight in society. Given that for Marx it is labour which creates surplus value (more value than labour needs to reproduce itself and certainly more than the wage it receives) and thus creates social wealth, it is no surprise to find that the *substance* of value which is found in commodities is congealed labour power, the capacity that is to transform materials and apply technologies and techniques. Labour is the common denominator, the parent to all commodities (nature is the other parent of course). But under capital it is not labour in all its diversity and specificity which is registered by value. 'As ... use-values, coat and linen, are combinations of special productive activities with cloth and yarn ... [but] as values, the coat and linen, are, on the other hand, mere homogenous congelations of undifferentiated labour' (Marx 1983:52). Just as formal rationality is indifferent to human contents, so capital is indifferent to the particularities of human labour and its outcomes. 'In order to act as ... a mirror of value, the labour of tailoring must reflect nothing besides its own abstract quality of being human labour generally' (Marx 1983:64). This abstraction is the central reason why the worker cannot 'reckon labour as part of his life, it is rather a sacrifice of his life' (Marx 1967:62). Along with the use-values of the product, the labour which produces them 'is nothing but the expenditure of human labour-power ... the value of a commodity represents human labour in the abstract, the expenditure of human labour in general' (Marx 1983:51). Thus labour becomes 'abstract, equal, comparable labour, measurable with increasing precision' (Lukács 1971:87). If human labour, practically conceived as homogeneous, uniform and abstract (without the detail of specificity) is the substance of value (Murray 2000), time is its measurement, the means by which the magnitude of value is expressed in the price or exchange value of the commodity, give or take fluctuations in supply and demand around the mean price. It is the average socially necessary time required for the production of labour (with particular skills) and the labour of production to make a given product which measures, quantifies and (via competition) equalises labour and the amount of 'value' stored in the commodity. As Marx writes in *The Poverty of Philosophy*,

[L]abour has been equalized by the subordination of man to the machine or by the extreme division of labour ... the pendulum of the clock has become as accurate a measure of the relative activity of two workers as it is of the speed of two locomotives ... Time is everything, man is nothing; he is at most, time's carcase. Quantity alone decides everything; hour for hour, day for day. (1967:151)

The carcase metaphor evokes the live human body as eviscerated by value relations, as a husk, a shell; emptied of bodily substance, labour is *possessed* by time, time conceived under the quantitative law of value; the body is time's host. Although the body is alive and has to be alive in order to be valuable to capital so that it can have some agency as labour power, the body is also dead, a carcase. Value inhabits the body (whether the body of a human being, an institution, an aesthetic practice) and retains its outer form in the same way that any commodity retains its use-value as an outer form, but it is colonised from within by another logic utterly antithetical to those use-values as use-values.

This logic is the logic of a remorseless quantitative proportionality which insists that everything can be made equivalent to everything else. In terms of consciousness of practice, quantitative proportionality is problematic because it smoothes over the details of social inequality. Money, for example, functions as the universal equivalent. It is supposed to signify that the value represented in a given quantity of numbers matches the amount of labour expended at work or exchanged for a commodity as a consumer. Of course, we can talk of 'unfair wages' or 'bad value' for money, but even this assumes that there is such a thing as 'fair wages' and 'good value' for the consumer, that, in other words, equal exchange (like market equilibrium) is a realisable ideal under capitalism. But, as Marx notes, if equivalents are always exchanged, there can be no surplus value and therefore no profit (1983:158). Let us now take an example of quantitative proportionality outside the economic sphere. In the UK the league tables of schools, which have been assembled ostensibly so that parents can measure their educational performance, are an operation of quantification and equivalence that purports to show how school A has a greater or lesser percentage of passes at a given level of exams than school B. By starting with the assumption that A and B are comparable according to quantitative proportionality, the logic of value rubs away such social questions as differences in funding, differences in the social composition of the students and the parents, and the learning of social values not measured by exam results. Penetrating deep into social practices and consciousness of practices, the logic of quantitativity dissolves social content by its presupposition that everything can in principle be made equivalent.

This process penetrates right into the structure of information itself. Information is the means by which the subject makes its calculations according to the classical economic theory of maximising its resources. The information is supposed to allow for an accurate assessment of performance. In other words the information is supposed to enact a mimetic exchange between data and the commodity in question. But the use-value of the performance indicators (signs) is in constant danger of being hollowed out by the very thing, value, which the indicators are supposed to measure. Thus it is hardly surprising that at the same time that exam results become crucial for the quantitative measurement of the performance of schools there are revelations that the results have been manipulated by teachers under pressure to perform. Nor is it then surprising that there is also a failure of equal exchange (between data and performance) in the private sector proper, with serious questions being asked about the accounts of multinational corporations such as Enron, WorldCom, Xerox, Vivendi and others, boosting profit margins on paper but failing to increase shareholder value in reality.

The gulf between appearance and reality, between claim and practice, between use-value and exchange value, between the outer form and the inner logic, inevitably widens as the competitive logics of commodity production increase and penetrate into the social and economic fabric. One cannot resolve this problem by trying to make performance indicators more transparent, more accurate or more realistic because the gulf between claim and practice, fantasy and reality, is generated up from the practices themselves, the ideological fantasy inheres in the practices themselves (Žižek 1989:30–33). Investors, for example, in the dot.com bubble were not misled by erroneous accounts of performance. Massive investments in high-tech companies were made in the knowledge that they were making little or zero profit now but in the hope that they would be profitable in the future. This claim/fantasy (where rational calculation and irrational faith converge) was one which was imposed collectively in the competitive scramble to achieve market share (and thus individual and corporate profits). The dynamic is nicely illustrated in this newspaper article:

Brian Ashford-Russell received a £6m bonus in 2000 – six months after the hi-tech companies he had backed began the wobble that became a nosedive. Mr Ashford-Russell invested £1.5bn of cash for millions of ordinary investors in the technology funds and investment trust he ran for City firm Henderson ... Mr Ashford-Russell warned his investors in December 1999 that the prices of technology stocks were getting high. But still they kept investing and Mr Ashford-Russell kept buying up the shares. He got his bumper bonus for a year's work in which his fund rose by 139% and earned his employer fees of £43m.[2]

The fantasy then that prices can never be too high is inscribed into investment fund practices irrespective of what people actually know to be the case. Is this fissure between what they know and what they do restricted to City investors, or is it a more generalised condition of life for the subject? I would suggest that the latter is the case and that commodity fetishism would help explain how, for example, the subject's sceptical knowledge of the nature of the performances they are engaged in as producer and consumer is contradicted by their complicities in those performances by virtue of their participation in them.

The subject comes to appreciate the pervasive pressures compromising data, information and indeed all messages and signs (including accurate ones). The subject knows, and, as the Leonard Cohen song has it, 'Everybody Knows',[3] that it is all just an act, a performance, a simulation and that all cultural spectacles lack authenticity. Judging from opinion polls, few people trust advertisers, journalists or politicians as far as they could launch them. Nevertheless people are still receptive to advertising campaigns, they still vote (although in declining numbers) and still use the media as a basis for their beliefs and entertainments. Thus the subject's cynicism alternates with the necessity to place credulous faith (even if well researched) in at least some of the signs designed to guide its calculations and actions in order to act as a subject at all, in order to participate in social practices at all. And by its necessary participation, the subject becomes complicit in the ideological fantasies of equal exchange, equivalence, competition, the rationality of what is, and the possibility of authenticity in cultural spectacles.

COMMODITY FETISHISM, POSSESSION AND SPECTRALITY

Capital ought not to be seen as a conventional work of economics, for it is as much about consciousness as it is about such questions as where profit comes from. Nor is the question of consciousness to be seen as a secondary derivation from economics. As Amariglio and Callari argue, a reified subjectivity is crucial to the everyday operation of the capitalist economy, it is not merely an effect of the economy but constitutive of it (1996:202–3); it is the oil which lubricates the machinery. Again and again Marx makes the distinction between how things appear and the real social relations which paradoxically generate these dissembling appearance-forms *and depend on them.* Thus for Marx, under capitalism, 'a definite social relation between men ... assumes, in their eyes, the fantastic form of a relation between things' (1983:77). And if they did not assume such fantastic forms, at least with some degree of systematicity, coherence and continuity, then those definite social relations would be a good deal more prone to economic and political crisis than they even are now. Yet on numerous occasions Marx has recourse to the imagery of ghosts, of phantasms, of capital's 'werewolf hunger for surplus labour' (1983:252) and the 'magic and necromancy that surrounds the products of labour as long as they take the form of commodities' (1983:80–81). Marx draws on discourses of the irrational, supernatural and the fantastic in order paradoxically to expose the irrational and inhuman qualities of capitalism. He also deploys the strategies of personification and animation beloved by advertising agencies, giving commodities brains and mouths with which to speak. But again, he does this to expose their real relations: commodities come alive in Marx's rhetorical strategies so that he can expose the absurdities of the power they have over humanity. Thus Marx deploys the imagery of fetishism against the rational appearance-forms, against the grain of the system. And this – albeit in more ambiguous and contradictory ways – is a feature of popular culture as well (Smith 2001). There are at least four ways in which the image of the ghost or spectrality can be invoked in relation to the Marxian critique of commodity fetishism:

> *Spectral Things.* In one mode the figure of the ghost represents the *appearance-forms* which social and economic reification generates up. The rubbing away of *social* materiality (relations) leaves only a physical materiality. Remembering the close association of ghosts with mists in the discourse of the gothic aesthetic, we find Marx arguing that under capitalism appearance-forms are like a 'mist through which the social character of labour appears to us to be an objective character of the products themselves' (1983:79). What

Marx evokes here is the way inanimate things such as money and commodities (from nuclear weapons to food mountains) acquire a supernatural agency and power *independent* of earthly human powers. At one level, the mist/ghost refers to an objective social process whereby a network of social relations (the 'social character of labour') is dematerialised and rematerialised as an immanent part of the products themselves. Yet, at another level, the reality of appearance-forms is unreal. The social character of labour, which capital itself develops, remains, and so this objectivity is also phantom-like, that is insubstantial. The spectrality of things is a popular current within mass culture. In the horror film *Thirteen Ghosts* (Steve Beck 2001 US), for example, a specially designed glasshouse becomes an autonomous entity trapping its occupants inside with a number of violent ghosts. The investment of physical things with a will hostile to human beings is the perfect allegorical expression of commodity fetishism. Within the horror genre, houses often acquire a certain phantom objectivity and this is not unrelated to the economic and ideological status of this form of property within consumer capitalism.

Spectral Simulation. Yet the metaphor undergoes a transformation in another usage when the solidity and independence of the appearance-forms (what is their ghostly 'objectivity' as spectral things) is actually undermined, when the spectre suddenly acquires an *insubstantial* rather than independent quality. Thus Jameson defines spectrality as having a directly critical impetus which 'makes the present waver', an experience where 'the massiveness of the object world – indeed of matter itself – now shimmers like a mirage' (1999:38). This is no mere subjective loss of grip, but, on the contrary, something like the beginnings of class consciousness where the sceptical subject senses that the appearance-form of reality is not 'as self-sufficient as it claims to be' (Jameson 1999:38). This dimension of spectrality, reality as shimmering mirage, is also now firmly entrenched within a *digitalised* popular culture where the subject/spectator/protagonist discovers that the world of appearances is the simulated and manipulated effect of disguised real relations (e.g. *The Truman Show* (Peter Weir 1998 US), *The Matrix* (Andy and Larry Wachowski 1999 US), *Pleasantville* (Gary Ross 1998 US) and *Dark City* (Alex Proyas 1997 US).

Spectral Repression. The ghost can also be invoked in the way it is at the beginning of *The Communist Manifesto* and in some of the films I have already discussed above. Here the ghost is the trace of something that is being repressed (use-value, history, the working class, women and children) and a clue to that which remains unacknowledged, the faint presence of something which cries out for redemption in the bourgeois social order and/or the faint presence of those other components of our lives and practices which cannot be 'lived' or experienced simultaneously – that fading or thinning of our full sociality at work in the formation of spectral things, but here now returning with the violent force of the repressed, as in *Urban Ghost Story* (Genevieve Jolliffe 2001 GB).

Spectral Possession. Finally the figure of the ghost can be invoked as a sign of the *real relations* of the value-form, its dissipation of the concrete diversity of practices, the displacement of the real living body by something dead and deadening. Spectral possession is not invoked by Marx explicitly, although, as we have seen, with the image of the human body becoming time's carcase, it is a trope bubbling away under the surface of his analysis of the law of value. It is an image which takes us to the heart of the economic dimension of capital's power and it gives us a purchase on the imagery of possession within popular culture. If in *The Communist Manifesto* it is the spectre of the proletariat that haunts the bourgeoisie, with the imagery of possession the situation is now reversed and we find the spirit/logic of capital to be haunting labour. This notion of capital as a spirit allows us to evoke the dematerialising materialism of capital, its movement (possession) of subjects and their labours, its infiltration of value into use-value.

Despite being insubstantial and lacking real concrete bodies, ghosts have the power to enter and possess the living, converting their autonomy and bodily presence into an expression of the will of the ghost. Indeed the spectre that possesses needs the concrete body in order to have some agency in the world. Similarly, Marx writes of how the particularities of a commodity and the labour which produces it become the 'bodily form' of value, the 'palpable embodiment of human labour generally' (1983:64). Taking a 'bodily form' capital makes everything equivalent: '[T]he manifold concrete useful kinds of labour, embodied in ... different commodities, rank now as so many different forms of the realisation or manifestation, of undifferentiated human labour' (Marx 1983:69). The sense of value moving from commodity to commodity (including labour of course), attaching itself to its use-value which is indispensable to it but simultaneously hollowing out that use-value, leaving only a shell behind which there lies value, is strikingly evocative of the imagery of possession in popular culture. One thinks, for example, of the bodily form of Professor Querrelle possessed (willingly although not unambiguously so) by the spirit of Voldemort in *Harry Potter and the Philosopher's Stone* (Chris Columbus 2001 US) or, more interestingly, the way the evil spirit moves swiftly from body to body in *Fallen* (Gregory Hoblit 1998 US), or the way the agents of the matrix can possess the simulated mental projections of the enslaved humans in *The Matrix* (Andy and Larry Wachowski 1999 US). Of course the logic of value is not mere 'spirit', it is the practical and institutionalised materiality of the capitalist market. But it acts *as if* it were spirit-like, transcending the material world and reducing it merely to the phenomenal form or manifestation of its homogeneous essence. We are then dealing with two kinds of materialism here. The materialism of use-value, with all its concreteness, richness and diversity, and the materialism of value which for all its real materiality is a kind of idealism, a kind of fantasy. It is ironic given the conceptual importance of difference or concrete sensuous particularity for Marx, that Marx and Marxism have been lambasted by critics for apparently not appreciating and being sensitive enough to diversity, plurality and heterogeneity. This is to confuse the critique with the object of the critique. It is not Marxism which reduces all social activity to the economics of quantification which characterises value relations, but capitalism. However, this reduction is never complete for the same reason that the mode of production does not pass through the social order in a uniform and homogeneous manner (see Chapter 5); instead the spirit/logic of capital encounters the 'resistances' of material practices, which, in their specificity, concreteness and historical development, adapt it even as they adapt to it. Yet capital behaves as if it really could assimilate everything to its homogeneous logic without any resistance or difference.

At this point we can make a link between Marx's gothic spirits as emblems of dematerialised materialism and Hegelian philosophy with its invocation of a World Spirit. In *The Holy Family*, Marx and Engels criticised the abstraction of Hegel's idealistic philosophy in terms that could stand equally as well for capital's own abstraction of human labour. For Hegel, the concrete, particular, material world, such as the state, is merely the vehicle or expression of a developing abstract collective Reason or World Spirit. Marx satirised Hegel's method as reproduced by some of his less able followers thus:

> If from real apples, pears, strawberries and almonds I form the general idea 'Fruit', if I go further and *imagine* that my abstract idea 'Fruit', derived from real fruit ... is indeed the *true* essence of the pear, the apple, etc., then – in the language of speculative philosophy – I am declaring that to be a pear is not essential to the pear, that to be an apple is not essential to the apple; what is essential to these things is not their real existence, perceptible to the senses, but the essence that I have abstracted from them and then foistered on them, the essence of my idea – 'Fruit'. (Marx and Engels 1956:78)

For Hegel, 'Fruit' is the higher concept because of its degree of abstraction, its capacity to subsume a variety of different particulars under it. Hegelian idealism abhorred what Marx and Engels comically call 'the base mass in all its massy massiness' (1956:21), in other words, the materiality of the material world. But then, so too do the abstractions of capital. If we replace apples, pears and strawberries with different kinds of labour and their products, we see the same process unfold at the economic level. The particularity of different kinds of labour/products is abstracted from them and foisted back onto them in the form of value. All the different kinds of labour and use-values are subsumed into the general category – in this case value, not the category 'Fruit'. In Hegelian philosophy: 'The different profane fruits are different manifestations of the life of the *one* "Fruit"; they are crystallizations of "Fruit" itself. In the apple "Fruit" gives itself an apple-like existence, in the pear a pear-like existence' (Marx and Engels 1956:80). The same is true of value which gives itself a film-like existence here, a newspaper-like existence there, a musical manifestation elsewhere. As Žižek notes, the bourgeois individual 'is definitely not a speculative Hegelian' in theory, but in practice they act otherwise (1989:32). In a suggestive passage in the *Economic and Philosophical Manuscripts*, Marx notes that: 'Private property does not know how to change crude need into human need. Its idealism is fantasy' (1972:147). Marx is arguing that capital cannot really engage with the materiality of human needs, it cannot develop them or can only develop them in a crude form. It is *as if the materiality of use-value and concrete sensuous human activity had no substantive materiality, only a 'bodily form' to be possessed*; this is the *fantasy* of capitalism, the roots of its peculiar *idealistic or dematerialising materialism*. This is why Marx can speak of the 'metaphysical subtleties' of the commodity form. And it is this fantasy which is on display, in an ambiguous mixture of critique and reaffirmation, in the film *Dark City*.

DARK CITY AS AN ALLEGORY OF REIFICATION

Dark City (Alex Proyas 1997 US) is a virtual compendium of motifs of alienation, fetishism and reification, something which, as we shall see, is not unproblematic. Let us start with the substance of the film's story. Our narrator at the start of the film is Dr Paul Schreber (Keifer Sutherland) who immediately informs us that the dark city of our story world is an elaborate laboratory where the Strangers conduct their experiments. The Strangers are an alien race who have mastered the ability to alter physical reality by will alone. They call this 'tuning'. Unbeknown to the humans who live out 'their' lives in the city, the Strangers engage in tuning every night at midnight, at which point the human subjects fall asleep as their lives and their world are reconstructed around them. The very description of the aliens as Strangers is as significant as their tuning powers. The concept of alienation means to 'make strange' that which once belonged to you: 'the worker come[s] to face the product of his activity as a stranger' (Marx 1972:110). The Strangers then can be seen as the collective embodiment of human alienation and their power to tune, to alter physical reality at will, is nothing less than an allegory of value and its idealistic materialism, the fantasy of capital to endlessly possess material life as if that materiality had no substance, no 'resistance'. We have seen that one crucial aspect of value relations is the quantification involved in the measuring of practically abstract labour by the average socially necessary time for the production of the commodity (labour and its products). The emphasis which the film places visually on time (Dr Schreber's old-fashioned pocket watch, the huge clock face in the Strangers' cavernous bunker) and on the grinding down of time as midnight approaches, recalls Marx's startling metaphor of deadening, hollowing possession when he writes of man as time's carcass.

The Strangers are, Schreber tells us, a declining race. The purpose of their experiments is to discover what it is that makes humans unique so that they can acquire (or reacquire) the quality of individual life which their collective homogeneous identity has robbed them of. Yet once again we are confronted here with subject-less subjects. The subjectless subject is not necessarily one whose power has been removed – their condition is more tragic than that. Rather their agency depends on internalising the very objectifying logics of the system which has hollowed them out in the first place. Thus the Strangers' experiments manifest a classic reified splitting between means and ends, with their goal of searching for the human 'soul' completely violated by their means of doing so. For what it means to be human is to be more than a mere object, a merely and infinitely manipulable object according to the behest of other powers. The humans have the appearance-form of what it is the Strangers seek but the Strangers themselves have reduced them to their own mirror image. Just as the product of the Strangers' mental labours becomes a reified thing (the humans) so the production process itself 'must be active alienation, the alienation of activity, the activity of alienation' (Marx 1972:110). Thus the tuning process is cast in the iconic imagery of industrial reification, with the Strangers working on production lines, assembling the articles which are to become part of the object world in the lives of the humans. As they do so, Dr Schreber manufactures the subjective life of the human population, mixing memories under the microscope, distilling them into serum form to be injected directly into the forehead. Here is the perfect imagery of formal rationality, or what the Frankfurt School called instrumental reason, subsuming human particularity into abstract science or philosophy. The Strangers need Schreber because they do not have the artistry to mix such serums; indeed their lack of emotional inner life is precisely what they seek to discover by observing their human subjects (who have of course become objects).

The film begins with one such subject waking up in the middle of the tuning process without any memory or identity. John Murdoch (Rufus Sewell) is one of those on whom the injection of new memories occasionally does not take. He awakes in a hotel room also occupied by a dead women on whom someone or something has inscribed into her flesh bloody spirals. This failure produces a crisis for the Strangers and is a signifier of the resistance of the material world to its endless quantitative manipulation by the Strangers (or value relations). This is the revolt of use-value (the return of the repressed) which takes the form of economic crisis within the capitalist economy. Here goods that pile up unused due to overproduction, such as semiconductors during the dot.com bust, are a 'revolting' reminder to capital that use-values cannot be endlessly manipulated for indefinite capital accumulation. Their use, in other words, *matters*. Use-value revolts in *Dark City* because of Murdoch's refusal to trade in his memories for a new set, his unconscious desire to hold onto the memories he has and not have them reduced to quantitative equivalence (that is, swapped with a new set of memories).

Murdoch goes on the run, pursued on the one hand by the Strangers and on the other by the police and in particular by Inspector Frank Bumstead (William Hurt). Bumstead is replacing another detective who has previously been working on a series of bizarre murders. But his predecessor, Walenski, has gone mad, and it appears that he too has discovered the truth of the world they occupy and their status within it. When Bumstead visits Walenski at home he is found drawing spiral circles on his walls in a room whose slanting ceiling and apparently curved structure recall the distorted perspectives of the classic German expressionist film *The Cabinet of Dr Caligari* (Robert Wiene 1919 Ger). And at that point the spectator may recall that spiral circles also featured in that film. German expressionism of course fed, via German émigrés fleeing Hitler, into the American film noir genre which is also the obvious intertextual reference point in a film literally without any natural light and swamped in perpetual darkness. We learn that the Strangers hate sunlight (like vampires) and water. The gaunt figures of the Strangers themselves are part Max Schreck from *Nosferatu* (F.W. Murnau 1922 Ger), while their leather clothing triggers a more contemporary memory trace from the sadistic figures of the *Hellraiser* series. We later learn that these figures are not the true form of this alien race, but that they have possessed human corpses, taken them as 'vessels', to give them (and the cadaverous shells they inhabit) some agency in the world. These intertextual references to the undead recall Marx's use of the gothic aesthetic to imagine the process by which something that was once human (labour power and its products) now confronts it as some ghostly independent spectral thing, some phantom object, no longer subject to earthly powers. It is significant that Murdoch starts to have brief flashbacks, residual traces of the memories the Strangers tried to exchange, of growing up on Shell Beach with his uncle after his parents had died in a house fire. Is this name a coincidence? After all these human subjectless subjects are themselves little more than shells, the 'palpable form' of the Strangers' instrumental experiments. Shell Beach meanwhile, the site of sunlight and water, exists only in the imagination, outside the physical parameters of the constructed city. Thus, despite the 1950s-style advertising hoardings for Shell

Beach which Murdoch sees around the city, with its sense of innocent leisure time consumption and an unavoidable hint of complacency associated with that decade, it appears totally inaccessible. Murdoch tries to get to Shell Beach via the subway, but the express train with Shell Beach as its destination, does not stop at any platform. With the iconography of the subway, we appear to have wandered out of 1940s film noir and into the 1970s, the period when this semantic terrain of the city began to enter a revitalised 'realistic' American cinema (the period of economic and cultural crisis for Hollywood) as a sign of the routines and violence of urban life in such films as *The French Connection* (William Friedkin 1971 US) and *The Taking of Pelham 123* (Joseph Sargent 1974 US).

Murdoch learns from Schreber that the entire city is manufactured out of memories from different periods which have been extracted from the kidnapped humans and mixed and matched into increasingly hybrid formations. The Strangers are thus postmodernist *bricoleurs*, endlessly rearranging their accumulated raw material with no regard to historical continuity or boundaries, compacting instead different cultural styles and historical periods simultaneously into the same space: that of the city. In this way the film itself tells us that its own postmodern style is in fact pure ideology, which is to say that it is the simulated construct of an exploiting elite whose power is concealed by those simulations. At this level, *Dark City* seems to be closely aligned with Fredric Jameson's view that postmodernism represents the cultural logic of advanced capitalism (1991).

Thus the very signs of reification drawn from the discourses of German Expressionism and its American noir cousin are themselves reified. The original aesthetic moments of expressionism and film noir were hardly lucidly in touch with the historical determinants impinging on their forms. They were more like the aesthetic version of the goldfish thrashing around on the bathroom floor amidst the debris of its shattered glass world, an early image in *Dark City*. The force of the existential crisis which German expressionism and American film noir discharged came partly from the incomprehension of the subject when confronted by an absurd and impenetrable world. By contrast, *Dark City* is hyperconscious of the politics of its intertextual cultural references, their status, function, history and reception (Collins 1992:335) and is deploying them in a manner more lucid than the originals ever were. In some ways the film could be read as a compendium of the cultural politics of various cinematic forms and periods. Yet there is also that sense – difficult to pin down empirically – that the aesthetics have become, like the subjects in the film, a shell or bodily form emptied of the emotional power and substantive historical content/context that originally motivated them. The film warns us of how memory is also an act of repression. Murdoch asks Bumstead when was the last time he remembered doing something during the day. Similarly, one wonders what is being repressed in the cultural memory of postmodern aesthetic strategies. Hyperconscious bricolage slots the signifers of alienation, cultural complacency, urban realism, etc., smoothly into place: Expressionism, Noir – you know the code, and one is left with the unsettling feeling of hermetic self-referentiality; it is after all, *only* a code, only a signifier, an aesthetic carcase robbed of its historical and cognitive power. Hence, postmodernism is characterised by a peculiar new 'emotional ground tone' which Jameson calls the waning of affect (1991:6–11). Yet the fact that alienation remains such a reiterated theme of popular cinema suggests that it is less a question that alienation is now merely a pleasing aesthetic for the eye, that all we have here is the simulation of alienation as Baudrillard would have it, than that there is a real *crisis* of representation, a deep cleavage between form and content and, like the Strangers themselves, between means and ends. Once again we find the subject split between a cynical reason, which already knows that capital is pernicious and the world exploitative, and a credulous self prepared to believe that this is just a convention, a form, a style with no political or ethical referent in the real world.

A similar contradiction between means and ends is evident in the film's plot which sees Murdoch acquire the Strangers' powers of tuning. This is the film's resolution to the problem of the Strangers' unnatural power, that it is instead invested in Murdoch, who brings sunlight to the city and makes it possible to really get to Shell Beach. This denouement feels unsatisfactory because Murdoch has in effect become god (immanence with a capital I). The *form* of power has changed, shifted now to the individual, the human, the 'good man', but the substance of power, the spirit of value or the power to tune, remains very much in place. A similar ambiguity is evident in how we read the film's bravura digital effects of the retuning process. This could at one level be read as an example of the kind of spectrality which Jameson defined as when the object world's apparent solidity and independence shimmers like a mirage. We see buildings grow out of the ground, others contracting, others folding and unfolding into new shapes, designs and combinations. Strangers mill around the streets, enter homes and rearrange the lives of the inhabitants. In one instance, a down-at-heel couple eating their evening meal are transformed (with the appropriate new environment) into wealthy members of the bourgeoisie. Does this sequence reveal the constructed nature of all social relations, their less than natural inevitability? Yet the very constructed nature is precisely what is coding the sequence as unnatural, alien and inhuman and thus by implication naturalising our more familiar day-to-day social relations whose constructedness is less visible. We have here the fantasy of equivalence, of a generalised commodification which the law of value pursues, played out as nightmare. At the heart of such digital aesthetics is a profound ambivalence, as Sobchack argues (2000:xii). If digitalisation offers glimpses of radically new modes of 'post-bourgeois' identity, shorn of their customary fixedness and monadic isolation and immense (if rather narrowly conceived) extension of human powers, as allegorical visions of the nightmare of equivalence, of a 'post-humanist' subject integrated absolutely into capital, it serves as both a warning of one possible historical trajectory and an affirmative shoring up of our more 'natural' (but really naturalised) world of everyday perception.

Commodity fetishism then derives from social relations which invest power into physical things which then acquire agency and independence from the human subject. As with possession, the spirit/logic of value hollows out the real materiality of the world, leaving just the shell, the bodily form. We have seen that this is not just an economic process, nor even just a social one. As a generalised but uneven process, this fetishism, or reification, burrows deep down into the subject, their consciousness, sense of self and the world and their culture. Where subjects feel that they are indeed agents is often the spot where they have been most hollowed out by value relations and turned into subjectless subjects. One manifestation of this drama is the splitting of the subject; on the one hand, the subject is forever sceptically exclaiming, in the popular vernacular, 'as if' when confronted by any set of signs; but, on the other hand, the subject credulously invests in those or other signs as authentic representations. In order to be a subject one has to participate in some social practices somewhere, there can be no opting out of social relations. Neither, though, can there be any definitive 'outside' of the very processes which generate scepticism. But the concept of the subjectless subject does not intend to continue the pessimistic trend of French thought (Lévi-Strauss, Althusser,

Foucault, Derrida, Lacan) whose theories of the subject (hollowed out by language) mime the subject's fate at the level of appearance-forms. The theory of commodity fetishism, I suggest, lays the basis for a Marxist theory of the subject, a historical and materialist account of the subject. I have tried to give some indications as to the fissures and contradictions of the subject under these conditions via the four concepts of immanence, splitting, inversion and repression. These constitute a differentiated unity of effects when the commodity becomes the subject and the subject becomes a commodity. But how far down does commodity fetishism/reification reach or penetrate? The transcendence of the social (immanence), the wrenching apart of what is a total social process (splitting, fragmentation), the dialectical flipping whereby a phenomenon turns into its opposite (inversion), and the necessary forgetting required to constitute the individual and collective self as a non-contradictory unity (repression) are confronted by the 'resistances' of the material world to its effective dematerialisation by value relations and the resulting crises which make it possible to grasp the real relations behind the fetishised appearance-forms. For much contemporary cultural theory, however, to talk of the real is a dangerous illusion or at best naive empiricism. On the other hand, without a sufficiently explicit and broad based social foundation for knowledge, the most radical theories are unable to ground their truth contents in anything other than a relativistic framework which leaves a more generalised basis for the emancipation of labour in the dustbin of history. It is to this question that we now turn.

8   Knowledge, Norms and Social Interests: Dilemmas for Documentary

If man draws all his knowledge, sensation, etc., from the world of the senses and the experience gained in it, the empirical world must be arranged so that in it man experiences and gets used to what is really human ... If correctly understood interest is the principle of all morals, man's private interest must be made to coincide with the interest of humanity ... If man is shaped by his surroundings, his surroundings must be made human.

Marx, *The Holy Family*

By virtue of the negativity that belongs to its nature each thing is linked with its opposite. To be what it *really* is it must become what it is not.

Marcuse, *Reason and Revolution*

The question of the impact of social interests on the explanatory power of knowledge is a central issue within the news, information and documentary traditions of the media. However, students of these signifying practices are bedevilled by the apparently irreconcilable antinomy that structures such media debates: the antinomy of objectivity and relativity. The problem with the claim of objectivity is that the role of language, culture and focalisation – in short the social situatedness of the cultural producer or consumer – in the construction of meaning is eradicated. Nothing short-circuits our critical faculties quicker than the claim that a text has acquired a serene *transcendence* of social influences that might have quietly shaped and limited lesser texts. This is one reason perhaps why the claim of objectivity tends to be associated with those institutions, such as the mainstream media, closest to dominant economic and political power blocs. The contrary claim, that there is no such thing as objectivity, that every statement, proposition or truth claim is relative, fragments communication into the merely subjective, into methodological individualism ('everyone has their own point of view') or relativism (postmodern style) – neither of which can provide the grounds for a theory of intersubjective communication (if everyone has their own point of view, how can we communicate with one another?) or a rationale for supporting alternative media practices such as Undercurrents. I have heard representatives of Undercurrents, the eco-video activists, attack the objectivity of the news in such terms – that all news has an agenda, or is biased; but this fails to explain why then we should accord what Undercurrents has to say with any greater veracity than a mainstream news programme. Any resolution to such an antinomy must start by arguing that while there is no such thing as *objectivity* (a disinterested position from which to speak) there is an objective world independent of conscious-ness 'out there', which media practices will be most able to deal with the more they speak from a position of the majority interests. The more social partiality (interests) represents the social majority (the majority, as we shall see, is not necessarily a quantitative calculation but a qualitative assessment of social location and interests), the greater the foundations for adequacy to the real. Conversely, the more social partiality represents minority exploitative interests, the greater the foundations for the production of ideology.

CLASS DIALECTICS AS A TRANSPOSABLE MODEL

What follows then is an exposition of the philosophical grounds for critically committed cultural practices and theories of practices. The theoretical apparatus which this book has mapped out – forces and class relations of production, mode of production, mode of devel-opment, media–industrial complex, the state, base–superstructure, ideology, commodity fetishism and reification – all have at their heart a normative argument for the emancipation of labour, for the free association of the producers. Marx insisted that this goal was inextricably tied to the generalisation of freedom throughout society. I want to offer the Marxist case for the grounding of social knowledge in the interests of labour in its struggle with capital in two overlap-ping ways. These class dialectics can be understood as both a *transposable model* in which the *form* of class struggle provides a template to other social and cultural movements, forces, agents and institutions; and as a *mediated causal determinant* on those others. Taking these together, as prototype or template of conflict and as a mediated determinant, we can start to excavate class from the other categories it is often buried deep inside. I have in mind here something close to what Fredric Jameson calls cognitive mapping.

This is Jameson's term for using class relations as 'allegorical grids' (1999:48–9) by which to decode various conflicts that may on the surface appear unrelated to class struggle. To take the labour–capital couplet as a mediated causal determinant on subcultures for example, we find, in their precarious living in the interstices of education and work, a complex dialectic between a struggle against the commodification of leisure (its resistance for example to transient fashion) and resistance to sporadic corporate interest and penetration, and certain inevitable dependencies on capital which the intense investment of identity *in* commodities (of dress, transport, music, etc.) brings.

The documentary maker/ethnographer of the mass culture/subculture tension will also learn something of the epistemological issues raised in their relation to their subject if they take class dialectics as a prototypical and transposable model. What class as a transposable model brings to the social researcher is a rich tradition of critical thinking about the dialectical relations between the social researcher/documentary maker on the one hand and the two poles of a whole range of dominant and subordinate positions (the master/slave dialectic as Hegel explored it) on the other (capital vs labour, mass culture vs subculture, men vs women, white vs black, West vs the Third World, Israeli vs Palestinians, city vs country, Christianity vs Paganism, reason vs superstition, work vs leisure, England vs the Celtic regions, society vs nature, and so on). We can identify four key characteristics of the class struggle as the prototypical form through which dominant/subordinate poles interact, and propose, cautiously and subject to revision depending on the concrete content of those poles, this dialectical form as a mapping mechanism.

1. Dominant and subordinate poles are in conflict with each other, necessarily so because the subordinate pole resists its subordination and the dominant pole seeks to reproduce its dominance within a given set of circumstances.

2. Dominant and subordinate poles are conflictual but also interdependent on each other, necessarily so because they are locked into a relationship in which each is the condition of the other's reproduction within a given set of circumstances. One area in which this insight has enriched cultural theory has been the whole question around the dynamic relations between self and other, or between any two terms which (necesssarily) mark some

difference or alterity between them. Each term relies on the other for its identity and any move or strategem by one is likely to cause some reciprocation, even if minute, by the other. So that, for example, if some agents of mass culture appropriate elements of a subculture, the latter tends to redefine its difference from the former with a new configuration of its own elements. Cultural theory has tended to lean overly heavily on the way positions rely on each other to construct their *differences*. This opens the way for the celebration of difference and plurality. But it has disguised the fact that if interdependence is responsible for the construction of difference, of boundary markers, interdependence also implies not only difference, but shared commonalities and assumptions. If two sides, for example, are in dispute over territory, then, underlying their antagonism is a shared assumption and agreement that the territory is important and significant. In other words, it takes some agreement to have a disagreement. The theorist most associated with trying to excavate the deeper consensual patterns underlying different positions is Jürgen Habermas. As we shall see, Habermas tries to orient social and cultural theory to the quality of the communication between speakers. In pointing to background patterns of consent which make difference and antagonism possible, he tries to orient us to the question of *intersubjectivity*, that is the subject-to-subject relations conducted through various linguistic, audio and visual communications. For a Habermasian influenced scholar such as Benhabib, intersubjectivity opens up a crucial realm of interpretive indeterminacy in the understanding of the meaning of actions and statements (1986:136). One can hardly deny her argument that Marxism has been very weak on this question of subject-to-subject relations, with the consequence that its commitment to political plurality (also a realm of interpretive indeterminacy) is rightly scrutinised and questioned by many non-Marxists. However, I will argue that Habermas' attempt to bracket off subject-to-object relations (traditionally Marxism's primary focus) tends to keep crucial aspects of the 'object', namely the capitalist mode of production, which powerfully shape the nature of our intersubjective relations with one another, pretty much in place.

3. Dominant and subordinate poles are internally divided, necessarily so because their conflict and their interdependence

penetrate into the heart of each pole. The crucial critical strategy which this gives rise to within Marxism is called *immanent critique*. Immanent critique works by revealing the self-contradictions of a social agent's actions, concepts or norms. It does not begin by imposing its own external criteria and find the action, concept or norm wanting. Instead it examines the ways an action thwarts an intention or leads to outcomes which undermine the agent of the action; it examines the way concepts or norms contradict one another or come into contradiction with the social relations they are embedded into. When, for example, the US government legitimises war in the name of peace, or first strike use of nuclear weapons in the name of defence, the immanent contradictions of the concepts and norms involved become farcically apparent. We shall explore this contradiction between concept/norm and actuality via Theodor Adorno's critique of identity thinking.

4. The dominant pole represents the conservative preservation of the dichotomy, the subordinate pole represents a position or perspective from which a new settlement that could overcome the contradictions structuring the dominant and subordinate pole might be developed. The latter does not entail, even in the instance of the prototype conflict, between capital and labour, the destruction of everything the dominant pole stands for or has achieved. Far from it, especially if the dominant pole is a category like 'society' (vs nature) or reason (vs the irrational). Instead the subordinate pole provides a clue for a way out of a structural blockage, a development of potentialities stiffled within the established polarities, an anticipation of a new settlement that would be a *synthesis* between the best elements of both poles. Thus even a post-capital society would be built on the back of the productive forces inherited from capital, as well as its cultural wealth and progressive political achievements (democracy, limited though it is in its present form).

These four characteristics, but particularly the fourth one, all raise important questions concerning the stance to be adopted by the social researcher/documentarist. The final characteristic could immediately be recuperated into that dominant media value, 'balance'. However, a synthesis is not the same as 'balance'. Balance implies that knowledge lies somewhere between two 'extremes'. It tends to leave the two poles exactly as they were and avoids a confrontation with the contradictions involved in the polarity. Balance is a much more passive and indecisive activity compared with the act of synthesis. Synthesis on the other hand requires an active investigation of foundations in order to select what is useful and discard what is regressive. It involves both a destructive and constructive process and it invokes a new formation on the basis of a coherent set of principles rather than hoping that a midway position between incompatible elements will do. Those principles might not be fully evident in either term of the polarity, which might need to be further mediated. For example, the widely observed polarity between commerce and spirituality could be mediated by another conflictual couplet, such as exchange value (the reduction of everything to a business proposition) and use-value (where something is valuable in relation to human needs outside and irrespective of the cash nexus). Above all, unlike balance, synthesis is not incompatible with aligning oneself with one pole or the other (depending on their content) and conducting the process of critique on *both poles from within one of them.*

THE OBJECTIVE OBJECT AND THE OBJECTIVE SUBJECT

Marxists belong to the philosophical tradition of realism which believes that there exists a world independent of our senses, our means and modes of apprehension and representation (Lovell 1983). It is this which Marxists refer to when they write of the 'objective' world or situation. As we saw in Chapter 6, there has been a strong idealist current within contemporary cultural theory which has pretty much absorbed this world independent of our senses back into discourse, signs, representation and the like. In doing so, the means by which knowledge can be generated about the world become logically impossible, since knowledge becomes *merely* the expression of social interests, none of which have any grounds for claiming a greater correspondence with the real than any others.

Now, I have suggested that Marxist epistemology grounds knowledge in social interests. But if this is all it did, then it would be indistinguishable from postmodern relativism. For Marxists, knowledge is not to be understood as merely the immediate expression of social interests in time or space (although neither can it be separated from social interests). Rather cognitions of the world are grounded in social interests and mediated by their spatio-temporal relations to this world that is independent of them. This 'world', the object world, is the outcome of the accumulated activities of subject-to-subject relations, which is why subject-to-object and subject-to-subject relations are inextricably entwined. No social interest exists in isolation. All social interests and the cognitions they generate about the world are mediated by other social interests. As we have seen from the prototype dialectical model outlined above, social agents are materially and culturally interdependent on other social agents with different locations within the social totality. The world is made up then of an accumulation of interests in social space with complex webs of interdependence and conflict linking them. It is for this reason that the relativist vision of a world of fragmented and non-commensurate discourses is deeply flawed. The object world is also independent of our modes of apprehension in a temporal sense in that it is the product of the accumulated activities of the generations who have come before us. We are born into a world and into its institutions (like the family, educational institutions, the market, the state, etc.) that are already up and running before we 'arrive' in them. Our dependence, as inheritors, on the prior activities of those who have come before us also gives a certain 'objectivity' to the world we find ourselves in. We can then legitimately speak of the *objectivity of the object (world)*.

However, this does not mean that there is a position or perspective on this objective world that *is objective*. To say that there is a world independent of *our* experiences of it and practical activities within it is not at all the same thing as arguing that *we* can be independent of that world, that we can rise above the social interests coursing through our social locations and identifications. Thus we can legitimately say that there is no such thing as an *objective subject*. Of course we can be critical of our social locations and culture, but that criticism in turn involves not the rising above of social interests *per se* but the mediation of our immediate social location by other social interests, via the intersubjective process of identification. Thus Marx criticised the interests of the intelligentsia and their academic/philosophical milieu which had also been his own social location as a student, via the interests and social location of the working class.

But we cannot bracket off from such subject-to-subject relations, subject-to-object relations, otherwise there are no good grounds for why some subjects of identification (George W. Bush, the Queen, the boss) are less preferable than others.

The belief in the possible *objectivity of the subject*, however, dominates the mainstream media. As Judith Lichtenberg argues, in defence of a version of this objectivity, 'Inextricably intertwined with truth, fairness, balance, neutrality, the absence of value judgements – in short, with the most fundamental journalistic values – objectivity is a cornerstone of the professional ideology of journalists in liberal democracies' (2000:238). Lichtenberg is here using the term ideology in its fairly neutral sense of 'ideas', although she is not uncritical of some versions of objectivity within the dominant media. She argues, for example, that journalists should not be afraid to question authority for fear of looking 'partisan': 'if facts are objective the objective investigator will not be neutral with respect to them' (2000:252). This is true but its limitation is that facts get mobilised within certain interpretive frameworks, while other frameworks (and their attendant facts) for questioning authority are not used.

Thus one problem with objectivity as an ideal is that it is simply not sophisticated enough to deal with the subtle means by which our own taken-for-granted assumptions, our own immediate and pressing cultural determinants, may shape our perceptions in ways that quietly bind us to unjust power complexes and blind us to the grievances and injustices of the oppressed. Take, for example, Kevin Macdonald's documentary *One Day in September* (2000 Sw/Ger/GB) which recounts the tragedy of the 1972 Munich Olympic Games. Eight members of the Palestinian Black September terrorist group took a number of Israeli athletes hostage. The incident ended in bloodshed and death for both the hostage takers and the hostages. The formal structure of the narrative in the first half hour appears to be 'balanced', alternating as it does between a focus on the Israeli athletes and Jamal Al-Hashey, one of the surviving terrorists. But it hardly takes a genius of semiotic analysis to see how the film quite clearly weighs towards the Israelis, the dominant pole in the conflict. It is their lives we learn about, their hopes, dreams, ambitions and characteristics. They are given a 'backstory', it is their narrative. While they are humanised, Jamal Al-Hashey provides the dramatic threat (complete with sinister music in the use of found footage and reconstructions). His discourse concentrates in recounting the planning behind and lead-up to the attack; he is defined in other words only by his actions as a terrorist. Crucially, where as the Israeli story is narrated with warmth and poignancy by Hollywood star Michael Douglas, this narration withdraws when Jamal Al-Hashey appears on screen, as if to say that Douglas' narration wants no association with this man.

In her defence of objectivity, Lichtenberg argues, against postmodern relativism, that people from different 'cultures' can engage in conversation. Our 'worldviews are not hermetic: others can get in and we can get out' (2000:243). This is an essential point which derives from the objectivity of the object (world). We can 'get out' because different world views are confronted by the same processes and phenomena whose independence from the way we see forces us to adapt, reformulate, dialogue with others and so forth. But because Lichtenberg does not distinguish between this and the objectivity of the subject, the latter is smuggled in. In fact this language of objectivity works to the detriment of either identifying with those outside our own social location or critically interrogating our own social location. The two are often closely connected which again makes the subjective, representational dimension so crucial. For what the media often do is block up our capacities for productive intersubjective *recognitions* with those whose interests, struggles and needs, while not identical with our own, nevertheless impinge on us; in an interdependent world, their well-being becomes our well-being.

Kevin Macdonald, in responding to criticism of the film by the Palestinian writer Edward Said, declared that the film was fair, that he had no case to answer and that it was a 'humanist not political' film.[1] *One Day in September* is a classic example of how simple-minded beliefs in objectivity short-circuit our critical faculties. Anyone from the West thinking about or representing the conflict between the Israelis and Palestinians would need, as a basic precondition to understanding the situation, to think very carefully and critically about how the West has traditionally represented the conflict, how the West has been complicit in causing and sustaining the conflict and how these power relations seep invisibly into signifying practices. Recalling the concept of synthesis from our dialectical model, it is not simply a question of identifying with the Palestinians, since the Palestinians are not a homogeneous, unified bloc, any more than the Israelis are. It is rather a question of *critical* identification which has to make certain evaluations of Palestinian politics, strategies, groups, interests, and so on, within that overall identification with an oppressed group (the subordinate pole of the polarity). Nor would the Western documentarist simply be rejecting everything from their own social and cultural location, since the 'West' too is not a homogeneous, unified bloc. Recalling the earlier argument concerning the dialectical transposable model and the way the two poles in any conflict are not self-identical but internally divided, it may be a case of taking certain concepts cherished by the West (and Israel), such as nation-states, and asking why the West is effectively happy for this particular form and norm of human organisation, so central to the political, economic and cultural life of modern capitalism, to be denied to the Palestinians. The sort of critical subjectivity I am trying to formulate here has affinities with what Paul Willemen describes, in relation to Third Cinema, as 'that sense of non-belonging, non-identity with the culture one inhabits' as a precondition for 'social intelligibility' (1989:28). It is not a question of being completely 'other' to one's social and cultural location, but mobilising a series of dialectical identifications and reciprocal critiques.

If believing in the objectivity of the subject is problematic however, Lichtenberg certainly skewers many of the arguments of the cultural relativists who destroy the objectivity of the object. Their reduction of knowledge to immediate social interests destroys any 'standpoint from which to adjudicate between conflicting accounts' (Lichtenberg 2000:240) including *their own* critique of the media. For to even complain about the bias of the media makes no sense 'except against the background of some actual or possible contrast, some more accurate statement or better description' (Lichtenberg 2000:242). The really crucial question, however, is from which standpoint may a 'more accurate statement' be made and assessed? Lichtenberg's defence of a version of the objective subject means that she must fall back on formal logic and methodological procedures as the guarantee of adequacy: 'We get more evidence, seek out other sides of the story, check our instruments, duplicate our experiments, re-examine our chain of reasoning' (2000:242). Of course the development of such criteria as empirical evidence and internal logical consistency are huge gains for reason which historically the bourgeoisie's practical activities helped to promote back in the eighteenth century and which we would not lightly relinquish today. But, as any spoof documentary implicitly tells us, there are limits to the conventions of formal and methodological logic. How would such an appeal provide a basis for explaining why, when confronted with competing claims, both of which can point to some formal logic, consistency and empirical proofs, we judge one to be more adequate than another? Facts, for example, can often be agreed on. It is their interpretation which divides. The appeal to formal reason is akin to the claim that people are intelligent just because they speak the Queen's English. In reality to understand the world often requires adjudicating between official documents or discourses, which have a formal rationality, and the diffuse vernacular cognitions of the marginalised, which generate greater understanding of the world because of their social locations *not* their adherence, or lack of it, to formal logic.

IDENTITY AND NEGATION

Identification, either with aspects of our immediate social and cultural location or across 'boundaries' to other social agents and cultures, involves an alignment between ourselves and that which we identify with, an alignment that also takes place through the indispensable medium of language and/or some signifying system. For example, we align the concept of 'historical grievance' or 'terrorists' with the referent 'Palestinians' according to our identifications on this and other issues. In *Negative Dialectics*, Adorno noted that thinking inevitably posits an identity between concept (or representation) and the real. Some unity between thought and the real is not only inevitable but also desirable, since without it there could be no social order that we would recognise. However, Adorno warned against the compulsion towards what he called *identity thinking*. This is characterised by the assumption that the unity or identity between thought and the real has achieved a consummate snugness in the here and now. If, for example, the Palestinians achieved their goal, the formation of a Palestinian state, and we then took that referent and made it fully identical to the concept of 'freedom', we would indeed be in the grip of identity thinking, as much as if we believed that 'freedom' and the reality of Western capitalism were identical. For Adorno, the purpose of dialectical thinking is 'to pursue the inadequacy of thought and thing' (1973:153). Adorno wants to prise open the gap between thought and thing, to see how the former 'lags behind itself as soon as we apply it empirically' (1973:151). In other words, if to think and to identify are closely interwoven, to think *critically* is to give a concept 'a turn toward non-identity', and this 'is the hinge of negative dialectics' (Adorno 1973:12). Contradiction 'indicates the untruth of identity, the fact that the concept does not exhaust the thing conceived' (Adorno 1973:5). One aesthetic mode which explores this gap between concept and thing as tragicomedy is satire. For example, the short film *The Luckiest Nut in the World* (Emily James II 2002 GB) combines animation, documentary footage and the musical genre to illuminate the yawning contradiction between what the discourse of neo-liberalism imposes on Third

World countries as a route out of poverty and the actual outcomes, which turn out to be more poverty. Our narrator is a singing American peanut, complete with boots, guitar and ten-gallon hat. The peanut has had his conscience pricked (and is thus a representative of the Western side of the anti-capitalist movement) by the evident inequities between his pampered and protected situation and the fate of Third World nut producers who have seen their industries implode after following World Bank and International Monetary Fund advice to open up their markets to international competition. The immanent critique of a concept like 'trade liberalisation' is also then a critique and reworking of the generic materials of mass culture whose 'innocence' and naivety are juxtaposed (with comic and tragic effect) with brutal realities. As Walter Benjamin famously noted, cultural documents of a civilisation, whether they be high art or 1950s newsreels, are also (disguised) documents of social barbarism. The task of critique is therefore 'to brush history against the grain' (Benjamin 1999b:248).

Adorno's critique of identity thinking has some similarities with the post-structuralist position, in which the concept of difference, rather than negation, serves as a means to call into question the relationship between representation and the real. However, there are fundamental differences between the Adorno of *Negative Dialectics* and contemporary cultural relativists (Dews 1995). Unlike post-structuralists, Adorno is unwilling to give up the ideals secreted in a concept even when the gap between the concept and its referent is laughably huge. Dialectics, he writes, 'means to break the compulsion to achieve identity, and to break it by means of the energy stored up in that compulsion and congealed in its objectifications' (1973:157). For example, the Walt Disney film *Lilo and Stitch* (Dean DeBlois and Chris Sanders III 2002 US) turns on the central normative ideal summed up in the Hawaiian word *ohana*, meaning nobody gets left behind or forgotten. A critique of the film would point out the non-identity between the normative concept and an empirical reality of capitalism which is premised precisely on forgetting people and leaving them behind (and even within the film, there are half-repressed clues as to this non-identity). At the same time, such a critique would recognise the 'energy stored up' in the concept of *ohana* and seek to transfigure that energy, cracking it open from the 'congealed' objectifications of the family and ground it in general social practices. Thus Adorno is looking to develop a dialectic between identity and negation, between being, or what is, and its incompleteness and/or dissolution as a prelude to a new configuration. Relativism, however, seeks the one-sided non-dialectical championing of difference which makes meaningful social solidarity difficult, to say the least.

If objectivity is the typical fallacy into which the mainstream media worker tips headlong, relativity, 'negativity' and the sheer celebration of 'difference' constitute the typical trap sprung, within the intellectual divisions of labour, for the academic and philosopher. Adorno thought that the 'tenacious vigor' of such relativising subjectivism

> is drawn from a misdirected opposition to the status quo, from opposition to its thingness. In relativizing or liquefying that thingness, philosophy believes it to be above the supremacy of goods, and above the form of subjective reflection on that supremacy, the reified consciousness. (1973:189)

We have already seen how structuralism and post-structuralism summarise this particular dichotomy: the former conceiving language as a fixed object independent of human agency, the latter attempting to 'liquefy' it in an act of 'misdirected opposition'. Underlying the epistemological split between objectivity and relativity is a philosophical split concerning what constitutes *critical* thinking. With *One Day in September* we see how leaning towards objectivity short-circuits our critical capacities in relation to our social location and its determining influences on our modes of apprehension. The relativists then, confronted with this evidently *uncritical* position, seek to 'liquefy' the thingness of the world and its unthinking internalisation of its norms. But – and here's the rub – the radical relativisation of reified objectivity escapes one aspect of bourgeois thinking, only to immediately collapse into its other side: the dissolution of the socialised basis of any activity, theoretical, political, ethical and practical, which could *challenge* this reified structure. For example, the United States currently spends 396 billion dollars on military arms while millions of its own citizens have no access to affordable healthcare. To question this distribution of resources requires tacit alignments with the needs of the poor and with norms which place those needs as higher than the needs of the military–industrial complex. All knowledge – if it is authentic knowledge and not faith or dogma – must have grounds for its qualification and negation. But grounding that critical provisionality in language (as the relativists do) is a coded grounding in the social interests of the intelligentsia *as the intelligentsia*, that is cut off from the more universal potentialities that lie dormant in the commodification of their labour. The grounds for the foundations (not guarantee) of knowledge (and its limits) should be explicitly located in the social interest with the broadest social base, that is in the historically specified meaning of structures rather than (exclusively) structures of meaning.

ŽIŽEK AND THE REAL

The German philosopher Jürgen Habermas is well known for his opposition to the postmodern turn towards relativity and the celebration of difference. His book *The Philosophical Discourse of Modernity*, produced in the early 1980s, is a sustained critique of the contradictions of various philosophers, such as Nietzsche, Heidegger, Bataille, Derrida and Foucault, who have tried to champion difference, relativity, the 'irrational' (sheer power, madness, repressed desire, linguistic indeterminacy) to bring some sort of disorder to the oppressive objectivity of the social order. During the 1990s, the work of Slavoj Žižek has exemplified the current emphasis in cultural theory towards a radical provisionality of knowledge that liquefies the grounds on which knowledge is constituted and undermines the possibility for making any sustained alignments with any particular social agents of social change. However, Žižek does occupy a curious position since he has been highly critical of postmodernism, multiculturalism and identity politics, largely it would seem because they do in fact try and reconcile their relativising philosophical underpinnings with some identification and alignment with certain social agents and political forces (Homer 2001). Žižek in effect pushes the question of relativity to its logical conclusion, but does not thereby escape its essentially contradictory nature. The concept central to Žižek's radical and perpetual negation of actually existing realities and their representations is, paradoxically, the Real. Žižek's concern is to resist the allure of ideology and sustain his (and our own) critical faculties. The motive cannot be faulted, but the method can be.

> [D]oes not the critique of ideology involve a privileged place, somehow exempted from the turmoils of social life, which enable some subject-agent to perceive the very hidden mechanism that regulates social visability and non-visability? Is not the claim that

we can accede to this place the most obvious case of ideology? (Žižek 1995:3)

In acknowledging the difficulty of stepping out from ideology, Žižek argues that it is only possible by refusing to identify with a 'positively determined reality' (1995:17). Thus, unlike Adorno, Žižek is conflating identification and alignment with identity-thinking. The position from which ideology critique is practised '*must remain empty, it cannot be occupied by any positively determined reality* – the moment we yield to this temptation, we are back in ideology' (Žižek 1995:17). Ideology critique is purely a negation of what is, never identification with *any* aspect of what is. This 'empty place' is what Žižek means by the Real – the concept he draws from Lacan. The Lacanian concept of the Real is precisely that which resists symbolisation, it is 'the void that makes reality incomplete/inconsistent, and the function of every symbolic matrix is to conceal this' (Žižek 2001:217–18).

The strength and appeal of this position is that it calls for never stilling our critical capacities in favour of projecting onto some favoured social movement or representation a completeness and consistency which it does not have. If a particular symbolic field, for example, a subculture, constitutes its identity as outsider, then a typical Žižekean move might be to reveal the extent to which this is a romantic concealment of how safely it is *inside* the social (Žižek would say, symbolic) order. If a particular symbolic order constitutes itself as self-determining – this is central to virtually all national identities – then the mischievous Žižekean move demonstrates that its Real is its hidden determination by exogenous determinants. In the hands of Žižek, the concept of the Real certainly allows for some ingenious dialectical inversions. However, by making his point of reference not 'reality' but the Real – the repressed – Žižek underestimates and undermines the possibilities of knowing and representing the social order; he makes knowledge the province of the highly specialised decoding skills of an elite and he lapses back into an ideology very familiar with the intelligentsia: the refusal of alignment with a collective social agent (other than the intelligentsia) – since that amounts to a 'positively determined reality'. Despite then the claim that there is no such thing as neutrality, no escaping the 'turmoils of social life', Žižek does imply a momentary, transient and elusive ascension to precisely just such a place every time he occupies the 'empty' place of the Real; for what is such a place unless it is emptied of all social situatedness?

A further problem with the Real at a normative rather than epistemological level, is that its negativity is based only on negation; its political and ethical compass is thus relative to that which it is seeking to undermine. Thus the Real could sanction a whole variety of politics including terrorism (I'm not suggesting Žižek himself does though). Terrorism disturbs liberal democratic capitalism by turning the invisible violence of everyday life which is its constitutive foundation into an explicit spectacle of violence that contravenes the liberal democratic symbolisations of itself as rational, civilised, fair and tolerant. In the case of *One Day in September* the Palestinian terrorists function as the Real in another related sense. Because Palestine does not officially exist, the Palestinians could only ever have been interlopers to the Olympic Games whose athletes compete as representatives of nation-states, the very identity and institutional apparatus denied to them. However, this symbolic critique (as with the terrorist attack on the World Trade Center towers), while subversive, hardly provides the ethical rationale for the act and neither does it make it a viable political strategy.

HABERMAS, KNOWLEDGE AND SOCIAL CONFLICT

The central target for the cultural relativist traditions critiqued by Habermas has been reason itself. For reason and rationality (the axial principles of the documentary) have been the watchwords of the social order's triumphant progress over all opposition since the Enlightenment. In the previous chapter we saw that rationality, knowledge and science have been integrated into the homogenising logic of value relations. However, the close relation between capitalist economics and formal rationality is severed to varying degrees by the relativists, since too close a link would logically imply some alignment with capital's potential antithesis: labour. Whatever social alignments postmodern relativists have gestured towards (the hybrid migrant is a favoured one at the moment), labour as a social agent has been comprehensively dismissed. Habermas for his part does not deny the oppressive uses to which reason has been put, but, like Adorno, he does not want to give up on the concept, but rather seeks through 'processes of self-reflection or of enlightened practice' (1987:103) to fulfil its liberating potential.

His central point is that, despite themselves, the 'anti-rationalists' operate, necessarily, within the parameters of the reason they seek to overturn. At the heart of the totalising critiques of reason practised by various writers lies a 'performative contradiction'. By what 'reason' can reason be comprehensively denounced? In the case of Foucault, for example, the argument is that the validity claims of a discourse are entirely confined to the life and parameters of that discourse. If that is true, however, any *study* of such a discourse must necessarily undercut its own validity or truth claims concerning other 'truth-regimes' (Habermas 1987:279). This contradiction undermines those gestures towards social alignment with oppressed groups made by the intelligentsia (prisoners, for example, in Foucault's case). Thus Habermas is arguing that the relativist denial of any possibility of grounding norms in subject–object relations presupposes those subject–object relations because they make propositions as to their true nature (namely, that the truth cannot be known, that discourse is all powerful, etc.).

For Habermas then, the relativists have failed to escape what he calls the philosophy of the subject. This is the tradition of thought which is overly obsessed with subject–object relations (as are even the relativists in their efforts to overturn a reified object world by the power of discourse). In its bourgeois variant it is fuelled by a powerful individualism that fantasises that it is autonomous from fellow human beings and conceives its own identity and self-consciousness in an aggressively domineering relation to them (they are reduced to objects). It is precisely intersubjectivity or sociality which Habermas will want to foster and sustain, against such relations of domination, with his own recommendations concerning a philosophy of communication. Subject-centred reason by contrast kills 'off dialogical relationships' and 'transforms subjects, who are monologically turned in upon themselves, into objects for one another, and only objects' (Habermas 1987:246).

Habermas' solution to the problem of subject-centred reason is to both break decisively with some of the terms of the discussion, and yet remain on much of the same terrain as his postmodern antagonists. The reduction of others to objects derives from the subject's desire to control and dominate the object world. '[T]he paradigm of the knowledge of objects has to be replaced by the paradigm of mutual understanding between subjects capable of speech and action' (Habermas 1987:295–6). In other words the relationship between concept and referent is less important than the conditions in which society constructs the means in which we debate differences. Habermas wants to shift communication away from the 'fixation on the fact-mirroring function of language' (1987:312) or, on the relativist's side, the failure of language to reflect anything other than immediate conditions and interests. Habermas' paradigm of communicative reason places emphasis on 'the performative attitude of participants in interaction, who co-ordinate their plans for action by coming to understanding about something in the world' (1987:296). In one sense then Habermas is following through the postmodern logic by downgrading the question of the importance of truth claims. Instead he seeks to locate rationality in the public mechanisms we have for discussion, debate and conflict resolution, in respecting differences but finding the means by which any antagonisms which they generate can be dissipated.

This is possible because the referential context of any interlocutors includes 'the unquestioned context for processes of mutual understanding' (Habermas 1987:314). No matter how degraded the content of a communication, no matter how antagonistic an exchange or how unequal the context in which it takes place (corporate and state dominance of the means of communication for example), there is, Habermas argues, a latent or embryonic impetus for rational dialogue in which agreement and mutuality can be detected. Habermas thus 'conceives of intersubjective understanding as the telos inscribed into communication in ordinary language' (1987:311). Take, for example, the pernicious and racist media discourse on immigration, now widespread throughout Europe. The explicit or implicit justification often given for fortifying borders against migrants is that the nation has finite resources which are scarce and which new (often poor) people are seen to be a drain on. However problematic this argument is, it at least takes place on a terrain, namely that of the question of resources, which permits a radical alternative discourse to engage with it, in order then to ask how resources are generated, how resources are distributed and which social forces are responsible for artificial scarcity. If the racist media discourse on immigration were purely incommensurable with a radical critique of such a discourse, then a radical critique would hardly be possible. While it is true that Habermas' concept of communicative rationality can spread the notion of consensus so wide that 'the essential condition of politics – antagonistic interest – disappears' (Aronowitz 1981:53) conversely it is clear that even antagonism requires some common ground.

Habermas thus tries to outflank the postmodernists by driving down deeper and wider than them into the structure of meaning (communication) and emphasising the taken-for-granted assumptions shared by antagonists. This contrasts with those postmodernists who tend to argue that the structure of meaning is characterised by the fragmentation and mutual incomprehension that result from what Lyotard called the proliferation of 'language games' (Norris 1992:70–81). Thus Habermas provides an elegant solution to the problem of reconciling universal norms tacitly encoded in communication with a recognition of difference and plurality.

We can practically apply Habermas' concept of consensual patterns lying behind religious, cultural, national and other differences to a critique of mainstream news and media representations. For example, wherever there are conflicts between communities of interest, such as between Catholics and Protestants in Northern Ireland, or Palestinians and Israelis in the Middle East, the news tends to only ever find spokespeople who speak for and recognise the legitimacy of claims attached to their 'own' communities. The idea that people from one constituency could recognise the claims of another constituency seems almost impossible to contemplate for the mainstream media. John Pilger's documentary *Palestine is Still the Issue* (2002), which incurred the anger of conservative Jews, was unusual for suggesting lines of consensus across the divided communities. Pilger interviewed an Israeli historian, an ex-soldier and a Israeli man whose teenage daughter was killed by a Palestinian suicide bomber. The moral courage of the last interviewee in particular stands out, for despite his grievous loss he could still ask *why* someone could do such a self-destructive act, wonder at the complicity of the Israeli state in generating such hatred, and recognise the legitimacy of Palestinian grievances. Articulating 'horizontal' lines of consensus and intersubjective recognition across conflicting constituencies also reveals the internal disagreements within the constituencies which the mainstream news agenda tends to present as a homogeneous bloc composed of a 'vertical' consensus in conflict with an equally homogeneous bloc. *Palestine is Still the Issue* was, however, screened at 11 p.m. on ITV, drawing an audience of around 1 million. It could perhaps have drawn six to eight times that number if it had been given a peak time slot. The sort of economic and political forces pushing this representation to the margins of the schedule have been discussed elsewhere in this book. The problem with Habermas' argument, to invoke Adorno's negative dialectics, is whether the non-identity between the concept of communicative reason and the actual organs for public debate that we have can be bridged *within* the capitalist mode of production.

Habermas' political position is sometimes hard to identify for it is ambiguous, complex and contradictory. He is regarded as a left philosopher, but whether his philosophy legitimises 'fashioning a participatory socialist democracy' as Terry Eagleton suggests (1991:130) seems questionable. To decode the politics of Habermas' philosophy and work out its practical implications, we might remember his earlier work, *The Structural Transformation of the Public Sphere*, which not only charted the rise and fall of the bourgeois public sphere, but also invested heavily in it. Habermas defines the bourgeois public sphere as 'conceived above all as the sphere of private people come together as a public' (1996:27). Such a definition may be appropriate for the bourgeois public sphere, but it should be noted that it screens out the collective (class) dimension of 'private' citizens and the antagonistic conflict between different collective forces. Indeed in *Structural Transformation* Habermas virtually equates the *collective* interests and bodies of the working class with the collective bodies and practices of the bourgeoisie (monopolies, cartels, business alliances) in his attack on the forces which put paid to the early 'heroic' bourgeois public sphere (1996:176) This hostility to collectivities whatever their class nature makes it unsurprising to find Habermas evaluating the embryonic workers public sphere which a working-class press was beginning to foster in the early nineteenth century as inferior to the bourgeois public sphere (1996:168). In *The Philosophical Discourse of Modernity*, written some two decades later, it is clear that the bourgeois definition of the public sphere is still the only definition Habermas is willing to countenance.

To put it bluntly, Habermas wants to retain the capitalist mode of production, but seeks to build up the organs of public communication (in the superstructure) that would ameliorate the conflicts which that mode of production gives rise to. In this sense Habermas has in no way broken with the bourgeois subject of reason, despite his emphasis on intersubjectivity. On the contrary, his philosophical architecture is designed to keep its deep material basis intact. Like the postmodernists', Habermas' explanation gets no further than the way we use language, that is its normative judgements concern the structure of meaning while bracketing off the meaning of structures. For Habermas, it is because we do not sufficiently mediate our knowledge and actions through the consensual potential of inter-subjective communication, but foreshorten and distort it by prematurely wanting to nail down what we know about the external world, make true statements and implement plans on the basis of those statements, that we suffer from a bad case of what he calls cognitive reductionism. For Habermas reason is defined not only by the power 'of representing states of affairs' (1987:311) but also by the qualitative nature of speech or communication; *how* we communicate is as important as *what* we communicate. But this is hardly earth-shattering stuff. The complex relationship between how and what, or form and content has been central to Marxian and other debates around aesthetics for a very long time (see Taylor 1988). And these debates did not, as Habermas seems to want to do, bracket the what off from the how. The political effect of separating the 'what' off from communicative reason is to in fact leave the 'what' – the dominant social relations responsible for conflict and impoverished forms of intersubjective mutuality – exactly as it was, and concentrate on dealing, somewhat therapeutically, with its after-effects.

Habermas thus associates the 'what' of communication, its propositional content, with cognitive-instrumentalism, and the 'how' with our moral and aesthetic sensibilities. In Habermas' model the subject is constituted as the individual subject with its own *private* interests who comes to the table with its cognitive instrumental one-to-one (subject-to-object) views of the world, but has these modified and tempered by the 'how' dimensions of communicative reason, which work to bind these private interests into some form of community, sociality or intersubjectivity.

In other words bourgeois private interests, their instrumental mastery over nature and labour, can be separated from the processes that will civilise these necessary social relations, binding them into intersubjective, communal responsibilities by language. Thus, for Habermas, the realm of material production can be co-ordinated

> by way of an *impoverished* and *standardized* language that coordinates functionally specialised activities – for instance, the production and distribution of goods and services – without burdening social integration with the expense of risky and uneconomical processes of mutual understanding. (1987:350–51)

This is a highly conservative defence of the priorities of capital accumulation which should not be 'burdened' with such uneconomical niceties as developing democracy in the workplace ('mutual understanding') but requires only the impoverished and standardised subjectivity required of work drones beavering away within hierarchical social relations and divisions of labour. For Habermas there can be no question of grounding any complex understanding of knowledge and reason in the activities of human labour since he conceives it entirely within the parameters of bourgeois philosophy as merely abstract labour, necessarily and irreducibly instrumental. Once the realm of production is conceived as *necessarily* instrumental, there can be no question of grounding the normative content of modernity in social praxis. Marxism itself, he argues,

> screens out of the validity spectrum of reason every dimension except those of truth and efficiency. Accordingly, what is learned ... can only accumulate in the development of the forces of production. With this productivist conceptual strategy, the normative content of modernity can no longer be grasped. (1987:320)

Admittedly, that now virtually extinct political dinosaur, Stalinism – with its prioritisation of catching up with the West – does or rather did conform to this model. But Stalinism, despite borrowing the rhetoric of Marxism, was always more bourgeois than revolutionary. To be sure one can find elements of productivism in Lenin and Gramsci, but any authentic Marxism cannot be assimilated to the productivist paradigm. For Marx and Marxism, increasing the forces of production provides only the essential *foundations* for the normative content of modernity – meeting social needs. However, the normative content of a Marxian modernity does not reside in increasing the productive forces *per se* but in developing the free association of producers, that is in emancipated social relations.

For Habermas then, the capitalist mode of production is an untranscendable datum and thus intersubjectivity which arises from the co-operative ethos of communicative action must be grafted *post-festum* onto a social order with a fundamentally antagonistic base. For Habermas, while it is unthinkable to develop modes of sociality, co-operation and intersubjectivity at the point of production, it is perfectly reasonable to expect that they can be successfully reconstructed elsewhere, through media and communication systems. Within the Habermasian model the subject is divided up between a realm which has to be pragmatically accepted as given and over which they can exercise little in the way of moral autonomy, and a realm of relative freedom (here communicative reason) where the subject can be reunited with their conscience and practical agency.

Can this model really be an advance on that of base–superstructure? Communicative reason for Habermas ultimately appears to be an intrinsic property of language. I argued in Chapter 6 that the deep structures of rationality in communication were grounded not in language as an autonomous entity but in our modes of practical social intercourse, interdependence and co-operation required for the reproduction of the human species on progressively higher levels of social surplus. It is this sort of grounding which the base–superstructure model sensitises us to. It also warns us against expecting aspects of the superstructure to work in ways diametrically opposed to the realm of social production. Habermas' model can hardly explain how social interests subordinated at the level of the mode of production will be able to access the realm of communicative reason on anything like equal terms with those interests which dominate the mode of production. Ditto for all the other forms of oppression complexly interwoven with class exploitation. Nor can Habermas' model explain what happens when economic power and political power refuse to recognise the superiority of the 'unforced force of a better insight' (Habermas 1987:305), or how one is to resolve fundamentally conflicting interests, such as the drive to accumulate wealth for a tiny minority of people at the expense of the majority, and the costs of such a drive to the environment. Above all the desire for intersubjective recognition, for reciprocity and mutuality between the two poles of capital and labour must necessarily diminish the capacities for intersubjective recognition within labour and other social identities struggling to emancipate themselves. One can appropriate Habermas to radical political ends by drawing the concept of communicative reason into such struggles. Radical aesthetic practices such as Third Cinema work precisely to develop such intra-class or inter-group intersubjectivities (a process which crucially involves the *how* as well as the what) of mutuality, recognition and sociality, drawing divided and separate groups into webs of knowledge, understanding, recognition and solidarity with each other on the basis of common interests as they confront, from their own mediated positions, the same multifaceted foe: capital and its institutions (Wayne 2001).

THE STANDPOINT OF LABOUR

When Marx identified the working class, labour, the proletariat, as the basis for overthrowing capitalism, his chosen social agent still represented a tiny proportion, in world terms, of the working population. To understand our relationship to that historical moment, we will have to differentiate between the terms we use to name this social agent and see the working class, labour and the proletariat not as interchangeable terms, but as representing a historical trajectory which broadly correlates to the past, the present and the future, although not in any simple linear manner. Rather all three are always simultaneously in play. Marx placed his wager on the future historical relevance of the working class not on quantitative criteria, but on the basis of qualitative ones: namely, that their objective location in the social relations of production gave them both the practical possibilities and incentives to know and change the world. Although the bourgeoisie sit at the helm of an economic system that extends in all directions, its position as a *minority* class and as an *exploiting* class within this system of production, imposes structural limits on its consciousness. As Andrew Feenberg puts it: 'for a class to be able to know the truth about its society, it must be, quite simply, in its interests to do so' (1980:159). Labour is installed in the heart of the production process, selling its labour power for a wage. Being simultaneously a commodity and a producer of commodities, labour occupies a social location from which it can grasp, in consciousness, the social totality *if* it strains towards the practical confrontation with its antithesis, capital. In the absence of that practical confrontation, labour sinks back into the commodity form, and consciousness correspondingly becomes narrower, more parochial as intersubjectivity is truncated in spatial and temporal terms; political consciousness (which is both a subject-to-subject relation and subject-to-object relation) goes into hibernation. Yet no matter how dimmed the antithesis between labour and capital may become in the consciousness and practice of the former, the latter's ceaseless drive to accumulate grinds on and into labour's texture of life, and, inevitably, periodically brings renewed confrontation at various scales of intensity. Although Adorno saw only critical theory and avant-garde aesthetics as the province of negative dialectics (Lunn 1984:240), and regarded the working class as fully integrated into a totally 'administered' society, labour is the self-divided, contradictory category that lives Adorno's dialectic between being and negation; as it produces itself safely within the parameters of capital, it negates what Marx called its *species being*, those normative ideals of autonomy, creativity and participation; as it struggles against capital, it struggles to negate not only what opposes it but its own identity as a class subject which has inscribed within it all the muck which ages of oppression have left.

A mature class consciousness for the dominated class was characterised by Lukács as one which strives to overcome the reified separation of the social totality into autonomous levels and practices. It brings production and consumption (routinely forced apart in recent discourses by the notion that 'producer interests' and consumers are two different species) into some mediated alignment, while drawing the disavowed connections between economics, politics, culture, the local and the global, which are all routinely fragmented and subdivided in the newspaper for example. Capitalism is of course a society constituted by mediations, but those mediations are asymmetrical and prone to dysfunctional crisis because the linkages and interconnections which hold society together turn on fundamental antagonisms (Mészáros 1995). A post-capital society would seek to develop symmetrical mediations and it would be characterised by developing, rather than stultifying, those elements within our present society which are striving towards a mode of practice and consciousness more orientated to the ethics of resource reciprocity and the issues of social justice which arise from our developing interconnectivity.

When Marx identified the working class as the central agency of social change, it was, precisely because of its relatively tiny numbers, a distinctly recognisable group, with precise geographical and industrial locations and clear identifiable cultural characteristics. But, while the term 'working class' still has some sociological and political significance, the generalisation of the wage relation, across nations, across 'classes' and occupations as they are ranked by sociologists, across ethnicities and the sexes, has radically transformed what that term used to cover. At the same time, across the political spectrum, the 'old' working class have retained a residual presence, as nostalgia for the left and as a reminder to the right that history, apparently, belongs to them. I prefer the term labour then because it is rather less encrusted with these cultural connotations and the sociological corruptions of the term 'working class', which would have us believe that white-collar jobs are somehow outside the dynamics of wage-labour commodification. Without disregarding the material and cultural differentials between them (in other words their mediated relations between each other and capital), radical cultural workers who identify with those suffering and struggling at the sharper end of exploitation and oppression can route that identification through their own experiences because of the frustrations and limitations which capital imposes on their own creative activities. It might be objected that the term 'labour' is too inclusive, failing to provide the necessary distinctions between senior managers for example, who after all earn a wage, and the workers below them. *Yet the ontology of labour is its collective, interdependent sociality.* The more labour is hierarchically organised with unequal powers and wage differentials, the more the labour of those who personify such inequalities represents the interests and logic of capital which, although it is contradictory and self-divided – it after all relies on and promotes, despite itself, sociality – will never escape its necessary compulsion to arbitrarily thwart and distort sociality and the ethics which interdependence implies.

The difficulties which the question of social interests and their relation to knowledge have caused many commentators, even those sympathetic to Marxism, are well illustrated in Bhikhu Parekh's book *Marx's Theory of Ideology.* Parekh's criticisms of the idea that Marx or Marxism aligns itself with, speaks or writes from the standpoint of labour are useful because they clarify what the formulation *cannot* mean if it is to sustain the critical provisionality of truth claims. Parekh argues that, on logical grounds, the idea that a social theorist gains something by studying society from a class point of view is incoherent:

> From what class point of view is the thesis advanced that society must be studied from a class point of view? If from the standpoint of a particular class, it obviously cannot claim universal validity. And if it is to claim universal validity, it cannot be advanced from a specific class point of view. (1982:171)

As we have seen, Marx identified the working class as the bearer of human emancipation because qualitatively, that is in terms of its position within the social structure, it represented the broadest social base and thus it could claim, not universal validity, but a universal *potentiality.* The concept of potentiality introduces temporality and on the one hand implies that there are objective social conditions which make certain desirable goals at least possible, but, at the same time, insofar as these are potentialities yet to be achieved, installs into the heart of the social agent a gap between what they are and what they could be. It is in that gap that critical provisionality installs itself, reconciling social solidarity with critique of the selfsame agents to whom the individual is aligned. The term proletariat can be used precisely to articulate this provisionality and potentiality. It has been usefully defined by Stephen Perkins as a 'politico-social category whose reality is in a state of becoming' (1993:169). Thus grounding knowledge in the standpoint of the working class/labour/the proletariat does not at all mean (as Parekh seems to think it means) either (a) simply reflecting and amplifying their experiences, opinions and values, whatever their merits; in other words, becoming a propagandist, or (b) restricting oneself to the experiences and knowledge of labour (Marx argued that labour had to reconfigure the philosophical, cultural and material inheritance provided by the bourgeoisie).

One can reverse the charge of circularity concerning the status of knowledge and the expression of point of view, back onto Parekh's own position. For from what *class* point of view can one judge that the working class 'point of view' is limited and partial?

> As a scientist Marx was not a class theorist but a 'free agent of thought'. He aimed to study the capitalist mode of production and human history from the most comprehensive and self-critical point of view possible. Accordingly he studied them not from the proletarian point of view, but from the standpoint of the social whole, critically constructed out of all the standpoints available to him, including the proletarian. (Parekh 1982:175)

Here we see the fear that the social theorist (or documentary maker) compromises their free agency of thought if they ground their knowledge claims in the social situation of a particular group of agents. But Parekh's answer to this – that Marx wrote from the standpoint of the social whole – turns Marx into a classic liberal figure, judiciously seeing things 'in the round' and balancing between conflicting (and ultimately incompatible) perspectives. Parekh's argument for the standpoint of the whole (a version of the objectivist fantasy) is not at all the same as a mediated knowledge or synthesis of the whole from the standpoint of labour. Parekh's argument is unable to answer the question, from which position can the competing claims, experiences, values and interests of the various parties be synthesised. It either acknowledges itself as a class position – in which case it will *know* itself as the class position of the intelligentsia – or it falls back into individualism, in which case it is a fantasy expressing (and disguising) the intelligentsia's class determined desire to transcend the class struggle (Ehrenreich and Ehrenreich 1979:22). To speak from the standpoint of the intelligentsia will at best produce a critique mediated by both capital and labour, as in the distinct positions of Žižek and Habermas, and at worst mediated wholly or largely by capital, as in the case of neo-liberal philosophers and economists.

For Lukács, the concept of mediation was central to understanding the interconnected but differential aspects of the social totality, and, for him, labour was the practical agent of mediation (1971:163). But the category of labour has to be considered subjectively in its concretely mediated relations with itself and other social identities. Marx famously made a distinction between a class that exists in itself and a class that exists for itself. In his analysis of the French peasantry in the mid-nineteenth century he argued that they had an objective existence as a class in itself. They 'live in similar conditions but without entering into manifold relations with one another' (1984:108–09). This isolation 'increased by bad means of communication' meant that the French peasantry, with their small holdings of land, were 'almost self-sufficient':

> A small holding, a peasant and his family; alongside them another small holding, another peasant and another family. A few score of these make up a village, and a few score of villages make up a department. In this way, the great mass of the French nation is formed by the simple addition of homologous magnitudes, much as potatoes in a sack form a sack of potatoes. (Marx 1984:109)

As an objective fact (independent of their modes of apprehension), the peasantry form a class and have therefore a passive weighting and influence in the outcome of political affairs. But they do not form a class *for itself*; their conditions of life work against their capacity to *recognise* themselves as a class and pursue their own interests independently. The lack of economic interdependence which constitutes their mode of production and its relatively limited productive forces means that, objectively, there is more about their conditions of life disabling the emergence of a class consciousness than enabling it. For wage-labour under capitalism, there are also disabling objective conditions militating against their capacity to recognise and identify with each other over extensive space–time relations (competition, division of labour, uneven development and so forth). However, these vie with enabling conditions which the capitalist mode of production also develops, namely extensive economic interdependence and elaborate possibilities for communication over space and time, which in turn politicise the use and distribution of resources. The notion of a class for itself suggests that a class (particularly a progressive class that does not want to rely on force) has to be (inter)subjectively constructed if it is to act on the objective potentiality in its conditions of life. For labour, the nature of that intersubjectivity is to recognise the *non-identity* between bourgeois rights and their universal application across all social groups and the *non-identity* between material and cultural needs and their universal satisfaction within capitalism.

For critics like Benhabib, the Marxian conception of class invokes a collective singularity and homogeneous intersubjectivity at best (1986:128). This in turn implies that the standpoint of labour is univocal and monological because of the unified nature of the class. But the unity of the proletariat (as opposed to labour) as a class is always a process of becoming and is indeed endlessly deferred because, by definition, as a class it is deeply marked by disabling conditions frustrating its intersubjectivity. This would suggest that along a temporal axis there is a tension to be negotiated. If the proletariat is a class always in the process of becoming, then any guides or compass as to what constitutes class consciousness (based on prior high points of revolutionary theory and practice) must remain provisionally open to being outstripped by such a process of becoming. Along a social axis labour does indeed often remain weirdly abstract (unmediated) in the work of many Marxists. 'Only the consciousness of the proletariat can point to the way that leads out of the impasse of capitalism' writes Lukács for example (1971:76). Both the exclusiveness of *whose* consciousness can point beyond the impasse of capital and the exclusive focus *on* consciousness is problematic here. For surely it is not primarily consciousness of the social order which leads out of the impasse of capitalism, but the concrete practices of participation, collective control, democratisation, symmetrical mediation and so forth. The problem with Lukács' overemphasis on consciousness is that a stipulated 'authentic' class consciousness can be appropriated by state elites who become its guardians and representatives whereas practical democratic developments are less easy to appropriate by an elite since by definition their 'representation' in the state negates their substance.

Lukács also errs in the exclusiveness he attributes to labour's role in developing radical consciousness. There are many sources outside labour from which legitimate emancipatory claims (consciousness) that point beyond capital have powerfully emerged. There is an

unfortunate tendency within some traditions of Marxism to acknowledge, say, claims concerning gender, race, or the environment where
they have been articulated by agents outside the organs and representatives of labour or Marxist theory, assimilate those claims,
rubbish the original spokespeople of them and point to some isolated
moments of theory or practice within the socialist tradition that have
addressed these claims in the past as proof that there is a sustained
unbroken line of continuity in addressing them. Such broken
dialectics should not be confused with the Marxist wager that only
by grounding such emancipatory claims in the generalised social
relations of labour can they acquire authentic universality as opposed
to being the preserve of sectarian or middle-class politics. Conversely
and dialectically, the potential universality of the proletariat can only
be achieved when this generalised category is de-homogenised,
escaping the abstract universalism of the value-form and extending
its emancipatory claims to each and every social group and identity
(black, gay, disabled, women) with which it intersects and of which
it is composed. This is not a question of bolting philosophies such
as liberalism or postmodernism onto Marxism. Rather, a conceptualisation of the proletariat as plural and diverse derives logically from
the Marxian critique of the law of value. For that law's remorseless
drive to make wildly different materials and use-values and practices
equivalent according to some quantitative proportion is necessarily
coupled with its drive to frustrate *equality*; abstract equalisation and
substantive inequality are the two sides of the law of value as capital
seizes on any and all social, culturally constructed or natural differences which it can opportunistically use to equalise upwards the rate
of profit. As Adorno argues: 'Barter as a process has real objectivity
and is objectively untrue at the same time, transgressing against its
own principle, the principle of equality' (1973:190). Not all oppres-
sions derive from economic motivations to be sure, but the law of
value sets the context in which culture, consciousness and the state
can develop an oppressive identity-thinking and hostility to
difference in all spheres of life. There is a mediated line of continuity
which links the instrumental thinking within the production process
that cannot tolerate any disruption, disturbance or unintegrated
matter in the smooth flow of output and those forms of thinking
which are hostile to any social group which does not 'fit' in with a
dominant identity.

I suggested earlier that a critical and dialectical social alignment
installs itself in the gap between labour as it is (fragmented, passive,

defensive, sexist, racist) and labour as it could be (the proletariat). Lukács made a similar distinction between actual and *imputed* class consciousness. The latter refers to the 'appropriate and rational reactions "imputed" to a particular typical position in the process of production' (Lukács 1971:51). The imputed class consciousness of the proletariat refers to a conciousness that would correlate to the emancipatory potential tacitly encoded in the socialised *practices* of labour. But, in that case, neither the practices nor the consciousness should be aligned with an achieved position in the here and now. One could indeed read the distinction between the actual and imputed class consciousness of labour as something akin to Adorno's negative dialectic (rather than, as it usually is, as a justification of the leading role of the vanguard revolutionary party which embodies this imputed consciousness). For it installs a non-identity and permanent critical deferral in even the most revolutionary movements, between ideals and practice, both in relation to labour and with regard to the continued existence of the state.

The *gap* between actual and imputed class consciousness within the subordinate class (and the necessary social transformation that implies) is reversed within the dominant class for whom actual consciousness is considerably closer to the appropriate and rational reactions tacitly encoded in their activities as personifications of capital. The gap between actual consciousness, with all its day-to-day distractions and confusions, and imputed class consciousness, which is the distilled representation of a class position, is therefore quite narrow because what is 'appropriate and rational' for them works with the *grain* of dominant social and economic relations. The class consciousness associated with capital is necessarily limited, capitalists' capacity for self-interrogation and critical understanding of the world around them truncated by their social location, which has no need or interest in enquiring too deeply into the nature of things.

This is nicely illustrated in *Startup.com* (Chris Hegedus and Jehane Nouaim 2001 US), a documentary that follows the fortunes of two childhood friends who attempt to corner a part of the online market in the heady days of the internet boom of the late 1990s. In one of the opening scenes in the film, Tom Herman is shown tying his daughter's hair into two pigtails with elastic bands. Unsatisfied that they are suffiently 'equal' or symmetrically positioned, he restarts the process despite her pleas for him to stop because it hurts. The 'equality' sought is akin to a rationalised penchant for design neatness blind to the more substantive issues involved. The camera closes in on the little girl's unhappy face as Herman dismisses her claims and continues his work. This rhetorical move on the part of the documentary opens up a discrepancy between what he thinks he is doing and what he is actually doing and a disjuncture between his own assessment of what is right and the counter-interpretation offered to the watching audience. This one scene sums up the strategy and structure of the entire film. Herman and his friend Kaleill Isaza Tuzman aim to set up a New York-based web site called govworks.com to provide an interface between government and citizens (particularly in the area of paying parking fines). Herman is the 'techno-geek' who focuses on the web site product while Tuzman, in charge of raising finance from venture capitalists, is ferociously competitive and egotistical.

In his literary criticism Lukács explored the question of imputed class consciousness via the concept of typicality. He defined typicality not in terms of statistical averages but in terms of those features of a situation or consciousness which crystallise and bring into relief the key contradictions and movements of social forces. Thus bourgeois or aristocratic characters who acquire such lucidity about their own class position tend to be quasi-tragic figures whose transcendence of the routine and mundane, merely 'average' consciousness of their class is unable of course to alter that class's structural position of decline or role as exploitor. However, because we are dealing here with documentary – whose stock and trade is precisely statistical averages since this is where its social relevance is frequently grounded (Winston 1995:130–37) – it is unsurprising to find that Herman and Tuzman are by no means typical characters in the Lukácsian sense. Instead they are two greedy wanabee entrepreneurs imbued with the American dream and desperately riding the dot.com boom to what they hope will be millionaire-dom. We – but not they – discover them to be hopelessly out of their depth. But if these utterly average characters are devoid of Lukácsian typicality, the documentary does make use of typicality of situation and events. As we saw in Chapter 2, the rise and fall of the dot.com bubble was a classic example of capital's cyclical expansion and contraction economy, in which the key socio-economic dynamics of the age are vividly delineated. The film charts this narrative curve and its moral critique reveals the discrepancy between what *we* learn of this world and what our two would-be capitalists fail to learn. The documentary form is part observational but it also has numerous direct-to-camera moments where the characters could have used this textual space for significant insight into their own lives and the world they have embraced. It is not a space they can make any productive use of. Herman and Tuzman are our vehicles into this world but their capacities for self critique or critique of the capitalist environment are virtually non-existent. We see the deleterious effects this world has on what little integrity they have, their friendships, self-respect, families, lovers and so forth and yet their capacities to recognise these let alone question them are extinguished as they try to work with the grain of the system and bend it to their own egoistic interests. The documentary illustrates that their stunted capacities for intersubjective recognition are closely tied up with their subject-to-object adherence to capitalism.

The cognitive insights generated by *Startup.com* have precious little to do with the consciousness of its principal protagonists but derive instead from the *ironic* discrepancy between spectator and subject. Compare this with *Injustice* (Ken Fero and Tariq Mehmood 2001 GB). This documentary investigates a handful of the instances where black people have died violently at the hands of the police in the last 30 years in the UK. Concentrating on recent cases, the documentary charts the struggles for justice and why those struggles are both necessary and thwarted due to the actions of the police and the legal apparatus. While over a thousand black people have died in police custody no police officer has been convicted in relation to these deaths. The documentary grounds its insights into the non-identity between justice and the empirical reality of the British state in the struggles of the bereaved families. In the combination of funerals, street demonstrations, public meetings and direct-to-camera interviews, we get a sense of how these struggles have consumed their lives and how they necessarily lead to their transformed and expanded understanding of the world around them. Thus the structure of the documentary is crucially built around parallel cases that are initially pursued separately, but gradually the campaigns converge, climbing higher and higher up the ladder of state power as the various groups *recognise in the circumstances of the other, their own pain and subordinate position.*

In *Injustice* we see how class as an epistemological category works as both a transposable model onto race and as a causally mediated determinant on the situation mapped out by the documentary. As a transposable model, strong parallels in the struggles of labour against capital are to be found in the protagonists' journeys of personal crisis, initial questioning, struggle, growing knowledge and practical critique of the *racist* state apparatus that confronts them. The power of the documentary derives from the proximate position it takes up in relation to the struggles of the subordinate pole in the polarity. The text clearly *recognises* their struggles (it was made over a period of several years which itself speaks of a significant level of commitment) in a way that places it outside the boundaries of 'balance' and 'objectivity' which regulates broadcast documentaries. *Injustice* has yet to be shown on UK television. The rich intersubjectivity which the documentary takes up in relation to its subjects in turn stimulates the spectator to recognise the breakdown of intersubjectivity between black people and the state apparatus. The challenge which *Injustice* poses to labour, white labour in particular, is to forge the imaginative analogy between its own position as object *vis-à-vis* capital and the reduction of black people to objects by the state. *Injustice* poses the question in the act of reception of a horizontal intersubjectivity among all the multiple and overlapping (but not homogeneous) social groups occupying the 'slave' position in the master–slave dialectic. As a causally mediated determinant, class is evident in the victims who are overwhelmingly *working-class* (not middle-class) and *black* (not white). This interlacing between class and race is complemented on the side of the perpetrators who are overwhelmingly white and working within the institutional state contexts of the dominant class.

Compare *Injustice* with the two-part BBC *Panorama* (2002) investigation by John Ware into collusion between the British army, intelligence services and Loyalist terrorists in Northern Ireland. Here the victims of state complicity and indifference to murder are recruited to the text in the form of interviews with the bereaved. The son of Pat Finucane, the solicitor murdered because he had taken on suspected IRA terrorists as clients, is allowed to talk of the night his father was killed in front of him and the scars that has left. But the struggles of the families to get justice, their campaigns, their questions, their knowledge, their speculations and their assessments of the context in which such killings occur have no space within the programme since to include them would place the text in a discursive proximity to a collective (the nationalists and Catholics in Northern Ireland) who have a similar status *vis-à-vis* the British state to black people in Britain. Certainly the programme was a brave departure from the norm, and was genuinely investigative, generating new information itself, but it conceals the extent to which the *Panorama* investigation arrives at the 'scene of the crime' as a *result* of all the campaigning done and questions raised by those immediately concerned with the murders. It keeps the bereaved family as 'victims', their grief apparently having no public transformational outlet, in stark contrast to *Injustice* which locates the bereaved in very public contexts (demonstrations, court appearances, etc.). It thus gives the impression of a class and national Establishment being the principal public investigators, 'objectively' turning a light on their own dark recesses and routing the spectator's identification and recognition of a problem through their dominant media communication apparatus. In terms of the 'how' aspects of communication which Habermas emphasises, it constructs a very impoverished opportunity for intersubjective recognition with the very community much of the British state has spent many years denying basic freedoms and rights to. In other words, the 'hows' of the *Panorama* programme and *Injustice* are closely related to their propositional power and orientations, the 'whats' of what they have got to say.

We have seen that in mapping out a philosophical base for committed, critical cultural practices and theories we have to navigate between a pseudo-objectivity of the subject (objectivism) and a pseudo-subjectivism of the object (relativism). In the case of the former, critical faculties concerning the social situatedness of the speaker and addressee and its effects are severely stunted. Within the philosophy of the objective subject, there is a tendency to entertain the fantasy of rising above social interests while the possibilities for immanent critique in order to diagnose conceptual contradictions or the gap between norms and reality are diminished to varying degrees. Generally, the objective subject cannot accommodate an understanding of the subject as internally divided and contradictory. In the case of relativism, where the objectivity of the object world is disavowed by relentless subjectivism, the complacency of objectivism regarding the object world disappears, but so too does the possibility of establishing any normative and epistemological grounds for preferring this or that method, politics, action or outcome from any other. We saw that Žižek's concept of the Real suffers from just such a problem. With both objectivism and relativism, sustained social alignment in theory and practice becomes difficult without entering into self-contradiction.

We can locate Habermas as trying to effect a synthesis between the polarities of objectivism and subjectivism (as we have seen, the dominance of one over the other depends on the institutional context, media industry or academia). Like the objectivists, Habermas believes that on the basis of methodological rigour and Enlightenment norms it is possible to establish underlying consensual agreements as to evidence and preferable values. He uses this to critique the relativists. However, like the relativists, he shifts attention away from the referential 'what' aspects of communication, to the 'how', emulating their own anti-mimetic thrust. In doing so Habermas opens up a space for considering intersubjectivity which neither the objectivists nor relativists can.

The problems with Habermas' attempt to find a route out of the philosophy of the subject are that it is insufficiently materialist and insufficiently dialectical. One cannot ground intersubjectivity and rationality in the structures of meaning alone (communicative reason) while bracketing off the meaning of structures (the mode of production). The resistance which Habermasian theory has to the deep materialism of the mode of production is evident in Seyla Benhabib's argument that labour as a process of transformation is quite different from the processes associated with 'communication, interpretation, dispute and organizing' (1986:156). The lack of dialectical mediation here should be evident as soon as we try to imagine the praxis of labour as something that could do without these essential features of intersubjectivity. Indeed, as we have seen in earlier chapters, capitalist management practices and ideologists have become increasingly concerned with the quality of communication within the corporate organisation as an essential resource in the battle for innovation and flexibility. Habermas himself is quite content to accept impoverished and standardised modes of communication in the sphere of material production as the base on which to build a theoretical and practical apparatus of communication where a fuller sociality can be developed. The non-identity between Habermas' 'base' and 'superstructure' is fatal to his own project while the acceptance of a stunted and limited intersubjectivity in material production, though deeply necessary for capital, is arbitrary as far as labour is concerned.

Yet grounding the concept of intersubjectivity in the Marxian social relations of production works as a double critique, not only of Habermasian idealism, but of Marxism itself, at least as it is often conceived and practised. Thus, to recall once more the dialectical model mapped out at the beginning of this chapter, between the poles of Habermas vs Marxism, it is possible to critique the latter as well as the former from within the pole of Marxism. An abstract and poorly mediated concept of labour leads to all sorts of problems, including an insensitivity to labour's mediation of and by other social identities, 'workerism' (where other issues and conflicts outside the immediate sphere of labour get marginalised) and an indifference or merely short-term tactical commitment to political diversity. The objective conditions of (wage) labour as the near universalisation of a particular social and economic relationship constitute the broadest possible foundations for grounding knowledge and norms – undistorted by economic or political force – in social interests. But for a class in itself to become a class for itself is a collective process of becoming which cannot be monopolised by one group or find adequate representation in a 'progressive' state (no matter how necessary the state might be in the medium term). For a class to recognise itself in all its diversity and multiplicity requires expanding our imaginative horizons far beyond what a capitalist public sphere can accommodate. A radical and committed aesthetics will seek to develop those modes of recognition. Such a cultural project is also a challenge to Marxist politics.

Conclusion:
Reflections on Key Concepts
and Contemporary Trends

> Value ... does not stalk about with a label describing what it is. It is value, rather, that converts every product into a social hieroglyphic. Later on, we try to decipher the hieroglyphic, to get behind the secret of our own social products.
>
> Marx, *Capital*

The hour is indeed getting late. And there is much at stake in how, if at all, we decipher the coded appearance-forms that confront us today. This book has argued that the best methodological tool we have available for deciphering the social hieroglyphic of value relations is Marxism. The theory of value is Marx's way of capturing the dialectic between labour and capital. Labour (along with nature which provides its raw materials) is a key generator of all socially-produced wealth. The development of labour as a general category of thought which could grasp labour as the source of wealth was, Marx noted, a great breakthrough in the development of political economy. Earlier forms of economic thought had passed through various stages in which wealth was at first located in material objects, then money, then a particular form of labour, namely agriculture, and finally, via Adam Smith, wealth was located in labour *in general*. As Marx argued, this breakthrough in forms of thought was in turn dependent on the development of the forces of production which capitalist social relations were engineering:

> The indifference as to the particular kind of labour implies the existence of a highly developed aggregate of different species of concrete labour, none of which is any longer the predominant. So the most general abstractions commonly arise only where there is the highest concrete development, where one feature appears to be jointly *possessed* by many and to be common to all. (1973:49 emphasis added)

But if capitalism develops the material conditions (namely our developing sociality) for grasping in abstract *thought* the shared

257

possession common to humanity in practice (labour power as a trans-formative wealth generating activity), it is also a contradictory two-sided process in which abstraction becomes a *practical* indiffer-ence to labour and the use-value of its products. Value thus returns to labour as capital, a material force dematerialising the specificity, particularity and concreteness of its use-values. Shared possession (human labour power, skills and knowledge) thus becomes possession in another altogether different sense: possession becomes seizure, property, control; the hollowing out of the authentic subject of wealth production. The other side to the spectre of the proletariat in *The Communist Manifesto* (the spectre of a repressed memory, of exploitation and injustice) is necessarily the spectre of capital possessing labour *as if* labour and its outcomes had no material body (use-values) of their own independent of accumulation and compe-tition. Capital's dematerialising materialism can never completely gut the subject and the object of its material content and weight however. Although the subjectless subject is torn by the fetishising dynamics of immanence, splitting, repression and inversion, there remains an essential friction even if it is only a half memory stubbornly lodged and resistant to its exchange or equivalence; an allegory of this general struggle between materiality (of memory and needs) and demateriality was evoked in the case of John Murdoch in *Dark City* (Alex Proyas 1997 US).

The implications of the friction between abstraction and the concrete for Marxism as a methodology for the analysis of the social totality are profound. For *critical* thought moves in the opposite direction to capital. The latter seeks to absorb all particulars and concrete specifics into abstract exchange. Concrete labour 'becomes the form under which its opposite, abstract human labour, manifests itself' (Marx 1983:64). Marxism seeks to invert this inversion and return the abstract principles implicit in a highly developed and interdependent economy back to the concrete and the particular so that the specificity of use-values can be fully developed. In the here and now, under social relations where abstraction remains dominant over concrete labour, the goal of being adequate to the concrete must be internalised in critical practice if it is to make a contribution to authentic change.

Marx's methodology then involves the development of abstract concepts that internalise within them sensitivity to social difference. How? The more complex abstractions are the more they can approx-imate to the 'rich aggregate of many determinations and relations' of the social order (Marx 1973:45). Complexity involves building up a network of conceptual relations – working through their internal dynamics and testing their explanatory power *vis-à-vis* historical and empirical referents.

> Population is an abstraction if we leave out for example the classes of which it consists. These classes, again, are but an empty word unless we know what are the elements on which they are based, such as wage-labour, capital, etc. These imply, in their turn, exchange, division of labour, prices, etc. Capital, for example, does not mean anything without wage-labour, value, money, price, etc. (Marx 1973:44)

The dialectical structure of the arguments in this book has often been woven around attempts to develop the sensitivity to the concrete in Marxian concepts. I suggested in Chapter 1 that the concrete speci-ficity of the intelligentsia within the struggle between labour and capital had to be developed within Marxian analysis. The specificity of being knowledge workers installs into the production process certain difficulties for capital in controlling and quantifying cultural labour and its output (ideas) and certain possibilities for resistance. For example, when Hollywood scriptwriters threatened to go on strike in 2001 over royalties for screenings of films on video, satellite and cable, they were laying claim to a portion of the surplus which workers involved in producing other (less cultural) kinds of goods and services cannot emulate. Of course the difficulties which capital faces in controlling cultural labour are not insuperable and capital develops all kinds of strategies to penetrate its controlling logic into the production process and make the creative process as economically and, to a contradictory degree, as ideologically safe as possible. I do not want to romanticise the autonomy of the intellectual in the least. But the difficulties are there and, arguably, there in ways which have not been true of production in general, although the culturalisation of production, itself not unrelated to the expanding production of cultural and communication goods and services, is perhaps general-ising these difficulties to wider social layers than ever before. I suggested as much in my discussion of software engineers, who see their work as a form of cultural expression, and corporate capital's attempts to keep the source code for computer software commer-cially confidential. Marxism cannot afford not to be very concrete in its analysis. It must get down to the very specific qualities of social practices because this goes to the heart of whether Marxism offers a credible emancipatory and democratic alternative to other kinds of political and cultural theory. Thought must negotiate a difficult balancing act between abstraction and the concrete. For example, the difference between film and music for black cultural workers is the different articulations of particular cultural labours within specific relations of production and consumption to the same multifaceted force: capital.

Lukács rightly notes that concrete analysis means, for Marxism, the analysis of the relation a particular practice has to the social whole, a relation, which, as we have seen, the dematerialising, decontextualising tendencies of capital rub away at the level of the appearance-forms. Yet, at the same time, the social whole has to be viewed in relation to the particular in such a way that the latter does not simply reflect or become the passive expression of the former. The base–superstructure apparatus and the concept of mediation are, I have argued, key conceptual tools for grasping this dialectic. But both have to be carefully defined and thought through. In Chapter 5 I tried to outline a model of the base and superstructure that would adequately represent both the abstractions of capital (accumulation, commodification, competition, control, etc.) and the concrete materiality (of different institutions and social 'levels'). I unpacked the traditionally somewhat monolithic base–superstructure model into seven levels of mediation. This involved differentiating the base into two conceptual levels: the mode of production, with its abstract postulation of the social relations and forces of production, and the mode of development, which sits inside the base, giving us greater purchase on some of the particular configurations of technology and social relations in specific historical conjunctures. The concept of the mode of development (specifically informationalism) thus lends the mode of production a greater sensitivity to historical changes, while the mode of production situates such developments within the fundamental continuities of struggle and contradiction which structure capitalism and helps guard against the sort of new paradigm fallacies discussed in Chapter 2. With the base differentiated into two levels I then unpacked the superstructure into five further levels for the purposes of media analysis, and these consisted of the state, the industrial context, the production context, the production process and finally the text.

Mediation is the key concept providing the necessary linkages between these different levels, between the parts and the social totality. Mediation, within the Marxian method, does not propose an identity between phenomena, since that would collude with the dematerialising fantasy of equivalence of capital itself; materialist mediation gives a proper weight, history, and due to the internal relations between connected but different phenomena. I proposed, against Althusser's dismissal of mediation and his own concept of overdetermination, that mediation involves a double process of internalisation and reconfiguration. Thus we have to track a process that emerges from the mode of production through the other levels of the social formation. That process comes to 'completion' in the cultural text not as an 'expression' of the mode of production, but as the compacting together of a variety of practices which do not 'converge' from some space autonomous from the mode of production (as with Althusser's concept of overdetermination), but instead reconfigure the mode of production in distinct and specific ways. At each stage of the process, within the different institutions and levels of the superstructure, social agents have made choices, within certain parameters to be sure, which, had they made other choices, would have to varying degrees, altered the outcome of the cultural text(s) or phenomena we are studying. *Big Brother* is thus to be understood as an intervention into a zone of commodification and struggle that can be tracked right back to the mode of production. The sense that, given a particular set of circumstances, *Big Brother* was inevitable is the retrospective effect of an analysis which links the part(s) to the whole, but this sense should not be confused with the actual historical process where there was no inevitable predetermination, but instead a series of reconfigurations of certain trends within wider contexts of production.

Every point of reconfiguration within the process of mediation is the site and stake of struggle. In Chapter 2 we explored this within new digital media technology, specifically, the Internet and linked technologies of music file swapping (P2P and MP3). We saw that particular aspects of such communications technologies opened up the potential for practices to emerge that (a) cut against the dominant forces within the mode of production (capital) in the here and now; and (b) prefigured practices and values that if generalised would spell the end of capital. Such struggles, and, with them, glimpses of alternative futures, can only emerge because of the contradictions within the mode of production and mode of development. Contradiction is indeed another absolutely central concept for us if we are to avoid sliding into some species of functionalism or pessimism.

Contradiction refers to the way in which a process, social force or agent negates certain aspects of itself and/or wider society in the course of pursuing its own reproduction within that society. In Chapter 2 I explored the contradiction between the socialisation of production and consumption which the capitalist mode of production develops (configured in the fixed capital of the new media) and the necessary perpetuation of private property, hierarchy, competition, commodity relations and price restricted access to culture and information. Napster and subsequent music file-swapping services (with their informal 'communist' culture of exchanging resources without attaching exchange value) sit at the intersection of precisely this fundamental contradiction.

Nevertheless, despite these contradictions, the penetration, by capital, of the public sphere – the realm of communication and dialogue – and the subordination of this sphere to the imperatives of capital, and therefore its selected voices and meanings, continue apace as technologies and companies converge, as companies diversify their interests and as capital extends its reach both in global space (penetrating the last remnants of the Second and Third Worlds) and in its intensive squeezing out of *more* surplus value from already commodified domains. In terms of corporate structures and strategies, value relations now take on an appearance-form diametrically opposite to the real relations. In Chapter 3 I examined the new organisational structures associated with post-Fordism. The inter-corporate relations around a plurality and diversity of subsidiaries and subcontractors allow Big Capital, still marching to the beat of its own concentration and centralisation, to be responsive to local and regional cultural tastes, trends and markets, on a global scale.

The growing powers of capital which Chapter 3 maps in turn impact upon the capitalist state, whose relations to the classes within the nation and to the international bourgeoisie have undergone dramatic shifts in the last 30 years or so. To borrow the phraseology of Marx who perfectly captures the paradoxes of capitalism, the state has the appearance of what it really is (at one level): a political organ separate from the economic relations of production. This appearance-form is the starting point for both Keynesians and neo-liberals, despite their different assessments of its meaning. For Keynesians, the reality of the appearance of such a separation allows them to invest in the supposed efficacy of the state to intervene in and resolve the inequalities and irrationalities of the economy. This represses the extent to which the state is shaped *by* the class relations of the economy and reproduces their irrationalities and inequalities. For the neo-liberals, the reality of the appearance of the state's separation from economic relations is an argument for it to keep its nose out of a sphere it is not competent to interfere with. This represses the extent to which capital's economic needs and relations are in fact serviced *by* and conditional *on* the state's continual 'interference'. Policy discussions framed by these parameters typically take the politics out of economics (neo-liberalism) and the economics out of politics (Keynesianism). The integration of national economies into the international economy has become the general goal of most states and thus media policy goals seek to lighten cultural obligations and intensify competition nationally and internationally. At the same time, because the state 'sits' inside the nation, such globalisation cannot entirely suppress the question of cultural values, cultural obligations and cultural demands without liquidating the state's own legitimacy in relation to the (class divided) nation. One fault line, between the national intelligentsia and cultural workers and the international bourgeoisie, is particularly sensitive. This was exposed once again in the UK in 2002 when a Joint Parliamentary Committee, chaired by David (Lord) Putnam, set up to scrutinise New Labour's Communications Bill, came into conflict with the government when it questioned the Bill's proposal to open up British television to American corporate ownership.

The apparent autonomy of the state, of technology, of culture and of texts is the recurrent leitmotif of capitalism. Thus it is no surprise to find Marxist cultural theory contesting the appearance-form of autonomy for the world of signs and meanings and theories of signs and meanings. Autonomisation generally derives from the real processes of a minutely honed specialisation and division of labour. The rubbing away of extensive social relations which this process facilitates is, as we have seen, a classic feature of commodity fetishism (immanence). As such extensive social relations become a faint ghostly trace from *within* any one particular domain of the social order, so those domains (whether the state or the social sciences) acquire that other feature of spectral fetishism: a phantom objectivity. Within linguistic theories, this leads to a *materialisation* of the sign. But what is meant here by materialisation is precisely that fetishistic foregrounding of its 'physical' materiality. That, even here, such materialism, with its structuralist vocabulary of langue/parole, signifier/signified, paradigm/syntagm, and so forth, is a form of progress as well as regression testifies to the contradictions of capitalist development. Yet the failure to rematerialise the materiality of signs as meanings that must be mediated by the mode of production has left much cultural theory championing the apparent one-way determination of language over the real. This has threatened the very usefulness of a concept such as ideology, which in some theories becomes the primary means for the reproduction of the social order (thus repressing more ontological forces such as mode of production). In other, more postmodernised theories, ideology's 'materiality', along with language in general, meant that it became an untenable concept for denoting some privileged (transparent) access to truth and knowledge (the non-ideological). Here the dominance of language over the real made any standard for judging discourse impossible or undesirable. I argued that the non-ideological remains an essential possibility if we are to think through signs and meanings as a contested dialogical space where the communicative rationality implicit in sharing information and resources, in making credible matches between sign and referent, in co-ordinating and co-operating for mutual benefit, entwines with the irrationality of ideology, where language and communication are pressed into the service of supporting relations of domination. The concept of hegemony, the moral and intellectual lead of the dominant classes, allows us to think through the world of signs across a wide range of issues within the public sphere. Hegemonic leads can, and, insofar as they want to minimise the use of force, must, accommodate difference, compromise and even contradiction. Clearly, to talk of hegemony, is to propose a highly uneven field and one that is constantly mutating, adapting and changing. In some areas, the hegemonic field might be particularly strong; consider, for example, the way the British state appears to be able to present itself (certainly without serious challenge within the UK) as an 'honest broker' between warring sides in the case of Northern Ireland. Yet, in other areas, particularly in such domains as personal behaviour such as sexuality or drug use, the hitherto dominant posture has been undergoing adaptation and change for several decades. But even in their 'liberal' manifestations, hegemonic formations find themselves on the defensive when the gap between 'liberal' theory and conservative practice is exposed (anti-gay legislation such as Clause 28 in the UK) or where liberalism runs up against the realities of widening social inequalities.

Within the philosophy of knowledge, hegemony splits into an antinomy between objectivity and relativity. In contrast to these dichotomous positions, Marxism does not start with the assumption that social interests are inimical to social knowledge, as both of these do, in different ways. For objectivists, social interests must be transcended and so are therefore inherently disabling; for relativists, we are inevitably mired in interests (the will to power in Nietzschean parlance) which construct a prison-house decorated by our own values, beliefs and perspectives that can have no claim to any general interests or consent with people living in different prison-houses. By contrast the potentiality for general interests to be grounded in the free association of the direct producers underpins the formulation of class dialectics as a two-fold decoding operation, namely: as a transposable model, prototype or form across a whole range of conflicting and self-divided phenomena or categories; and, a mediated causal determinant (or content) on those phenomena. In both its form and its content, class is often buried within other more visible categories and it is this political unconscious which this two-fold decoding operation (or cognitive mapping as Jameson calls it) seeks to bring out into the open light of day.

Take, for example, the proposition that there is a widespread cultural trend splitting the subject between a deep-seated scepticism and a credulous naivety within advanced capitalism. Recent reports have found that while young urban shoppers are well aware that many of their favourite brand goods are manufactured in exploitative conditions in developing countries, this knowledge does not detract from the appeal of those brand goods.[1] At one level they 'know' that the brand images are hugely discrepant with the real conditions of production of the material goods they are attached to. But this knowledge is combined with the credulous knowledge and identifications inscribed into their actual practices, in this case, buying the brand goods and all the promises of happiness and contentment they sell. This rift between what we know and what we do (and the ideas tacitly inscribed into what we do) is generated by the self-alienating fetishising dynamic of capital in which we are at once the authors of our own subordination to that which we do not control.

This split subject was first mooted in my analysis of *Big Brother* and developed more fully in the chapter on commodity fetishism. Typically, the split subject switches between scepticism and credulity without resolving the antinomy which structures the splitting in the first place. The most immediate forces mediating this polarity in the instance of *Big Brother* are of course media culture and media communications technology. The ideologeme of surveillance makes sense of this particular dichotomy. On the one hand, *Big Brother* is evidently a field of massive manipulation, of both contestants and audiences, and sporadic awareness of this dark undertow of surveillance often breaks through. On the other hand, the appeal of *Big Brother* depends on the credulous investment that real time monitoring is an innocuous means by which the consumer's real desires can be tapped and presented back to them, or, as in the specific case of *Big Brother*, that judgements can be made as to the authenticity of character and emotions on the basis of the audio-visual panopticon. Thus, in both its form and its content, the scepticism/credulity dichotomy is a mediated moment in the class struggle.

If we juxtapose *Big Brother* with the Adorno of *Negative Dialectics*, we see that the scepticism/credulity polarity bears a striking resemblance to our major rift in the philosophy of knowledge between relativity and objectivity or between negation and identity-thinking. Adorno, as we saw, offered a critique of credulous identity-thinking, but he did not fall into the opposite error of simply championing negativity. A high theory concept such as Žižek's notion of the Real, as with an undialectical popular scepticism, rapidly makes any prospect of aligning oneself with particular social forces, particular ideals and values, illogical. Some credulity then or some willingness to entertain the provisional correspondence or identity between concept/representation and the real is inevitable and certainly necessary for effective social action.

The practical dialectical synthesis of the antinomy which structures the philosophy of knowledge (as well as the documentary tradition) and the split subject lies in the social force (labour) which carries within it the seeds or potentiality of its own critical transformation (negation). This means that, as an achievement, the normative goal of the free association of the direct producers must be assumed to be perpetually deferred, on pain of extinguishing that reflexive immanent critique. This is one interpretation of what Trotsky called, permanent revolution. Central to this critical transformation and endlessly deferred goal is the whole question of intersubjectivity. Here I mobilised Marxism and Habermas in a dialectical critique of each other, while nevertheless locating myself firmly in the former pole of this particular antinomy. Intersubjectivity takes us into the realm of subject-to-subject relations and the qualitative modes by which we communicate with each other and recognise in the other the same basis for rationality, reason and universal rights as we recognise in ourselves. Marxian aesthetics, I suggested, has long recognised the importance of 'how' we construct meanings. Habermas' concept of intersubjectivity extends this 'aesthetic' dimension into communication and its public organs, but does so at the cost of bracketing off the 'what' dimension of subject-to-object relations, which effectively leaves the mode of production intact. Developing democratic social and political practices, which is to say the symmetrical mediations of a post-capital order, is the prerequisite to developing the subject-to-subject relations in which we recognise ourselves in the other, an intersubjectivity that would require a public sphere very different from the one we have today. In trying to develop a philosophy of intersubjectivity Habermas wants the philosophy of the subject to open itself up, to turn away from a monologically closed subject in which other subjects are merely objects or, we may add, invisible. A new aesthetics of recognition is called for, fostering not the 'vertical' identifications with dominant institutions, as in the case of *One Day in September* (Kevin Macdonald 2000 Sw/Ger/GB) or the *Panorama* (2002) programme I analysed in Chapter 8, but the 'horizontal' identifications generated by a documentary such as *Injustice* (Ken Fero and Tariq Mehmood 2001 GB). We can juxtapose Habermas and documentary practices with the spectral dialectics explored in the chapter on commodity fetishism and reification. For it is precisely the ghostly, insubstantial, thin and elusive quality of our present mode of intersubjectivity under capitalism that is evident in those films where special characters acquire or have the optical and sensory organs to see, to recognise, ghosts. What the boy Cole Sear in *The Sixth Sense* (M. Night Shyamalan 1999 US) has is precisely a painful awareness of all the pain, histories and misfortunes in time and space which others have suffered but which our contracted, foreclosed, privatised and monologically inward intersubjectivities so easily screen us from.

The Marxist theory of commodity fetishism, it should be noted, is thus very much concerned with the manner in which our subject-to-subject relations, our 'direct social relations' (Marx 1983:78), fade into a ghostly trace, becoming a hieroglyph in which we struggle to recognise our *interdependence* on each other. Sociality under capitalism is only established in the sphere of exchange, not at the point of production itself. The exchange of signs and meanings cannot possibly remedy the negative effects which the truncated and thwarted sociality of the capitalist mode of production produces. At best, the realm of communication and representation can explore the negative effects of this thwarted sociality, point to their irresolvable nature within capitalism and provide a forum for debating and prefiguring alternative forms of sociality. Marxist (cultural) theory is our best guide and hope in getting 'behind the secret of our own social products'.

Notes

INTRODUCTION

1. Dominic Thomas, 'TV's bad credit rating', *Guardian* (New Media), 5 August 2002, pp. 30–31.
2. Dominic Thomas, 'TV's bad credit rating'.

CHAPTER 1

1. Paul Abbott, 'Culture clash', *Guardian* (Media), 28 May 2001, pp. 16–17.
2. <http://freedevelopers.net/press/faq/>.
3. <http://www.gnu.org/philosophy/free-sw.html>.
4. Heather Sharp, 'A world without Microsoft', *Red Pepper*, April 2001, p. 25.
5. Matt Wells, 'Cold Feet over a fifth series', *Guardian*, 27 December 2000, p. 9.
6. Walter Murch, 'Touch of evil', *Guardian* (Review), 25 September 1998, p. 6.
7. David Hughes, 'The massacre of my movie', *Guardian* (Review), 13 September 1996, p. 2.
8. Ekow Eshun, 'The rap trap', *Guardian*, 27 May 2000, p. 8.
9. Ekow Eshun, 'The rap trap'.
10. Toby Young, 'Rappers aspire to nicer class of ghetto', *Observer*, 5 September 1999, p. 25.

CHAPTER 2

1. Jamie Doward, 'Meltdown', *Observer*, 9 September 2001, p. 13.
2. Jamie Doward, 'Meltdown'.
3. Jon Snow, 'Old MacDonald had a modem ...', *Guardian* (G2), 25 April 2001, p. 5.
4. Mark Simpson, *Independent*, 5 August 2001, p. 15.
5. Edward Helmore, 'P2P – is it pirate to pirate?', *Guardian*, 19 October 2000, pp. 2–3.
6. Peter H. Lewis, <www.nytimes.com/libr...tech/00/06/circuits/articles/29pete.html>.
7. <www.mtv.com/news/articles/1439602/20010220/story.jhml>.
8. Chris Arthur, 'Huge increase in music swaps over the Net despite demise of Napster', *Independent*, 8 November 2001, p. 15.
9. Ronald Grover and Tom Lowry, 'Can't get no satisfaction', *Business Week*, 3 September 2001, pp. 78–9.

CHAPTER 3

1. Larry Elliot, 'Rise and rise of the super-rich', *Guardian* (G2), 14 July 1999, pp. 2–3.

2. See *BFI Film and Television Handbook, 2002* (p. 44), *2001* (p. 43), *2000* (p. 35) and *1999* (p. 35) edited by Eddie Dyja and published by the BFI.
3. Edward Helmore, '"Wicked" Disney accused of plot to eat the world', *Observer*, 24 May 1998, p. 18.
4. Paul Betts, 'Disneyland enlists the Hunchback', *Financial Times*, December 1996, p. 8.
5. Benedict Carver, *Screen International*, no. 974, 9–15 September 1994, p. 8.
6. David Teather, 'Magic kingdom under siege', *Guardian*, 15 January 2002, p. 24.
7. See Disney's annual report at <http://disney.go.com/corporate/investors/financials/annual/2001/keybusinesses/studioentertainment/bvinternational.html>.
8. Christopher Grimes, 'TV mogul with finger on the button', *Financial Times*, 18 December 2001, p. 28.
9. James Harding, 'Messier's feast', *Financial Times*, 18 December 2001, p. 22.
10. James Harding, 'Disney's Eisner admits rival is at peak of perfection', *Financial Times*, 6 February 2002, p. 15.
11. See Disney's 2001 annual report at <http://disney.go.com/corporate/investors/financials/annual/2001/financials/pdf/wdw2k1ar_financials.pdf>.
12. Christopher Grimes, 'Disney's income drops 55% despite job cuts', *Financial Times*, 1 February 2002, p. 31.
13. Oliver Burkeman, 'Why the TV chiefs think Letterman is worth $71m', *Guardian*, 8 March 2002, p. 3.
14. Ed Vulliamy, 'Outrage as American TV giant sends for the clown', *Observer*, 3 March 2002, p. 23.
15. Matt Wells, 'ITN cuts jobs and shifts towards lifestyle news', *Guardian*, 22 November 2001, p. 1.
16. Kamal Ahmed, 'Kids TV "dumbing down"', *Guardian*, 5 November 1997, p. 3.
17. Roy Greenslade, 'The new standard bearer', *Guardian* (Media), 21 January 2002, p. 8.
18. Leo Lewis, 'GE boss on mission to be big in China', *Independent on Sunday*, 3 February 2002, p. 5.
19. John Hazelton, 'China opens doors to Hollywood', *Screen International*, no. 1261, 2–8 June 2000, p. 8.
20. Danny Gittings and Julian Borger, 'Homer and Bart realise Murdoch's dream of China coup', *Guardian*, 6 September 2001, p. 3.

CHAPTER 4

1. UNESCO website: <http://www.unesco.org/culture/policies/index.sht>.
2. *InterMedia*, May 1997, vol. 25, no. 3, p. 6.
3. Paul Brown, 'Printers pulp Monsanto edition of Ecologist', *Guardian*, 29 September 1998, p. 5.
4. Adrian Cooper, 'My tears will catch them', *Sight and Sound*, October 2001, pp. 30–31.
5. Mike Davis, 'Great and glorious days', *Socialist Review*, no. 262, April 2002, p. 23.

6. <http://europa.eu.int/eur-lex/en/lit/dat/1997/en_397L0036.html>.
7. Eurimages website: <http://culture.coe.fr/eurimages/eng/eeurprof.lm. html>.
8. John Hazelton, 'China opens doors to Hollywood', *Screen International*, 2–8 June 2000, p. 8.
9. Peter Chapman, 'Turn on, tune in, opt out', *Screen International*, 19 November 1999, p. 14.
10. John Hooper, 'Politicians prepare to pay for Kirch rescue', *Guardian*, 30 March 2002, p. 20.
11. Mark Milner, 'Murdoch frozen out of Kirch', *Guardian*, 6 April 2002, p. 25.
12. John Hooper, 'Minister says Kirch should stay German', *Guardian*, 5 April 2002, p. 24.
13. Gurinder Chadha, 'Call that a melting pot?', *Guardian* (2), 11 April 2002, p. 11.

CHAPTER 5

1. Christopher Dunkley, 'It's downhill from here: Christopher Dunkley despairs as he surveys the increasingly populist schedules', *Financial Times*, 20 September 2000, p. 20.
2. Ed Martin, 'Toss out the script', *Advertising Age*, vol. 71, no. 21, 15 May 2000, p. 26.
3. Peter Thal Larsen, 'Spanish were watching as *Big Brother* stole the show', *Financial Times*, 18 March 2000, p. 10.
4. Paul McGann, 'Web reaps the benefits of TV', *Media Week*, 25 August 2000, p. 8.
5. Kate Watson-Smyth, 'Would you pay to watch TV on your computer?', *Guardian* (New Media), 15 July 2002, p. 40.
6. Kate Watson-Smyth, 'Would you pay to watch TV on your computer?'.
7. Kate Watson-Smyth, 'Would you pay to watch TV on your computer?'.
8. Paul McGann, 'Web reaps the benefits of TV'.
9. Kathryn Flett, 'Only a gameshow? TV's theatre of cruelty', *Observer*, 20 August 2000, p. 15.

CHAPTER 6

1. *The Times*, 19 July 2002, p. 1.
2. Kevin Mitchell, *Observer* (sport), 21 July 2002, p. 3.
3. Dea Birkett, 'Remember Jade and Keiren?', *Guardian* (2), 13 December 2001, pp. 6–7.
4. Dea Birkett, 'Remember Jade and Keiren?'.

CHAPTER 7

1. Yvonne Roberts, *Observer*, 5 May 2002, p. 30.
2. Jill Treanor and Nils Pratley, *Guardian*, 5 July 2002, p. 4.
3. *Everybody knows that the dice are loaded, everybody rolls with their fingers crossed, everybody knows the war is over, everybody knows the good guys lost.*

Everybody knows the fight is fixed, the poor stay poor, the rich get rich, that's how it goes, everybody knows. Everybody knows that the boat is leaking, everybody knows the captain lied, everybody got this broken feeling, like their father or their dog just died ... Leonard Cohen, 'Everybody Knows'.

CHAPTER 8

1. Kevin Macdonald, 'My film is not biased against Palestinians', *Guardian*, 27 May 2000, p. 23.

CONCLUSION

1. Felicity Lawrence, 'Sweatshop campaigners demand Gap boycott', *Guardian*, 22 November 2002, p. 8.

Bibliography

Abercrombie, Nicholas, Stephen Hill and Bryan S. Turner, 1980, *The Dominant Ideology Thesis*, George Allen & Unwin, London.

Adorno, Theodor, 1973, *Negative Dialectics*, Seabury Press, New York.

Adorno, Theodor and Max Horkheimer, 1977, 'The cultural industry: Enlightenment as mass deception' in *Mass Communications and Society*, eds J. Curran, M. Gurevitch and J. Woolacott, Open University Press, London.

Aglietta, Michael, 1979, *A Theory of Capitalist Regulation: The US Experience*, translated by David Fernbach, New Left Books, London.

Alderman, John, 2001, *Sonic Boom, Napster, MP3, and the New Pioneers of Music*, Fourth Estate, London.

Althusser, Louis, 1971, *Lenin and Philosophy and Other Essays*, Monthly Review Press, New York.

—— 1996, *For Marx*, Verso, London.

Amariglio, Jack and Antonio Callari, 1996, 'Marxian value theory and the problem of the subject: The role of commodity fetishism' in *Fetishism as Cultural Discourse*, ed. Emily Apter and William Pietz, Cornell University Press, New York.

Amin, Ash, 1997, 'Post-Fordism: Models, fantasies and phantoms of transition' in *Post-Fordism: A Reader*, ed. Ash Amin, Blackwell, Oxford.

Anderson, Perry, 1976, 'The antinomies of Antonio Gramsci', *New Left Review*, no. 100, December–November.

—— 1980, *Arguments Within English Marxism*, Verso, London.

Annan, Lord, 1977, Report of the Committee on the Future of Broadcasting, HMSO, London.

Aronowitz, Stanley, 1981, *The Crisis in Historical Materialism: Class, Politics and Culture in Marxist Theory*, Praeger, New York.

Askoy, Asu and Kevin Robins, 1992, 'Hollywood for the 21st century: Global competition for critical mass in image markets', *Cambridge Journal of Economics*, vol. 16, no. 1.

Bagdikian, Ben H., 1997, *The Media Monopoly*, Beacon Press, Boston.

Bakhtin, M.M., 1992, *The Dialogic Imagination*, University of Texas Press, Austin.

Barker, Colin, 1997, 'Some reflections on two books by Ellen Wood', *Historical Materialism, Research in Critical Marxist Theory*, no. 1, Autumn.

Barthes, Roland, 1986, *Mythologies*, Paladin, London.

—— 1990, *S/Z*, Blackwell, Oxford.

Baudrillard, Jean, 1994, *Simulacra and Simulation*, University of Michigan Press, Ann Arbor.

Benhabib, Seyla, 1986, *Critique, Norm, and Utopia: A Study of the Foundations of Critical Theory*, Columbia University Press, New York.

Benjamin, Walter, 1999a, *The Arcades Project*, translated by Howard Eiland and Kevin McLaughlin, Harvard University Press, Cambridge, Massachusetts.

273

—— 1999b, *Illuminations*, Pimlico, London.

Bennett, Tony, 1997, 'Towards a pragmatic for cultural studies' in *Cultural Methodologies*, ed. Jim McGuigan, Sage, London.

Best, Steven and Douglas Kellner, 1991, *Postmodern Theory, Critical Interrogations*, Macmillan Press, London.

Bordwell, David, Janet Staiger and Kristen Thompson, 1988, *The Classical Hollywood Cinema, Film Style and Mode of Production to 1960*, Routledge, London.

Bottomore, Tom, (ed.), 1988, *A Dictionary of Marxist Thought*, Blackwell, Oxford.

Bourdieu, Pierre, 1996, *Distinction, A Social Critique of the Judgment of Taste*, Routledge, London.

Braverman, Harry, 1974, *Labor and Monopoly Capital: The Degradation of Work in the Twentieth Century*, Monthly Review Press, New York.

Brecht, Bertolt, 2000, 'A short organum for the theatre' in *Marxist Literary Theory*, ed. Terry Eagleton and Drew Milne, Blackwell, Oxford.

Briggs, Asa, 1961, *The Birth of Broadcasting*, Oxford University Press, Oxford.

Buck-Morss, Susan, 1989, *The Dialectics of Seeing, Walter Benjamin and the Arcades Project*, MIT Press, Cambridge, Massachusetts.

Byrne, Eleanor and Martin McQuillan, 1999, *Deconstructing Disney*, Pluto Press, London.

Castells, Manuel, 1996, *The Rise of the Network Society*, Blackwell, Oxford.

—— 1997, *The Power of Identity*, Blackwell, Oxford.

Caughie, John, (ed.), 1990, *Theories of Authorship*, Routledge, London.

Chanan, Michael, 1983, 'The emergence of an industry' in *British Cinema History*, ed. James Curran and Vincent Porter, Weidenfeld and Nicolson, London.

Christopherson, S. and M. Storper, 1986, 'The city as studio; the world as back lot: The impact of vertical disintegration on the location of the motion picture industry', *Environment and Planning D: Society and Space*, no. 4.

Clarke, John, 1991, *New Times and Old Enemies: Essays on Cultural Studies and America*, HarperCollins/Academic, London.

Clarke, Simon, (ed.), 1991, *The State Debate*, Macmillan, London.

Clarke, Simon, et al., 1980, *One Dimensional Marxism, Althusser and the Politics of Culture*, Allison and Busby, London.

Cohen, G.A., 1978, *Karl Marx's Theory of History: A Defence*, Clarendon Press, Oxford.

Cohen, Nick, 1999, *Cruel Britania, Notes on the Sinister and Preposterous*, Verso, London.

Collins, Jim, 1992, 'Television and postmodernism' in *Channels of Discourse*, ed. Robert C. Allen, Routledge, London.

Collins, Richard, 1999, 'European Union media and communication policies', in *The Media in Britain, Current Debates and Developments*, ed. Jane Stoke and Anna Reading, Macmillan, London.

Collins, Richard and Cristina Murroni, 1996, *New Media, New Policies*, Polity Press, Cambridge.

Coward, Rosalind and John Ellis, 1977, *Language and Materialism: Developments in Semiology and the Theory of the Subject*, Routledge and Kegan Paul, London.

Cowling, Keith, 1982, *Monopoly Capitalism*, Macmillan, London.

Creed, Barbara, 1993, *The Monstrous Feminine, Film, Feminism, Psychoanalysis*, Routledge, London.

Crofts, Stephen, 1998, 'Concepts of national cinema' in *The Oxford Guide to Film Studies*, ed. John Hill and Pamela Church Gibson, Oxford University Press, Oxford.

Curran, James and Jean Seaton, 1997, *Power Without Responsibility, The Press and Broadcasting in Britain*, Routledge, London.

Debord, Guy, 1983, *Society of the Spectacle*, Black and Red, Detroit.

—— 1990, *Comments on the Society of the Spectacle*, Verso, London.

Derrida, Jacques, 1994, *Spectres of Marx, the State of the Debt, the Work of Mourning and the New International*, Routledge, London.

Dews, Peter, 1995, 'Adorno, post-structuralism and the critique of identity' in *Mapping Ideology*, ed. Slavoj Žižek, Verso, London.

Dijk, Jan Van, 1999, *The Network Society*, Sage, London.

Doane, Mary Anne, 1996, 'The Economy of desire: The commodity form in/of the cinema' in *Movies and Mass Culture*, ed. John Belton, Rutgers University Press, New Jersey.

Dorfman, Ariel and Armand Mattelart, 1991, *How to Read Donald Duck: Imperialist Ideology in the Disney Comic*, International General, New York.

Dovey, Jon, 2000, *Freakshow, First Person Media and Factual Television*, Pluto Press, London.

Downing, John, et al., 2001, *Radical Media, Rebellious Communication and Social Movements*, Sage, London.

Dyer, Richard, 1985, 'Utopia as entertainment' in *Movies and Methods Vol. 2*, ed. Bill Nichols, University of California Press, Berkeley.

Eagleton, Terry, 1986a, *Against the Grain*, Verso, London.

—— 1986b, *Criticism and Ideology*, Verso, London.

—— 1989, 'Base and superstructure in Raymond Williams' in *Raymond Williams, Critical Perspectives*, ed. Terry Eagleton, Polity Press, Cambridge.

—— 1991, *Ideology: An Introduction*, Verso, London.

—— 1993, *Literary Theory*, Blackwell, Oxford.

—— 1997, *The Ideology of the Aesthetic*, Blackwell, Oxford.

—— 2000, *The Idea of Culture*, Blackwell, Oxford.

Eckert, Charles, 1996, 'The Carole Lombard in Macy's window' in *Movies and Mass Culture*, ed. John Belton, Rutgers University Press, New Jersey.

Ehrenreich, Barbara, 1995, 'The silenced majority: Why the average working person has disappeared from American media and culture' in *Gender, Race and Class in Media: A Text-reader*, ed. Gail Dines and Jean M. Humez, Sage, London.

Ehrenreich, Barbara and John Ehrenreich, 1979, 'The professional-managerial class' in *Between Capital and Labour*, ed. Pat Walker, Harvester Press, Hassocks.

Enzenberger, Hans Magnus, 1999, 'Constituents of a theory of the media' in *Media studies: A Reader*, ed. Paul Marris and Sue Thornham, Edinburgh University Press, Edinburgh.

Feenberg, Andrew, 1980, *Lukács, Marx and the Sources of Critical Theory*, Oxford University Press, Oxford.

Ferguson, Robert, 1998, *Representing 'Race', Ideology, Identity and the Media*, Arnold, London.

Fleming, Dan, 2000, 'The ghost citizen and class' in *Formations, A 21st Century Media Studies Textbook*, ed. Dan Fleming, Manchester University Press, Manchester.

Friedman, Milton, 1982, *Capitalism and Freedom*, University of Chicago Press, Chicago.

Gardiner, Michael, 1992, *The Dialogics of Critique, M.M. Bakhtin and the Theory of Ideology*, Routledge, London.

Garnham, Nicholas, 1990, *Capitalism and Communication: Global Culture and the Economics of Information*, Sage, London.

—— 1997, 'Political economy and the practice of cultural studies' in *Cultural Studies in Question*, ed. Marjorie Ferguson and Peter Golding, Sage, London.

—— 2000, *Emancipation, the Media, and Modernity: Arguments About the Media and Social Theory*, Oxford University Press, Oxford.

Giddens, Anthony, 1999, *Runaway World, How Globalization is Reshaping Our Lives*, Profile Books, London.

Golding, Peter and Graham Murdock, 2000, 'Culture, communications and political economy' in *Mass Media and Society*, ed. James Curran and Michael Gurevitch, Arnold, London.

Goodwin, Peter, 1999, 'The role of the state' in *The Media in Britain, Current Debates and Developments*, ed. Jane Stoke and Anna Reading, Macmillan, London.

Gramsci, Antonio, 1967, *The Modern Prince and Other Writings*, Lawrence and Wishart, London.

—— 1971, *Selection from the Prison Notebooks of Antonio Gramsci*, ed. Quintin Hoare and Geoffrey Nowell Smith, International Publishers, New York.

Grantham, Bill, 2000, *'Some Big Bourgeois Brothel', Contexts for France's Culture Wars with Hollywood*, University of Luton Press, Luton.

Grover, Ron, 1997, *The Disney Touch, Disney, ABC and the Quest for the World's Greatest Media Empire*, Irwin Publishing, Chicago.

Habermas, Jürgen, 1976, *Legitimation Crisis*, Heinemann, London.

—— 1987, *The Philosophical Discourse of Modernity*, Polity Press, Cambridge.

—— 1996, *The Structural Transformation of the Public Sphere*, Polity Press, Cambridge.

Hall, Stuart, 1997, *Representation, Cultural Representations and Signifying Practices*, ed. Stuart Hall, Sage/Open University Press, London.

Hall, Stuart, Chas Critcher, Tony Jefferson, John Clarke and Brian Roberts, 1978, *Policing the Crisis, Mugging, the State and Law and Order*, Macmillan, London.

Hall, Stuart and Martin Jacques, 1989, *New Times: The Changing Face of Politics in the 1990s*, Lawrence and Wishart, London.

Hamacher, Werner, 1979, 'Lingua Amissa: The Messianism of commodity-language and Derrida's *Spectres of Marx*' in *Ghostly Demarcations, A Symposium on Jacques Derrida's Spectres of Marx*, ed. Michael Sprinker, Verso, London.

Haralambos, Michael, 1985, *Sociology: Themes and Perspectives*, Unwin Hyman, London.

Harvey, David, 1984, *The Limits to Capital*, Blackwell, Oxford.

—— 1990, *The Condition of Postmodernity: An Enquiry into the Origins of Cultural Change*, Blackwell, Oxford.

Heffernan, Nick, 2000, *Capital, Class and Technology in Contemporary American Culture*, Pluto Press, London.

Herman, Edward S. and Noam Chomsky, 1994, *Manufacturing Consent, The Political Economy of the Media*, Vintage, London.

Herman, Edward S. and Robert W. McChesney, 1997, *The Global Media: The New Missionaries of Corporate Capitalism*, Cassell, London.

Hesmondhalgh, David, 2002, *The Culture Industries*, Sage, London.

Higson, Andrew, 2000, 'The limiting imagination of national cinema' in *Cinema and Nation*, ed. Mette Jort and Scott Mackenzie, Routledge, London.

Hobsbawm, Eric J., 1968, *Industry and Empire, An Economic History of Britain Since 1750*, Penguin/Weidenfeld and Nicolson, London.

Hogenkamp, Bert, 1986, *Deadly Parallels: Film and the Left in Britain 1929–1939*, Lawrence and Wishart, London.

Holloway, John, and Sol Picciotto, 1991, 'Capital, crisis and the state' in *The State Debate*, ed. Simon Clarke, Macmillan, London.

Homer, Sean, 2001, 'It's the political economy, stupid! On Žižek's Marxism', *Radical Philosophy*, no. 108, July–August.

Hoskins, Colin, Stuart McFadyen and Adam Finn, 1997, *Global Television and Film, An Introduction to the Economics of the Business*, Oxford University Press, Oxford.

Humphreys, Peter J., 1996, *Mass Media and Media Policy in Western Europe*, Manchester University Press, Manchester.

Hutton, Will, 1996, *The State We're In*, Vintage, London.

Jackson, Leonard, 1994, *The Dematerialisation of Karl Marx: Literature and Marxist Theory*, Longman, London.

Jameson, Fredric, 1974a, *Marxism and Form, Twentieth-Century Dialetical Theories of Literature*, Princeton University Press, Princeton.

—— 1974b, *The Prison-House of Language, A Critical Account of Structuralism and Russian Formalism*, Princeton University Press, Princeton.

—— 1988, 'Reflections in conclusion' in *Aesthetics and Politics*, ed. Ronald Taylor, Verso, London.

—— 1989, *The Political Unconscious*, Routledge, London.

—— 1991, *Postmodernism: Or, the Cultural Logic of Late Capitalism*, Verso, London.

—— 1992, *Signatures of the Visible*, Routledge, London.

—— 1999, 'Marx's purloined letter' in *Ghostly Demarcations, A Symposium on Jacques Derrida's Spectres of Marx*, ed. Michael Sprinker, Verso, London.

Jessop, Bob, 1991, 'Thatcherism and flexibility: the white heat of a post-Fordist revolution' in *The Politics of Flexibility*, ed. Bob Jessop et al., Edward Elgar, Aldershot.

—— 1997, 'Post-Fordism and the state' in *Post-Fordism: A Reader*, ed. Ash Amin, Blackwell, Oxford.

Jhally, Sut, 1987, *The Codes of Advertising, Fetishism and the Political Economy of Meaning in the Consumer Society*, Routledge, London.

Keenan, Thomas, 1996, 'The point is to (ex)change it: Reading *Capital* rhetorically' in *Fetishism as Cultural Discourse*, ed. Emily Apter and William Pietz, Cornell University Press, New York.

Kellner, Douglas, 1997, 'Overcoming the divide: Cultural studies and political economy' in *Cultural Studies In Question*, ed. Marjorie Ferguson and Peter Golding, Sage, London.

Klein, Naomi, 2000, *No Logo*, Flamingo, London.

Korsch, Karl, 1972, *Marxism and Philosophy*, New Left Books, London.

Kroker, Arthur, 1996, 'Virtual capitalism' in *Techno Science and Cyber Culture*, ed. Stanley Aronowitz, Routledge, London.

Kuhn, Annette, 1990, *Alien Zone: Cultural Theory and Contemporary Science Fiction Cinema*, Verso, London.

Lash, Scott and John Urry, 1987, *The End of Organized Capitalism*, Polity Press, Cambridge.

Lenin, V.I., 1996, *The State and Revolution*, Foreign Language Press, Beijing.

Leslie, Esther, 2000, *Walter Benjamin, Overpowering Conformism*, Pluto Press, London.

—— 2002, *Hollywood Flatlands, Animation, Critical Theory and the Avant-Garde*, Verso, London.

Lichtenberg, Judith, 2000, 'In defence of objectivity revisited' in *Mass Media and Society*, ed. J. Curran and M. Gurevitch, Arnold, London.

Lipietz, Alain, 1987, *Mirages and Miracles, The Crises of Global Fordism*, Verso, London.

Lodziak, Conrad, 1995, *Manipulating Needs, Capitalism and Culture*, Pluto Press, London.

Lovell, Terry, 1983, *Pictures of Reality, Aesthetics, Politics and Pleasure*, BFI, London.

Lukács, Georg, 1971, *History and Class Consciousness, Studies in Marxist Dialectics*, Merlin Press, London.

Lunn, Eugene, 1984, *Marxism and Modernism, An Historical Study of Lukács, Brecht, Benjamin and Adorno*, University of California Press, Berkeley.

Macherey, Pierre, 1978, *A Theory of Literary Production*, Routledge and Kegan Paul, London.

MacKinnon, Kenneth, 1998, 'Bare necessities and naked luxuries: The 1990s male as erotic object' in *Dissident Voices, The Politics of Television and Cultural Change*, ed. Mike Wayne, Pluto Press, London.

Mandel, Ernest, 1978, *Late Capitalism*, Verso, London.

Marcuse, Herbert, 1955, *Reason and Revolution: Hegel and the Rise of Social Theory*, Routledge and Kegan Paul, London.

Mattelart, Armand, 1991, *Advertising International, The Privatisation of Public Space*, Routledge, London.

Marx, Karl, 1967, *Essential Writings of Karl Marx*, ed. David Caute, Panther, London.

—— 1972, *The Economic and Philosophical Manuscripts of 1844*, International Publishers, New York.

—— 1973, *Marx's Grundrisse*, ed. David McLellan, Paladin, London.

—— 1980, *The Thought of Karl Marx*, ed. David McLellan, Macmillan, London.

—— 1983, *Capital Vol. 1*, Lawrence and Wishart, London.

—— 1984, *The Eighteenth Brumaire of Louis Bonaparte*, Lawrence and Wishart, London.

Marx, Karl and Friedrich Engels, 1956, *The Holy Family or Critique of Critical Critique*, Foreign Languages Publishing House, Moscow.

—— 1985, *The Communist Manifesto*, Penguin, London.

—— 1989, *The German Ideology*, Lawrence and Wishart, London.

McArthur, Colin, 2000, 'The critics who knew too little: Hitchcock and the absent class paradigm', *Film Studies*, no. 2, Spring.

McCarthy, Cameron, 2000, 'Reading the American popular: suburban resentment and the representation of the inner city in contemporary film and television' in *Formations, A 21st Century Media Studies Textbook*, ed. Dan Fleming, Manchester University Press, Manchester.

McLennan, Gregor, 1996, 'Post-Marxism and the "four sins" of modernist theorizing', *New Left Review*, no. 218, July–August.

McQuail, Denis, 1997, 'Policy help wanted: Willing and able media culturalists please apply' in *Cultural Studies In Question*, ed. Marjorie Ferguson and Peter Golding, Sage, London.

—— 1998a, 'Changing media and changing society' in *Media Policy: Convergence, Concentration and Commerce*, ed. Denis McQuail and Karen Siune, Sage, London.

——1998b, 'Commercialization and beyond' in *Media Policy: Convergence, Concentration and Commerce*, ed. Denis McQuail and Karen Siune, Sage, London.

Meier, Werner A. and Josef Trappel, 1998, 'Media concentration and the public interest' in *Media Policy, Convergence, Concentration and Commerce*, ed. Denis McQuail and Karen Siune, Sage, London.

Mepham, John, 1979, 'The theory of ideology in *Capital*' in *Issues In Marxist Philosophy, Epistemology, Science, Ideology Volume 3*, ed. John Mepham and D.H. Ruben, Harvester Press, Hassocks.

Merriden, Trevor, 2001, *Irresistible Forces, the Business Legacy of Napster and the Growth of the Underground Internet*, Capstone, Oxford.

Mészáros, István, 1995, *Beyond Capital*, Merlin Press, London.

Miliband, Ralph, 1987, *The State in Capitalist Society*, Quartet Books, London.

Moran, Albert, 1996, *Film Policy: International, National and Regional Perspectives*, Routledge, London.

Mulvey, Laura, 1996, 'The carapace that failed: Ousmane Sembene's *Xala*' in *Fetishism and Curiosity*, ed. Laura Mulvey, BFI, London.

Murdock, Graham, 1997, 'Base notes: The conditions of cultural practice' in *Cultural Studies In Question*, ed. Marjorie Ferguson and Peter Golding, Sage, London.

—— 2000, 'Reconstructing the ruined tower: Contemporary communications and questions of class' in *Mass Media and Society*, ed. James Curran and Michael Gurevitch, Arnold, London.

—— 2001, 'Against enclosure: Rethinking the cultural commons' in *British Cultural Studies*, ed. David Morley and Kevin Robins, Oxford University Press, Oxford.

Murray, Patrick, 2000, 'Marx's "Truly social" labour theory of value: Part II. How is labour that is under the sway of capital *actually* abstract?', *Historical Materialism*, No. 7, Winter.

Negus, Keith, 1997, 'The production of culture' in *Production of Culture/Cultures of Production*, ed. Paul du Gay, Open University Press/Sage, London.

Nichols, Bill, 1996, 'Reality TV and social perversion' in *Media Studies, A Reader*, ed. Paul Marris and Sue Thornham, Edinburgh University Press, Edinburgh.

Noble, David, 1979, 'The PMC: A critique' in *Between Capital and Labour*, ed. Pat Walker, Harvester Press, Hassocks.

Norris, Christopher, 1992, *Uncritical Theory, Postmodernism, Intellectuals and the Gulf War*, Lawrence and Wishart, London.

Palmer, Bryan, D., 1990, *Descent into Discourse, The Reification of Language and the Writing of Social History*, Temple University Press, Philadelphia.

Parekh, Bhikhu, 1982, *Marx's Theory of Ideology*, Croom Helm, London.

Penley, Constance, 1989, 'Time travel, primal scene and the critical dystopia' in *Fantasy and the Cinema*, ed. James Donald, BFI, London.

Perkins, Stephen, 1993, *Marxism and the Proletariat, A Lukácsian Perspective*, Pluto Press, London.

Petley, Julian, 1999, 'The regulation of media content' in *The Media in Britain, Current Debates and Developments*, ed. Jane Stokes and Anna Reading, Macmillan, London.

Pietz, Willaim, 1996, 'Fetishism and materialism: The limits of theory in Marx' in *Fetishism as Cultural Discourse*, ed. Emily Apter and William Pietz, Cornell University Press, New York.

Pinker, Stephen, 1994, *The Language Instinct*, Penguin, London.

Piore, Michael and Charles Sabel, 1984, *The Second Industrial Divide*, Basic Books, New York.

Porter, Vincent, 1983, 'The context of creativity: Ealing Studios and Hammer Films' in *British Cinema History*, ed. James Curran and Vincent Porter, Barnes and Noble Books, New Jersey.

Prusak, Laurence, (ed.),1997, *Knowledge in Organizations*, Butterworth Heinemann, Oxford.

Puttnam, David, 1997, *The Undeclared War, The Struggle for Control of the World's Film Industry*, HarperCollins, London.

Rees, John, 1998, *The Algebra of Revolution, The Dialectic and the Classical Marxist Tradition*, Routledge, London.

Reich, Robert, 1991, *The Work of Nations: Preparing Ourselves for 21st-Century Capitalism*, Simon and Schuster, London.

Rigby, S.H., 1998, *Marxism and History: A Critical Introduction*, Manchester University Press, Manchester.

Ritchie, Jean, 2000, *Big Brother: The Official Unseen Story*, Channel Four Books, London.

Roos, Johan, (ed.), 1997, *Intellectual Capital: Navigating the New Business Landscape* Macmillan Business, Basingstoke.

Rustin, Michael, 1989, 'The trouble with "new times"' in *New Times: The Changing Face of Politics in the 1990s*, ed. Stuart Hall and Martin Jacques, Lawrence and Wishart, London.

Sabel, Charles F., 1997, 'Flexible specialisation and the re-emergence of regional economies' in *Post-Fordism: A Reader*, ed. Ash Amin, Blackwell, Oxford.

Said, Edward, 1978, *Orientalism*, Routledge and Kegan Paul, London.

Sardar, Ziauddin, 2002, 'Walt Disney and the double victimization of Pocahontas' in *The Third Text Reader on Art, Culture and Theory*, ed. Rasheed Araeen, Sean Cubitt and Ziauddin Sardar, Continuum Press, London.

Schiller, Dan, 1999, *Digital Capitalism, Networking the Global Market System*, MIT Press, Cambridge, Massachusetts.

Schiller, Herbert, 1989, *Culture, Inc.: The Corporate Takeover of Public Expression*, Oxford University Press, Oxford.

Schlosser, Eric, 2001, *Fast Food Nation*, Allen Lane, Penguin, London.

Sinclair, John, 1989, *Images Incorporated: Advertising as Industry and Ideology*, Routledge, London.

Smith, Andrew, 2001, 'Reading wealth in Nigeria: Occult capitalism and Marx's vampires', *Historical Materialism, Research in Critical Marxist Theory*, vol. 9, Winter.

Sobchack, Vivian, (ed.), 2000, *Metamorphing: Visual Transformation and the Culture of Quick-Change*, University of Minnesota Press, Minneapolis.

Soper, Kate, 1986, *Humanism and Anti-Humanism, Problems of Modern European Thought*, Hutchinson, London.

Storper, Michael, 1997, 'The transition to flexible specialisation in the US film industry: External economics, the division of labour and the crossing of industrial divides' in *Post-Fordism: A Reader*, ed. Ash Amin, Blackwell, Oxford.

Strinati, Dominic, 1995, *An Introduction to Theories of Popular Culture*, Routledge, London.

Tapscott, Don, Alex Lowy and David Ticoll, 1998, *Blueprint to the Digital Economy: Creating Wealth in the Era of E-business*, McGraw-Hill, London.

Taussig, Michael T., 1980, *The Devil and Commodity Fetishism in South America*, University of North Carolina Press, Chapel Hill.

—— 1996, 'Maleficium: State Fetishism' in *Fetishism as Cultural Discourse*, ed. Emily Apter and William Pietz, Cornell University Press, New York.

Taylor, Ronald, (ed.), 1988, *Aesthetics and Politics*, Verso, London.

Thompson, E.P., 1978, *The Poverty of Theory and Other Essays*, Merlin Press, London.

Thompson, John B., 1990, *Ideology and Modern Culture: Critical Social Theory in the Era of Mass Communication*, Polity Press, Cambridge.

Thrift, Nigel, 1999, 'Capitalism's cultural turn' in *Culture and Economy After the Cultural Turn*, ed. Larry Ray and Andrew Sayer, Sage, London.

Tracey, Michael, 1998, *The Decline and Fall of Public Service Broadcasting*, Oxford University Press, Oxford.

Vološhinov, V.N., 1996, *Marxism and the Philosophy of Language*, Harvard University Press, Cambridge, Massachusetts.

Wallerstein, Immanuel, 1989, *Historical Capitalism*, Verso, London.

Wasko, Janet, 1994, *Hollywood in the Information Age, Beyond the Silver Screen*, Polity Press, Cambridge.

Wayne, Mike, 1997, *Theorising Video Practice*, Lawrence and Wishart, London.

—— 2000, '*Who Wants To Be A Millionaire?* Contextual analysis and the endgame of public television' in *Formations, A 21st Century Media Studies Textbook*, ed. Dan Fleming, Manchester University Press, Manchester.

—— 2001, *Political Film: The Dialectics of Third Cinema*, Pluto Press, London.

—— 2002a, *The Politics of Contemporary European Cinema: Histories, Borders, Diasporas*, Intellect Books, Bristol.

—— 2002b, 'Constellating Walter Benjamin and British cinema: A study of *The Private Life of Henry VIII* (1933)', *Quarterly Review of Film and Video*, vol. 19, no. 3, July–September.

—— 2002c, 'Utopianism and film', *Historical Materialism, Research in Critical Marxist Theory*, vol. 10, no. 4.

Webster, Frank, 1995, *Theories of the Information Society*, Routledge, London.

Wilkin, Peter, 2001, *The Political Economy of Global Communciation*, Pluto Press, London.

Willemen, Paul, 1989, 'The Third Cinema question: Notes and reflections' in *Questions of Third Cinema*, ed. Jim Pines and Paul Willemen, BFI, London.

Williams, Raymond, 1980, *Problems in Materialism and Culture*, Verso, London.

—— 1988, *Keywords, A Vocabulary of Culture and Society*, Fontana Press, London.

Winston, Brian, 1995, *Claiming the Real: The Griersonian Documentary and its Legitimations*, BFI, London.

—— 1998, *Media Technology and Society, A History: From the Telegraph to the Internet*, Routledge, London.

Wollen, Peter, 1970, *Signs and Meanings in the Cinema*, BFI/Thames and Hudson, London.

Wright, Erik Olin, 1979, 'Intellectuals and the class structure' in *Between Labour and Capital*, ed. Pat Walker, Harvester Press, Hassocks.

Wyatt, Justin, 1998, 'The formation of the "major independent": Miramax, New Line and the new Hollywood' in *Contemporary Hollywood Cinema*, ed. Steve Neale and Murray Smith, Routledge, London.

Žižek, Slavoj, 1989, *The Sublime Object of Ideology*, Verso, London.

—— (ed.), 1995, *Mapping Ideology*, Verso, London.

—— 2001, *Enjoy Your Symptom! Jacques Lacan In Hollywood and Out*, Routledge, London.

Index

Abbott, Paul, 19
Abercrombie, Nicholas, 179
abstraction, 33, 34, 35, 36, 37, 204, 211–12, 249, 257–8, 260
Ackre, Jane, 82
Adorno, 28, 124, 200, 224, 230–3, 234, 235, 238, 243, 249, 250, 260
advertising, 71, 77, 78, 81, 83–4, 109, 110, 111, 207, 208
Afghanistan, 30, 97
Affleck, Ben, 75
Aglietta, Michael, 41, 66, 70, 71
Ali, Muhammad, 172
Alien (film), 7–11, 15
Al Jazeera, 97
Althusser, Louis, 127, 138–41, 184, 218, 261
Amariglio, Jack, 208,
American Beauty (film), 195
Annan Report (Broadcasting), 106, 109
Antitrust (film), 16, 55–6
appearance-forms, 62, 86, 94, 103, 107, 108, 116, 117, 125, 126, 184–5, 190, 193–4, 198, 208, 209, 214, 219, 257, 260, 262, 263
Aristotle, 34
Arts Council, 96
AT&T, 65–6, 76, 95
Austen, Jade and Keiren, 181

Bakhtin, Mikhail, 170–3, 181
balance, 163, 169, 224–5, 227, 246, 253
Balibar, Etienne, 127
BBC, 81, 109, 110–11, 146, 253
Barthes, Roland, 7, 160, 170, 171, 172
Baudrillard, Jean, 194, 217
Bean (film), 65
Beauty and the Beast (film), 74
Beaverbrook, Lord, 109

Bend it Like Beckham (film), 115
Benhabib, Seyla, 223, 248, 255
Benjamin, Walter, 47–8, 54, 199, 231
Bennett, Tony, 93–4, 104, 120
Bentley, Marcus (*Big Brother*), 149
Berlusconi, Silvio, 98, 114
Bertelsmann, 55, 58, 97
Bhaji on the Beach (film), 115
Big Brother (television), 5, 119, 127, 132, 133, 141, 142, 143, 144, 145–54, 177, 199, 261, 265–6
Big Brother's Little Brother (television), 147
bin Laden, Osama, 30, 97
black film, 30–1, 32
Blair, Tony, 157–8, 162, 177
Blob, The (film), 34
Blue Collar (film), 7
Bourdieu, Pierre, 18, 28
Boyz N the Hood (film), 32
Brando, Marlon, 29
Braverman, Harry, 19
Briggs, Asa, 90
Broadcasting Act (1990), 80, 105
Broadcasting Standards Commission, 81
BskyB, 105, 108, 146
Bush, George W., 97–8, 121, 177, 226
Byrne, Eleanor, 80

Cabinet of Dr Caligari, The (film), 215
Callari, Antonio, 208
Canal Plus (television), 98
Candyman (film), 201
Capital (Marx), 107, 123, 185, 189, 192, 203, 207
capitalist class (personifications of capital), 10, 12–13, 23, 24, 33–4, 35, 64, 68, 70, 95–6, 99, 104, 124, 135, 170, 175, 177, 178, 191–2, 201, 203, 229, 239, 243, 245, 246, 250, 259, 262–3
see also class

Carlton (television), 105
Castaway (television), 146
Castells, Manuel, 40, 44–5, 49, 59, 127
Chadha, Gurinder, 115
Channel Five, 81, 146
Channel 4, 81, 110, 146, 147
children, 179–82, 196–7, 210
Chomsky, Noam, 63, 80
Christopherson, S. 72
Clarke, John, 20
Class,
    signifiers of, 7–10, 16, 149–50
    class struggle, 13, 52, 53, 54, 60, 62, 70, 105–6, 129, 189, 203, 221, 222, 246, 266
    class struggle and signs, 143, 148–9, 154, 168
    Marxist definitions, 11–17, 36, 244–5
    sociological definitions, 8–10, 13–14, 15, 16, 35, 244
    transposable cognitive model, 221–5, 228–9, 252–3, 265
    see also capitalist class, middle class, intelligentsia, petit-bourgeoisie
Clocking Off (television), 19
Cohen, G.A. 53
Cold Feet (television), 27
Collins, Richard, 92–3
Communist Manifesto, The (Marx), 4, 201, 210, 258
competition, 43, 63–7, 69–70, 71, 78, 88, 92, 95, 98–102, 104, 105, 151, 204, 206, 247, 262
consent and coercion, 95–7, 106–7, 115–16, 134, 178–9
    see also hegemony
Conservative government, 99, 105
contradiction, 3, 7, 16, 27, 39, 43, 46, 48, 50, 52, 62, 67, 86, 88, 92, 103, 104, 105, 111, 123, 125, 224, 260, 261–2, 263, 264
    within consciousness, 183
    between thought and thing, 230
    between base and superstructure, 131, 132, 154

between modes of production and development, 145
    in ideology, 176, 224
    representations of children, 196
    repression of, 133, 142, 172
    the subject, 185
Coup, The (music), 31–2
Cowling, Keith, 70–1
Crofts, Stephen, 115
culturalisation, 21, 23, 24, 44, 259

Daily Mail (print), 168–70, 174–5
Daily Mirror (print), 176–7
Dark City (film), 194, 209, 213–18, 258
Davis, Mike, 97
Debord, Guy, 42, 148
Derrida, Jacques, 162–4, 172, 219, 233
Devil's Backbone, The (film), 196–7, 201
discourse theory, 163–6, 225, 264
Disney, 63, 65, 73–8, 80, 85, 86, 97
division of labour, 7, 8, 14–15, 17–19, 27–8, 30, 187, 232, 240, 247, 263
Douglas, Michael, 227
Dr Dre, 31, 57
Dunkley, Christopher, 131–2, 133, 144

Eagleton, Terry, 112, 138, 161, 175, 239
East is East (film), 115
Ecologist, The (print), 96
Economic and Philosophical Manuscripts (Marx), 212
Ehrenreich, Barbara, 15–16, 20
Ehrenreich, John, 20
Eighteenth Brumaire of Louis Bonaparte, The (Marx), 203
Eisner, Michael, 73–4, 85
end credits, 1–3, 72
Endemol Entertainment, 145, 147
Engels, Friedrich, 122, 132–3, 135, 136, 137
ER (television), 110
Ermo (film), 114
Eurimages, 102–3

European Commission, 100
European Union, 100
Evening News (print), 83–4
Evening Standard (print), 83–4

Fallen (film), 211
family, 179–82
Fanning, Shawn, 55–6
Federal Radio Commission, 91
Feminism, 200
Fight Club (film), 195
Film Council, 96, 102
Financial Times, (print), 131, 132, 133
Fininvest, 98, 115
Finucane, Pat, 253
fixed capital, 42, 46–50, 59
Fordism, 44, 62, 66–70, 72, 77, 86, 105, 106, 107, 110, 114, 117, 153, 160, 161
    see also post-Fordism
Foucault, Michel, 163, 219, 233, 236
Free Software Foundation, 25–6
Friedman, Milton, 65
French Connection, The (film), 216

Garnham, Nicholas, 21, 124
GATS, 95
GATT, 114
General Electric, 65, 73, 84–5, 86
General Public License, 25–6
German Ideology, The (Marx and Engels), 122, 135, 137
ghosts, 11–12, 152, 184, 194, 197, 201–3, 205, 208–13, 258, 263, 267
Goldsmith, Teddy, 96
Goody, Jade (*Big Brother*), 153
Granada (television), 105
Green, Michael (Chairman of Carlton), 35

Habermas, Jürgen, 78–9, 83, 106, 163, 169, 170, 223, 233, 235–42, 254–5, 266–7
Hackman, Gene, 75
Hall, Stuart, 164–5

Harry Potter and the Philosopher's Stone (film), 130, 152, 211–12
Harvey, David, 63, 66, 71
Hegel, G.W.F., 104, 122–3, 136, 139, 168, 182, 184, 211, 222
hegemony, 135, 143, 155, 177–8, 264
    counter-hegemonic, 182
Hellraiser (film), 215
Herman, Edward, 82, 63, 80
Hesmondhalgh, David, 28
hip hop, 31–2
History and Class Consciousness (Lukács), 158, 188
Holy Family, The (Marx and Engels), 211–12
Hoskins, Colin, 64
Hughes, David, 29
Hunchback of Notre Dame, The (film), 75
Hutton, Will, 109

idealism, 120, 122–3, 136, 211–12, 225, 255
ideologeme, 9–10, 143, 148–9, 265
ideology, 21, 155, 168, 169, 173–82, 190–1, 206, 221, 227, 233–4, 259, 264
Immelt, Jeff (General Electric CEO), 85
ITV (television), 80–1, 99–100, 105, 146, 238
Independent Television Commission, 81, 110
ITV Digital (television), 98, 105, 199
Injustice (film), 96–7, 175, 252–4, 267
intelligentsia, 17–19, 21, 23–26, 32, 36, 38–9, 69, 101, 120, 123, 129, 135, 233, 234, 236, 246–7, 259, 263
    see also class
interdependence,
    social and economic, 7, 15, 23, 164, 226, 242, 244, 245, 247, 258, 267
    of base and superstructure, 139
    denial of, 194

interdependence *continued*
  and gender, 195
  and identification, 228, 238, 242,
    247
  of language, 137, 159, 168, 170,
    182, 223
  master and slave, 222
  see also intersubjectivity
International Monetary Fund, 1, 61,
    187, 231
Internet, 5, 24–6, 39, 49, 50–1, 54,
    56, 58, 59, 140–1, 250, 261
  dot.com crash, 39–44, 198,
    206–7, 214, 251
  and *Big Brother* (television),
    146–7, 148
intersubjectivity, 223, 225–6, 228,
    236, 237, 238, 239, 240, 241,
    242, 243, 248, 252, 253, 254,
    255, 266–7
  see also interdependence; the
    subject
Island of Dr Moreau, The (film), 29

Jackson, Leonard, 136
Jameson, Fredric, 4, 9, 130–1, 133,
    141–5, 209, 216, 217, 221–2,
    265
Jolie, Angelina, 75

Keenan, Thomas, 203
Kellner, Douglas, 124, 126
Kilmer, Val, 29
Kirch, Leo, 114
Koppel, Ted, 78
Korsch, Karl, 156–7
Korzun, Dina, 198
Kotto, Yaphet, 7
Kroker, Arthur, 52

labour power, 11, 14, 17, 18, 27, 33,
    39, 121, 204–5, 258
Lacan, Jacques, 164, 219, 234
Lash, Scott, 72
Last Resort (film), 198
Lawrence, Stephen, 174–5
Lawson, Nigella, 155
Lenin, V.I. 241
Letter To Brezhnev (film), 13

Letterman, David, 78
Lévi-Strauss, Claude, 160, 218
Lichtenberg, Judith, 226–9
Lilo and Stitch (film), 231
Lodziak, Conrad, 179
Lovell, Terry, 173
Luckiest Nut in the World, The (short
    film), 230–1
Lukács, Georg, 158, 159, 184,
    187–8, 194, 197, 224, 247, 248,
    250, 251, 260
Lyotard, Jean-François, 238

Macdonald, Kevin, 227–8
MAFF, 51, 112
Maher, Bill, 97
Malone, John (Liberty Media), 66
Mandel, Ernest, 20, 22
Marconi, 41
Marx, Karl, 4, 11, 14–15, 20, 33–5,
    41, 46–51, 52, 55, 59, 60, 71,
    98, 104, 107, 121–3, 135, 136,
    137, 139–40, 166, 179, 182,
    183, 184, 185–6, 187, 192–3,
    199, 201, 202, 203–5, 208–13,
    214, 221, 226, 241, 242–7, 258,
    262
Marx's Theory of Ideology (Parekh),
    245
*Marxism and the Philosophy of
    Language* (Vološinov), 159
materialism, 121–3, 136–8, 140–1,
    159, 161, 165, 166, 197, 263–4
  capital's dematerialising logic,
    184, 194, 199, 201, 208–9,
    210–13, 214–15, 219, 258, 260,
    261
Matrix, The (film), 1, 209, 211
Mattelart, Armand, 110
McCall, Davina, 108
McChesney, Robert, 82
McQuail, Denis, 108
McQuillan, Martin, 80
mediation, 49, 90, 105, 123, 124,
    125–6, 127, 133, 134, 138–41,
    148, 150, 163, 194, 196, 221–2,
    225, 239, 242, 244, 246, 247,
    249, 255, 256, 260–1, 264, 266
MEDIA programmes, 102

media structures, 62, 63, 66, 67, 69, 70–3, 76–7, 88, 94, 107, 109, 147, 262
Mészáros, István, 99
middle class, 10, 11, 13–30, 84, 130, 198, 249, 253
see also class
Milosevic, Slobodan, 94
Miramax, 75–6
mode of development, 23, 40, 44–5, 62, 66, 86, 107, 113, 119, 127–9, 131–3, 144, 148, 149, 153, 160, 221, 260
mode of production, 23, 40, 43, 45, 48, 59, 67, 68, 86, 89, 97, 107, 113, 118–22, 124, 127–35, 136–7, 138, 141, 143, 145, 148, 151, 153, 165, 185, 189, 211, 221, 239, 241, 247, 255, 257, 260, 261, 262, 267
   definition, 38–9
   feudal, 48, 130, 186
   forces and relations of, 50–4, 129
   Inuit, 165
   and language, 168, 223, 242, 264
   socialist mode, 35, 131, 144, 187
money, 12, 166, 205
monopoly, 16, 31, 55, 57, 62–73, 78, 86, 91, 92, 94, 105, 127, 158, 160
Monsanto, 96
Monsters, Inc. (film), 75, 76
Mulan (film), 75
Murdoch, Rupert, 82, 85, 98, 105, 114–15
Murdock, Graham, 59, 124–5, 141
Murroni, Cristina, 92–3
Mussolini, Benito, 177
Mutiny on the Bounty (film), 186–7
Mythologies (Barthes), 60

nation-state, 61, 69–70, 88, 95, 101–2, 111–16, 153, 229, 235, 263
Napster, 40, 47, 48, 54–9, 203, 262
Negative Dialectics (Adorno), 230, 231, 266
neo-liberalism, 70, 73, 88–9, 94, 103, 108–9, 116, 230, 263

New Jack City, (film), 32
New Labour, 105
New York Post (print), 171
News Corporation, 65, 66, 76, 82, 85, 98
News of the World (print), 153
Nichols, Bill, 148,
Niggaz With Attitude (music), 31
Nosferatu (film), 215

OFCOM, 96
Open Source, 96
One Day In September (film), 227–8, 232, 235, 267
Others, The (film), 201–3

Palestine is Still the Issue (television), 238
Panorama (television), 253–4, 267
Parekh, Bhikhu, 245–6
Payne, Sarah, 181
Perkins, Stephen, 246
petit bourgeoisie, 16, 17, 23, 32, 39, 79, 101, 129
see also class
PI (film), 192–3, 200
Picasso, Pablo, 197
Pilger, John, 238
Piore, Michael, 67
Philosophical Discourse of Modernity, The (Habermas), 233
Pleasantville (film), 209
Pocahontas (film), 74
Political Unconscious (Jameson), 142
Politically Incorrect (television), 97
Popstars (television), 28
Porter, Vincent, 28
post-Fordism, 44, 62–3, 66–70, 77, 86, 106, 132, 160, 262
see also Fordism
postmodernism, 132, 142, 144, 145, 151, 153, 194, 216–17, 220, 225, 228, 233, 235, 236, 237, 238, 239, 249, 264
post-structuralism, 161–2, 171, 231, 232
proletariat, 242–3, 245–6, 248, 249, 250, 258
Propp, Vladimir, 160

public service broadcasting, 88–92, 96, 101, 105, 108–9, 110, 146, 153
public sphere, 78–86, 110, 152, 153, 237, 238, 239, 256, 262, 264, 267
Puttnam, David, 90, 263

Quinn, Carol, 181

Rage Against The Machine (music), 27
RAI, 98
Recording Industry Association of America, 40, 57, 58
Reich, Robert, 29, 71, 77
reification, 97, 156, 183, 184, 187–9, 194, 213, 214, 216, 218, 219, 221, 232, 236, 244
Reith, John, 109
Representation (Hall), 164
Rigby, S.H. 52–4
Ring (film) 201
Ring 2 (film) 201
Rustin, Michael, 70

Sabel, Charles, 67, 71, 77
Said, Edward, 163, 228
Sartre, Jean-Paul, 197
Saussure, Ferdinand de, 155, 157, 159, 174
scales of determination, 80, 126–8, 148
Schiller, Dan, 51
Schröder, Gerhard, 114
Second Industrial Divide, The (Piore and Sabel), 67
Sex and the City (television), 200
Signatures of the Visible (Jameson), 142
Sixth Sense, The (film), 75, 267
Smith, Adam, 257
Smith, Will, 75
Snow, Jon, 51
Sobchack, Vivian, 218
Sony, 55, 58, 65
Stallman, Richard, 25
Stanley, Richard, 29–30
Startup.dom (film), 250–2

Storper, Michael, 72
Straight Out of Brooklyn, 32
Strinati, Dominic, 120–1
Structural Transformation of the Public Sphere (Habermas), 239
structuralism, 141, 158–61, 171, 232
  see also post-structuralism
subject, the, 132–3, 144, 153, 163, 184–6, 189–203, 206–7, 214, 215, 216, 217–19, 236–7, 240, 254, 258, 265, 267
  objective subject, 226–9
  subjectivism, 232–4, 254
Survivor (television), 145, 158

Taking of Pelham 123, The (film), 216
Taussig, Michael, 184, 194
technological determinism, 39–40, 59, 90–1
Telefonica, 148
terrorism, 94, 176, 195, 227, 235, 253
TF1, 110
Thatcher, Margaret, 169
Third Cinema, 229, 242
Thirteen Ghosts (film), 209
Thompson, John, B. 173
Time-Warner/AOL, 55, 58, 65, 66, 85, 86, 97, 147
Times, The (print) 157, 162, 168
Touch of Evil (film), 28
Toy Story (film), 75, 80
Toy Story 2 (film), 75
Trotsky, Leon, 266
Truman Show, The (film), 209
Turn of the Screw, The (James) 202

Undercurrents (video), 221
UNESCO, 89, 103
Urban Ghost Story (film), 210
Urry, John, 72

Value, 34–5, 58, 78, 133, 143, 186, 189, 195, 203–6, 210–13, 214, 218, 235, 249, 257–8, 262
  celebrity value, 132

surplus value, 11–13, 20, 21,
   26–7, 34, 46–7, 107, 191, 259
use-value, 140, 141, 203–5, 206,
   210, 211, 214–15, 249, 258

Viacom, 65
Vivendi, 58, 65, 66, 77, 97
Volŏshinov, V.N. 170, 173, 181

Ware, John (*Panorama*), 253
Wasko, Janet, 67
Weber, Max, 187
Weinstein, Bob, 76
Weinstein, Harvey, 76
Wells, Orson, 28–9
Who Wants To Be A Millionare?
   (television), 146
Willeman, Paul, 229
Williams, Raymond, 119, 124, 135,
   137–8, 139, 144

Willis, Bruce, 75
Wilson, Steve, 82
Winston, Brian, 52, 58
Woods, Tiger, 171–2
working class, 7, 8, 9, 10, 13, 15, 16,
   17, 22, 23, 27, 30, 31, 36, 70,
   83, 101, 176, 177, 178, 201,
   202, 210, 226, 239, 242–46,
   253
   see also class
World Trade Organisation, 61, 85,
   95, 113, 114
Wright, Eric Olin, 17, 18

You Have Mail (film), 16

Zapatistas, 50
Žižek, Slavoj, 185, 191, 212, 233–5,
   254, 266